COMPUTER-SUPPORTED SPECTROSCOPIC DATABASES

ELLIS HORWOOD SERIES IN ANALYTICAL CHEMISTRY

Series Editor: Dr. R. A. CHALMERS and Dr. MARY MASSON, University of Aberdeen
Consultant Editor: Prof. J. N. MILLER, University of Technology, Loughborough

S. Allenmark — **Chromatographic Enantioseparation — Methods and Applications**
G.E. Baiulescu & V.V. Coşofreţ — **Application of Ion Selective Membrane Electrodes in Organic Analysis**
G.E. Baiulescu, P. Dumitrescu & P.Gh. Zugravescu — **Sampling**
G.E. Baiulescu, C. Patroescu & R.A. Chalmers — **Education and Teaching in Analytical Chemistry**
S. Bance — **Handbook of Practical Organic Microanalysis**
H. Barańska *et al.* — **Laser Raman Spectrometry**
K. Beyermann — **Organic Trace Analysis**
O. Budevsky — **Foundations of Chemical Analysis**
J. Buffle — **Complexation Reactions in Aquatic Systems: An Analytical Approach**
D.T. Burns, A. Townshend & A.G. Catchpole — **Inorganic Reaction Chemistry Volume 1: Systematic Chemical Separation**
D.T. Burns, A. Townshend & A.H. Carter — **Inorganic Reaction Chemistry Reactions of the Elements and their Compounds: Volume 2, Part A: Alkali Metals to Nitrogen and Volume 2, Part B: Osmium to Zirconium**
S. Caroli — **Improved Hollow Cathode Lamps for Atomic Spectroscopy**
E. Casassas — **Trends in Solvent Extraction**
R. Czoch & A. Francik — **Apparatus Effects in Homodyne Electronic Paramagnetic Resonance Spectrometers**
T.E. Edmonds — **Interfacing Analytical Instrumentation with Microcomputers**
J.K. Foreman & P.B. Stockwell — **Automatic Chemical Analysis**
Z. Galus — **Fundamentals of Electrochemical Analysis**
J. Gasparič & J. Churáček — **Laboratory Handbook of Paper and Thin Layer Chromatography**
S. Görög — **Steroid Analysis in the Pharmaceutical Industry**
T S. Harrison — **Handbook of Analytical Control of Iron and Steel Production**
T.F. Hartley & T.W.Huber — **Computerized Quality Control**
Saad S.M. Hassan — **Organic Analysis using Atomic Absorption Spectrometry**
M.H. Ho — **Analytical Methods in Forensic Chemistry**
Z. Holzbecher, L. Diviš, M. Král, L. Šůcha & F. Vláčil — **Handbook of Organic Reagents in Inorganic Chemistry**
A. Hulanicki — **Reactions of Acids and Bases in Analytical Chemistry**
David Huskins — **General Handbook of On-line Process Analysers**
David Huskins — **Quality Measuring Instruments in On-line Process Analysis**
J. Inczédy — **Analytical Applications of Complex Equilibria**
Z.K. Jelínek — **Particle Size Analysis**
M. Kaljurand & E. Kullik — **Computerized Multiple Input Chromatography**
R. Kalvoda — **Operational Amplifiers in Chemical Instrumentation**
Editor: I. Kerese — **Methods of Protein Analysis**
S. Kotrlý & L. Šůcha — **Handbook of Chemical Equilibria in Analytical Chemistry**
J. Kragten — **Atlas of Metal-ligand Equilibria in Aqueous Solution**
A.M. Krstulovic — **Quantitative Analysis of Catecholamines and Related Compounds**
C. Liteanu & S. Gocan — **Gradient Liquid Chromatography**
C. Liteanu & I. Rîcă — **Statistical Theory and Methodology of Trace Analysis**
Z. Marczenko — **Separation and Spectrophotometric Determination of Elements**
M. Meloun, J. Havel & E. Högfeldt — **Computational Methods in Potentiometry and Spectrophotometry**
O. Mikeš — **Laboratory Handbook of Chromatographic and Allied Methods**
J.N. Miller & J.C. Miller — **Statistics for Analytical Chemistry**
J.N. Miller — **Fluorescence Spectroscopy**
J.N. Miller — **Modern Analytical Chemistry**
J. Minczewski, J. Chwastowska & R. Dybczyński — **Separation and Preconcentration Methods in Inorganic Trace Analysis**
V. Sediveč & J. Flek — **Handbook of Analysis of Organic Solvents**
R.M. Smith — **Derivatization for High Pressure Liquid Chromatography**
R.V. Smith — **Handbook of Biopharmaceutic Analysis**
K.R. Spurny — **Physical and Chemical Characterization of Individual Airborne Particles**
K. Štulík & V. Pacaková — **Electroanalytical Measurements in Flowing Liquids**
O. Shpigun & Yu. A. Zolotov — **Ion Chromatography in Water Analysis**
J. Tölgyessy & M. Kyrs — **Nuclear Analytical Chemistry**
J. Urbanski, *et al.* — **Handbook of Analysis of Synthetic Polymers and Plastics**
M. Valcárcel — **Flow Injection Analysis**
J. Veselý, D. Weiss & K. Štulík — **Analysis with Ion-Selective Electrodes**
F. Vydra, K. Štulík & B. Juláková — **Electrochemical Stripping Analysis**
N. G. West — **Practical Environment Analysis Using X-ray Fluorescence Spectrometry**
F.K. Zimmermann & R. E. Taylor-Mayer — **Mutagenicity Testing in Environmental Pollution Control**
J. Zupan — **Computer Supported Spectroscopic Databases**

COMPUTER-SUPPORTED SPECTROSCOPIC DATABASES

Editor:
JURE ZUPAN, B.Sc., M.Sc., Ph.D.
Senior Researcher, Boris Kidrič Institute of Chemistry
Ljubljana, Yugoslavia

ELLIS HORWOOD LIMITED
Publishers · Chichester

Halsted Press: a division of
JOHN WILEY & SONS
New York · Chichester · Brisbane · Toronto

First published in 1986 by
ELLIS HORWOOD LIMITED
Market Cross House, Cooper Street,
Chichester, West Sussex, PO19 1EB, England
The publisher's colophon is reproduced from James Gillison's drawing of the ancient Market Cross, Chichester.

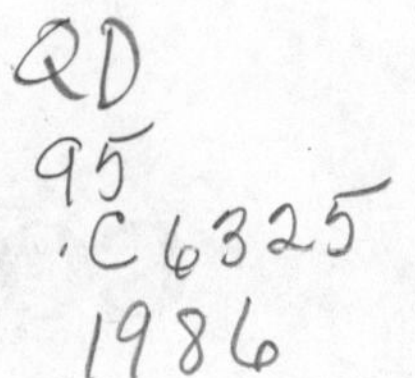

Distributors:
Australia and New Zealand:
JACARANDA WILEY LIMITED
GPO Box 859, Brisbane, Queensland 4001, Australia
Canada:
JOHN WILEY & SONS CANADA LIMITED
22 Worcester Road, Rexdale, Ontario, Canada
Europe and Africa:
JOHN WILEY & SONS LIMITED
Baffins Lane, Chichester, West Sussex, England
North and South America and the rest of the world:
Halsted Press: a division of
JOHN WILEY & SONS
605 Third Avenue, New York, NY 10158, USA

British Library Cataloguing in Publication Data
Zupan, J.
Computer-supported spectroscopic databases. —
(Ellis Horwood series in analytical chemistry)
1. Spectrum analysis — Data processing
I. Title
535.8′4′0285 QC451.6

Library of Congress CIP data also available

ISBN 0–85312–941–X (Ellis Horwood Limited)
ISBN 0–470–20730–2 (Halsted Press)

Typeset in Times by Ellis Horwood Limited
Printed in Great Britain by R.J. Acford, Chichester

Table of contents

Introduction

Spectroscopic data banks, either computerized or not, in many respects resemble icebergs. In both, the public (or the users) always see only a small (but the most shiny) part, whether in movies and slides or in scientific papers and instrument exhibitions. The larger they grow the more dangerous they become if approached from the wrong direction. Unfortunately, it is the larger data banks which attract most attention, in spite of the fact that they are mainly obtained by simple merging of smaller ones. As a rule, the parts differ in quality, and consequently the quality of the collection as a whole is judged in the best case by the worst part, and in the worst case by the best one. There are many reasons why a number of people consider computerized spectroscopic databases to be of little value. In his contribution, C. A. Shelley summarizes this attitude nicely: "Although many spectral databases have been created, few are of high quality and many are useless"! Some scientists have even stronger feelings against contemporary computerized spectroscopic databases: the contributions of some very competent people are missing in the present book. In spite of being asked to express their point of view they did not accept the challenge. Their argument was that the warnings have been made so many times that there is almost nothing left to say to prevent people from getting entangled in computerized spectroscopic databases.

Meanwhile, thousands of spectroscopists in many laboratories throughout the world are using different types of databases daily. Their position on the issue of the quality of spectroscopic databases is very pragmatic: they are all aware of the shortcomings but feel it is better to have a database with errors than nothing at all.

As always, the truth may be found somewhere between the two opposite views. Let us inspect the positions again. Is the real dilemma "to use or not to use" or is the dilemma something else or can it be expressed differently? Could the 'pragmatists' and 'rejectionists' be reconciled on the issue: "When is the database acceptable and when not"? There are many complex questions to be answered before the final judgement can be made. Are there ways and means for extraction of information out of the database that are less prone to error than the standard ones? Are there cross-tests and additional data that can make the data more reliable? The answers to these questions depend on the type of errors we are talking about, on the percentage of wrong entries in the entire database and, above all, on the type of information we would like to extract from the database.

Let us leave aside for the moment the type and number of errors in the database. The purpose for which the database is intended to be used will decide (i) which data are to be collected and stored, and how accurate they should be, and (ii) the methods for handling these data. There is a big difference between using the database for identification of standard samples by designing spectroscopic methods, and a multispectroscopy database to be part of an automatic chemical structure-elucidation system. Once the purpose is known, the data structure and afterwards the tolerance on the data items can be agreed upon.

One of the purposes of this book is to show different possibilities for the use of spectroscopic databases. In the last few years the ultimate aims of collecting spectroscopic data have changed dramatically. The once innovative retrieval for identification of unknown compounds is now more or less a routine utility, being a by-product of a far more complicated evaluation of probabilities for the presence of structural fragments and substrucures in unknown chemical compounds. While the chemical name or ID number is sufficient information for identification of the compound sought, both are far from enough for the structure-elucidation process. The unanimous opinion of the contributing authors is that a spectroscopic database without accompanying connection tables (i.e. the full topology of molecular structures) for each spectrum can hardly be regarded as useful. A very important but much more subtle shift in spectroscopic database policy concerns the size of the database. The time when the most significant characteristic of spectroscopic databases was their size is not so far in the past, but it is now at least recognized that instead of "how many" the question should be "how good". Unfortunately, a very important aspect of the first question is that it is routinely asked, not by the spectroscopists, but by the administrators or those responsible for the budget of research on spectroscopic databases. Once the second question replaces the first at this decision level a lot of problems that are now inherent in databases will be solved in a short time.

It has to be generally recognized that in chemical information, as in materials science, better products will emerge not only because of better processing, but mainly from better starting material!

Until now, our attention has been focused on the quality of the data. The next most important aspect is the search for better and more flexible methods of handling not only single-spectroscopy but also multi-spectroscopy data. To achieve this goal several problems have to be solved. The problem of overlap of different spectroscopic data was described in S. R. Heller's lecture during the VIIth ICCCRE Conference in Garmisch-Partenkirchen in June 1985. The following figure showing the overlaps of three different spectroscopic databases (mass, ^{13}C NMR, and infrared) containing 39827, 5815, and 2866 spectra, respectively, is borrowed from his lecture.

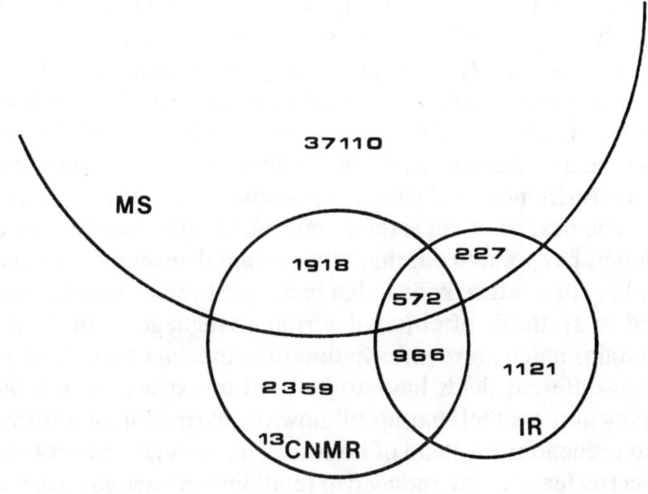

Fig. 1.

In a collection of almost 50000 spectra, all three types were available for only 572 compounds. The number 572 is not as small as it looks, however, because although the infrared database contains only 2886 spectra it was created with the intention of making the overlap as large as possible. To make this example even more illustrative, when the crystallographic database for 27727 compounds was checked against the other three collections, only 100 compounds were found to be listed in all four. The largest overlap between two databases was not between the largest but between the mass and ^{13}C NMR databases.

For a significant improvement of the structure-elucidation process consideration of the multispectroscopy data for the *same* structural entities is essential but, as shown in Fig. 1, quite hard to achieve without the collaboration of many laboratories. As can be seen from the literature on spectroscopic information systems and from this book as well, the authors of such systems are mainly experts in one type of spectroscopy and usually consider, apply, and implement (if at all) the other methods less skilfully than 'their own' spectroscopy. The results can be improved relatively easily by intensifying the collaboration between experts in different spectroscopic fields and with information and computer scientists.

Another very important aspect, raised by some of the contributors to this book, is the manipulation of spectroscopic data (spectra and subspectra), chemical structures (sub- and super-structures), correlations between spectroscopic data and chemical structures, as well as many other additional sources of information such as images, lists, etc. Owing to the large amount of collected data the handling has become so complicated and perplexing that it calls for some sort of high-level solution. In our opinion the design and implementation of an 'operating system' for manipulation of chemical information would be very desirable. It should be transparent to the user and enable him to manipulate easily such chemical information as spectra, structures, properties, or combinations of them, in any form (e.g. numerical data, images, text). The operating system should make it easy to update and maintain the databases as well as to extract the information needed by chemists. Some of the larger systems such as DARC have already implemented user-friendly dialogue but there is still a long way to go before a truly 'chemist-friendly and chemistry-oriented' operating system will emerge.

The next problem is the organization and processing of databases. J. E. Dubois has pointed out that "the potential developer of a chemical database and . . . of a future knowledge bank must return to taxonomy, to grammar, and to synthesis of object-describing languages". In short, each database contains much more information than the data alone and, various methods from different fields have to be used to extract the relevant information. Many authors feel that up till now the extraction of information was much too reductionist instead of holistic. The correlations between structural and spectral features are reduced to relations between substructure and subspectra in an attempt to narrow the size and scope of particular questions and the relevant information. Instead of such a reductionist view, they argue, the data and answers should be treated as whole objects carrying much more information than meets the eye. In the chapter on hierarchical ordering of spectral data, such a holistic attempt is proposed.

The book consists of eight chapters ordered according to the authors' 'holistic *vs.* reductionist' approach. The first three chapters deal with general aspects of spectroscopic database organization, and are followed by four describing information systems based on a single type of spectroscopy: infrared, mass or nuclear magnetic resonance, and finally a short survey of problems in multispectroscopy chemical information systems.

In the first chapter C. A. Shelley gives a concise and sharp description of the state of the art of chemical databases and gives guidelines according to which such systems should develop in the future. The Kodak spectroscopy network is given as an example of a modern approach to a multilevel spectroscopy information system. Additionally, he calls for moderation when hopes are high that a c omputer will replace the chemist. In the second chapter J. E. Dubois, the main author of the DARC system, and Y. Sobel raise a very interesting aspect of fuzzy situations in complex spectroscopy data systems. They describe optimal organization of data banks as 'federated data banks' in which even the dormant information can be invoked in the structure-elucidation process. The third chapter describes a hierarchical organization of a spectroscopic database. Here J. Zupan and M. Novič argue that a holistic approach can yield good prediction of structural features, i.e. the information buried in single spectra or *groups* of spectra is obtained from the whole representation of these objects. The idea behind the automatic hierarchical clustering of spectra is that the clusters should be formed on the basis of representation of whole spectra and not on the subspectral features of some preselected hierachy of structural fragments. In the fourth chapter H. Somberg describes the problems encountered with infrared spectroscopic databanks and the solutions to some of them from an instrument manufacturer's (Bruker) point of view. It is interesting to note that even on the microcomputer level the spectroscopic database has to be accompanied by connection tables, i.e. by the full structural information on the compounds in the collection. The next chapter is on the same topic, by H. Passlack and W. Bremser of BASF. This company's research on spectroscopic databases, notably for ^{13}C NMR, is very well known to all working in this field. This time they present an information system based on 17000 infrared spectra. What makes this infrared spectra collection specially interesting is the link with connection tables *and* with the $_{13}C$ NMR spectra (for some of the compounds). The computerized mass spectra collection and the associated mass spectra search system of the NIH/EPA chemical information system is now almost a classic in this field. Its main author and promoter, S. R. Heller, focuses his chapter on the quality control and quality evaluation of mass spectra. We can only regret that such rigorous procedures for evaluation of spectra quality are not endorsed and standardized for all spectroscopic techniques. Finally, he warns that "the QI (quality index) is not really an indicator that a spectrum is good. Rather it is an indicator of the problems with the spectrum". The last type of spectroscopic database included in the book is that of nuclear magnetic resonance spectra. S. I. Sasaki and his co-workers describe their effort to link ^{13}C and ^{1}H nuclear magnetic resonance spectra and topological structures. The resulting system is incorporated in the expert system CHEMICS. Finally, Z. Hippe addresses and briefly discusses the role of artificial intelligence (AI) in a structure-elucidation process based on the use of different types of spectrometry.

At this point I would like to thank my co-workers Dr. Marko Razinger and Dr. Marjana Novič for creation of an extremely friendly and stimulating atmosphere, whether in the laboratory, the computer room, or on the high mountains and the ski slopes. The creative environment that evolved through hard work, hundred of discussions, and thousands of cups of coffee, was the medium in which our research and contribution to this book became possible.

Special thanks go to Professor Dušan Hadži who introduced me to the field of computerized spectroscopy-based information systems twelve years ago and gave me the opportunity to work in his laboratory in the Boris Kidrič Institute of Chemistry, and to Professor Morton E. Munk from Arizona State University in Tempe, whose broad knowledge and conceptual firmness gave me the necessary push in my work when it was needed.

Jure Zupan
Ljubljana, October 1985

1

Problems that prevent computer-assisted structure elucidation from becoming a practical tool

C. A. Shelley
Eastman Kodak Company, Research Laboratories, Rochester, New York 14650

1.1 INTRODUCTION

Since the mid-sixties, a few scientists have been developing computer programs that make the structure-elucidation process more efficient. Interest in this software has increased in the eighties as some researchers and the media have popularized 'expert systems' in the field of 'artificial intelligence'. The ability of these expert systems to accomplish tasks in their area of specialization has often been exaggerated. For example, a popular book on developing expert systems makes the following statement about the DENDRAL program [1], a program which attempts to elucidate the structure of chemicals: "DENDRAL surpasses all humans at its task and, as a consequence, has caused a redefinition of the roles of humans and machines in chemical research." [2]. The actual progress in computer-assisted structure elucidation, in contrast to this quotation, is not overwhelming.

For the computer to be able to analyse infrared, mass, nuclear magnetic resonance, and ultraviolet/visible spectra, the ultimate goal of computer-assisted structure elucidation, some fundamental and practical problems must be solved. An important fundamental problem is the lack of innovative ideas for efficient and effective computer representation of spectroscopic knowledge. Simplistic correlation-table-like representations do not even begin to incorporate in a program the spectroscopist's knowledge and ability to handle the ambiguity and vagueness inherent in spectral analysis. The use of existing expert systems (e.g. CASE [3], CHEMICS [4], DENDRAL [1], and PAIRS [5]) in industry is limited, in part, because the most important problem facing industrial spectroscopists, the verification of a proposed structure, is not addressed. More work needs to be directed towards this gap in research on computer-assisted structure elucidation. A second fundamental problem is the representation and use of chemical structures in programs. In contrast to the representation of spectroscopic knowledge, there is a wealth of research on this topic, and many subproblems have been solved but some remain.

There are also important practical problems preventing computerized spectral analysis from becoming routine. The most challenging is the lack of quality reference spectral databases, which are required for obtaining structure–spectrum correlations efficiently. In addition, expert systems must have access to routine sample data, chemical structure and all available spectral data. Expert system and sample-management software must be integrated into one system. Large corporations require not only integrated software but software that will integrate independent spectroscopic facilities in a network to share tools and resources.

These problems, and undoubtedly others, must be solved before computer-assisted structure elucidation becomes a practical tool for industrial spectroscopists. This chapter presents the author's viewpoint with regard to these problem areas. The chapter's four sections deal with the spectral database, knowledge representation, software integration, and the problem of handling chemical structure. Software and database developments at Eastman Kodak Company that are beginning to tackle some of these problems will be described where applicable.

1.2 SPECTRAL DATABASES — AN IMPORTANT RESOURCE

The lack of good databases for infrared, mass, nuclear magnetic resonance, and ultraviolet/visible spectra will, at the least, slow the development of expert systems for computer-assisted structure elucidation. These databases are a vital resource for obtaining and testing empirical structure–spectrum correlations efficiently. A reference database-management system can also be used by the spectroscopist to obtain useful model compounds quickly. In addition, a sample-management system integrated with a reference database can eliminate redundant work by automatically informing spectroscopists about the existence of a reference spectrum for the same or a similar structure.

Reference spectra can be obtained from commercial sources, the literature, or in-house measurements. Obtaining data from any of these sources has its associated problems. There are a few useful commercial and public databases. A carbon-13 nuclear magnetic resonance database is available from FIZ [6]. This is one of the few databases with connection tables, a necessary computer representation of chemical structure, but these connection tables do not contain stereochemical information. The database contains a fair amount of redundant data. Many chemicals have several nearly identical spectra. Some structures have an entry with ambiguous assignments, even though there may another reference to use of the same solvent, and all the shifts are assigned. It is also common to find only one or two spectra extracted from a published paper that contains many spectra. Despite these problems, this database is undoubtedly the best commercially available ^{13}C NMR collection. For other nuclei there are no NMR databases with interpreted information, i.e., shifts and coupling constants with assignments to specific atoms.

There is no commercially available condensed-phase infrared database with high-resolution digitized spectra and connection tables. An infrared database of moderate resolution with no connection tables is available from Nicolet Instruments [7]. An electron-impact mass-spectral database is available from the National Bureau of Standards [8]. The associated connection tables can be obtained from Fein-Marquart [9].

It is practicable to obtain NMR shifts, coupling constants, and relaxation times from the literature to create a reference database. At Kodak, we have been collecting literature NMR data in this fashion for the last three years. The user enters the chemical structure with the program CHEMwriter at a graphics terminal (see Section 1.5). After structure entry, a data-entry menu appears. The user positions the graphics cursor over an atom and then 'accesses' the atom by depressing the pen on the tablet. Next the chemical shift is entered by accessing menu items in the 'graphical numeric keypad'. Coupling constants and relaxation times are entered in the same way. An EQUIVALENCE command speeds the entry of assignments for structures that contain symmetry, by automatically making the assignments. We have found this program useful for acquiring reference NMR spectra from literature sources.

Most academic or industrial researchers will not be able to justify the expense of obtaining the spectra of pure, known chemicals directly from instruments for the sole purpose of generating a reference database. An alternative is the establishment of sample-management software that would allow information to be obtained on data quality for routinely analysed chemicals. The sample-management software would also need to collect spectral data and connection tables for all samples (see Section 1.4).

Although many spectral databases have been created, few are of high quality and many are useless. A number of problems have plagued reference spectral databases. Many databases have a substantial number of errors. A common problem, especially with old collections, is the exclusion of important information. Connection tables are often not included, though they are essential. Another common error of database developers is to discard some or most of the spectral data simply because the full spectrum search procedure does not require it or "the complete data set will require too much storage." Because search techniques are always changing, reduced spectra should not be relied on as sufficient; information contained in the original spectrum may be important for later search routines. This problem is especially common for infrared databases, for which spectra of 'binary' peak/no-peak type or with only the *N* most intense peaks saved are common but rather useless formats for a general-purpose database. Infrared data should be stored with the entire high-resolution curve in the database. Mass storage is inexpensive and should no longer be a consideration in determining whether the complete spectrum or a reduced format should be used. Another problem with many databases is the lack of structural diversity. Often many of the data are redundant. Commercial or public databases may not contain data relevant to a company's business.

Databases can be improved or new ones can be established. Our experience suggests that the job should be done correctly the first time; it is generally more time-consuming to correct errors than to make the original entry. Unfortunately, we must make the best possible use of existing databases in addition to creating new ones. The quality of reference databases can be improved by decreasing errors, increasing structural diversity, and increasing relevance. Routines to add spectra should provide immediate feedback to the user. The user should be informed about potential errors whenever this is practicable. Messages should be sent immediately to the user when there are other spectra for the same structure. There must be an easy mechanism for users to correct errors they detect. This means that the reference database system must be transaction-oriented, i.e. it must provide concurrent write-access to multiple users. A historical log of database changes for each entry would add a measure of security against undesired changes.

Many transcription errors could be reduced by extracting data directly from primary sources. This may be feasible for NMR shifts, coupling constants, and relaxation times reported in the literature. The tabular data could be 'read' directly from the journal article. It may become possible to implement software to directly 'read' chemical structures contained in literature articles. The important ability of the CHEMwriter program to parse chemical symbol strings brings this goal a step closer to reality (see Section 1.5).

The relevance of the database may be increased by integrating sample-management and reference-database systems. The sample-management system would also be an important method in determining the quality of the data. In an integrated system it would require little effort to transfer a routine spectrum with its associated connection table to the reference system. These transfers to the reference system could, perhaps, be done automatically by the sample-management software.

The spectral data manager (SDM) is software that is being developed at Kodak to establish and access a reference database. This software has been in use by spectroscopists for more than two years, but it is constantly being changed and refined. The major function of the SDM is to provide spectroscopists and developers of expert system software with empirical structure–spectrum correlations.

A substantial effort has been made to improve the quality of spectral data and increase the diversity of chemical structures in the reference database. Spectral data have been acquired from several sources and merged into a common database. All entries contain the chemical structure in addition to the spectral data. For NMR (mainly ^{13}C NMR), the chemical shifts, coupling constants, and T_1 relaxation times are entered. For infrared, the digitized spectrum (for which resolution is variable because most spectra have a point in the vicinity of every wavenumber) and peak table are stored. The peak table, which can be regenerated from the digitized data if the peak-picking procedure is changed, classifies the peaks (sharp, average, and broad) and shoulders with an intensity range from 0 to 15. The mass spectra are stored as mass and intensity pairs.

The SDM has many commands to search the database. These commands can be categorized into five broad types: full structure, substructure, full spectrum, partial spectrum, and Boolean (logical) expressions combining substructure and partial spectrum search results. For ^{13}C NMR data there are three possible substructure search methods. The data can be searched with the standard substructure search command, which is applicable to structures with any type of associated spectral data. There is also a substructure search command, C13_SSS which will return the chemical-shift range, average, and standard deviation for each carbon atom in the substructure. A third command, C13_ACS, will retrieve all atom-centered substructures (shells) for each carbon atom in a given chemical structure. The *n*th shell for a carbon atom includes all atoms within *n* bonds of it, any atoms that have a resonance influence on these atoms, hetero and charged atoms that are $n+1$ bonds from the central carbon atom, and any atom multiply bonded to an atom that is *n* bonds from the central atom. The chemical-shift range, average, and the standard deviation for the shifts assigned to each shell are listed in a tabular format. At the user's option, the references containing these retrieved shells can be examined.

At present, the SDM can search ^{13}C NMR data only by full spectrum. This interpretive search retrieves all substructures in the reference database that contain shifts that match a subset of the observed chemical shifts. The procedure has been published [10].

The SDM has facilities to search the infrared peak tables to obtain references to a peak of given wavenumber, intensity, and width characteristics. References with more than one required peak can be retrieved by using the Boolean query facility. For example, to get all reference infrared spectra with both the symmetric and asymmetric bands for a sulphone, the IR_PEAK_SEARCH command could be used to retrieve all spectra with a sharp or an average band between 1120 and 1200 cm^{-1}, of intensity greater than 5. The reference structure numbers associated with these spectra would be saved in a file, with the name '1150' (the name can contain any character except a blank). The file format is a binary bit map, which is an efficient structure for Boolean operations. The IR_PEAK_SEARCH command could be used again to obtain all spectra with a sharp or an average band between 1300 and 1380 cm^{-1}, of intensity greater than 5. The associated structure numbers would be saved in file '1330'. The FILE EXPRESSION command could be used to create a file with the name '1150_and_1330' by entering the Boolean expression '1150 and 1330'.

The following example illustrates how the SDM can be used to test and develop structure–spectrum correlations. An infrared spectroscopist has an interest in obtaining the correlations for the sulphonamide group. First, he would search the database by substructure to create a file, SULPHONAMIDE, containing all sulphonamides with a known infrared spectrum. The utility of a hypothesized correlation, for example, of the SO_2 symmetric and asymmetric stretch bands, could be examined. The FILE_EXPRESSION command could be used to create a file (called DIFFERENT) of sulphonamides that lack one or more of the bands, expressed as 'S and not 1150_and_1330'. The file names can be shortened, as in the preceding expression, if they are unique. The spectra of these counter-examples could then be examined to determine why the bands are missing. After these references have been examined, the correlation may be modified; e.g. a wavenumber range may be increased.

IR_COMPOSITE and IR_HISTOGRAM are useful commands to extract the database. IR_COMPOSITE can be used to create the average digitized spectrum for an existing file, e.g. the SULPHONAMIDE file. This is especially useful in obtaining correlations for large substructures for which the correlations are unknown. Once an approximate correlation is suggested, the wavenumber range, the intensity range, and the shape may be investigated with the IR_HISTOGRAM command. This command will create histograms of probability *vs.* wavenumber for bands of given intensity and shape characteristics, for the spectra associated with a structure file. For example, the likelihood of the sulphonamide symmetric stretch band having an intensity less than 12 could be determined.

1.3 THE KNOWLEDGE–REPRESENTATION BOTTLENECK

The knowledge–representation problem is the most fundamental challenge in development of practical expert systems in computer-assisted structure elucidation. The correlation-table-like representations and simplistic models used so far are not likely to be sufficient. These knowledge data structures do not necessarily need to model how the chemist approaches structure elucidation. They must be easily modifiable and ideally rather dynamic to accommodate mechanisms for the software to change itself. Expert systems should explain how a conclusion is reached; the knowledge representations may influence the ability of an expert system to generate such explanatory messages. Perhaps expert-system software should be closely integrated with reference databases so that the program can search for models to justify conclusions that appear to be abnormal.

The practical application of expert systems in industry requires that the problem of structure–spectrum verification be addressed. This problem is similar to the interpretation of a spectrum of an unknown, but has the advantage that the process may be either spectrum- or structure-driven. The ideal structure–spectrum verification routine would also suggest alternative interpretations of the data. For example, if the structure is that of a synthetic product, the routine could predict side-products of the reaction mechanistically and compare their data with the observed data. Salatin and Jorgensen have been developing CAMEO, a program to predict reaction products mechanistically [11]. A similar routine could perhaps serve this proposed role for the structure-verification software.

The knowledge representations must be able to accommodate the ambiguity and vagueness inherent in structure-elucidation problems. The representation must not limit the ability to express correlations. An example is the CONCISE language used in the PAIRS program [5], which interprets infrared spectra. In the CONCISE language, infrared correlations are expressed as conditional, if-then-else, statements (called production rules in the literature on artificial intelligence). Table 1.1 lists a section of a

Table 1.1 — Part of a pyrrole infrared correlation written in CONCISE

```
. . .
  IF ANY INTENSITY 1 TO 10 SHARP TO BROAD PEAKS ARE IN RANGE 3530
  TO 3460
$
  THEN BEGIN
  SET PYRROLE TO 0.25
  IF ANY INTENSITY 4 TO 10 SHARP PEAKS ARE IN RANGE 3530 TO 3460
$
  THEN BEGIN
  ADD 0.25 TO PYRROLE
  IF ANY INTENSITY 4 TO 10 SHARP PEAKS ARE IN RANGE 3500 TO 3475
$
  THEN BEGIN
  ADD 0.25 TO PYRROLE
  DONE
  DONE
. . .
```

CONCISE routine for pyrrole. These CONCISE statements describe a probability distribution with several conditional statements. Note how the later conditional statements modify the first in arriving at the score for the pyrrole prediction. It may be possible to describe the probability distribution for any correlation, given enough conditional statements; however, such routines obscure the correlation and are awkward, at the least. Most likely, because of the limitations of CONCISE, the optimal correlation will not be expressed. In addition, the probability distribution will be obscured. This makes the routine difficult to understand.

The numerical actions of CONCISE rules, which are typical of many expert systems, are based on the experience of an expert. The problem with this is that spectroscopists do not function with this kind of numerical scoring system. This 'foreign' language forces the spectroscopist to do things the computer's way. People are poor at guessing these pseudo-probabilities. The result is inconsistent prediction. A prediction of '70' for a nitro group is not equivalent to a prediction of '70' for pyrrole. This does not mean that numerical actions should be excluded from knowledge representations. It means that numerical actions, if required, should be derived by a program.

Trulson and Munk suggested an alternative representation in which the correlation is directly related to probability-based histograms [12]. This simplifies the representation of the correlation and includes the fine detail of the entire probability distribution for the histogram. The correlations are also based on empirical evidence. In spite of these improvements, the relative predictions are still not correct. The identical nitro group and pyrrole predictions of '70' are not equivalent. The probabilities must include the chance that a spectrum of a structure may not contain the substructure with the same spectral feature. This is accommodated in part by Trulson and Munk's 'weighting factors'. For example, these authors consider the peak for the carbonyl stretch as 'essential' but not as important as some other bands in arriving at the final score for a given substructure, because carbonyl stretch bands occur in approximately the same region for many different substructures.

Using probabilistic correlations derived directly from an infrared database solves some problems, but not all. First, if the database lacks diversity, then misleading correlations will be generated. It is assumed that the database is representative of the structural universe that the expert system will encounter. It is safe to assume that this is never true; it is an approximation that may not even be close to reality for some databases. This emphasizes the need to have databases relevant to the chemistry performed in the expert-system environment. Secondly, probabilistic correlations for predefined substructures are too localized. For example, a routine to predict sulphonamides may not perform well if the sulphonyl group has a fluoro substituent. In addition, probabilities generated without consideration for other substructures will not be based on the optimal correlation. For example, if it is known that a nitro group is unlikely, the significance of a sulphonamide-like band near 1350 cm^{-1} is increased, since the nitro group has a band that frequently occurs in the same region. An expert system that can access the database may be able to improve its prediction by analogy. Noticing the fluoro group in the example above, it might suspect that this group changes the normal position of the symmetric and asymmetric stretch bands. It could look for an example in the database to provide empirical evidence that the bands are indeed shifted. The program might also dynamically generate probability functions 'on the fly' from the database to improve the sulphonamide prediction when the nitro group is known to be absent or unlikely to be present. It might be advisable to supplant probabilistic empirical correlations with more fundamental information on the process. For example, information on how changes in structure influence vibrational frequencies in infrared spectroscopy would be useful.

Ambiguity in a spectrum may be more apparent than real. The interpretation of a spectrum may appear ambiguous because some of the available information is not being considered. Expert systems must fully exploit this condition whenever it exists. The program does not need to operate in the same way as a spectroscopist. Certainly the computer has better ability than a spectroscopist to recall information, but fails, often miserably, in its ability to make the best use of the information. It may be possible to give the computer a competitive edge in the process by giving it access to more pieces of information than would normally be considered or used by a chemist. The detailed probability-based correlations, including the fine structure of the histogram, would be one source of detailed information that the chemist does not use. For sulphonamides we have found that the distance between the symmetric and asymmetric stretch bands is an extremely important correlation. In addition, the relative intensity of the two bands is important; they normally have about the same intensity. Theoretical predictions may also be of aid in using weak bands in the correlation, in contrast to the case with spectroscopists, who often use just the strong and moderate intensity bands in most regions.

In addition to making better use of existing spectra, it may be reasonable to employ computerized analysis in conjunction with instruments that generate a large amount of detailed information. The computer should analyse those data for which it can do the best job. For example, low-resolution mass spectra are perhaps too ambiguous, but high-resolution data, perhaps from an FT–MS instrument, are full of additional detail. At least in an industrial environment, the cost of an expensive instrument may be justified if the computer can analyse routine samples automatically. A 400-MHz NMR instrument rather than an inexpensive low-field instrument may be a requirement for computerized ^{1}H NMR analyses.

1.4 SOFTWARE INTEGRATION AND NETWORKING

Several times in this chapter we have emphasized the importance of integrating sample-management, reference database-management, and expert-system software. The need for such integration is substantial. The ultimate goal of computer-assisted structure elucidation, to analyse spectral data automatically, will not be realized until this integration occurs. Large corporations require not only integrated software but software that will integrate independent spectroscopic facilities in a network to share tools and resources. The resultant savings will also offset the cost of developing the network software.

The networking should improve communication between independent spectroscopic groups that often work in similar or identical problems, and provide immediate access to current data. This improved communication would be expected to reduce redundant work and increase the quality of the results. The network would also be a major step in acquiring more and better reference data on chemicals relevant to the company, and allow software techonology, especially expert systems, to be developed and promptly sent to other sites.

Network site-hardware, small microcomputers without special electrical or cooling needs, could be placed in the spectroscopy groups they service. These self-sufficient sites, in the domain of the spectroscopic laboratories, could provide rapid response to user commands. They should be able to perform most functions even during down-time of the network or remote sites. Network redundancy would also help to maximize up-time of each site. The network software should be implemented with anticipation of future hardware capabilities; too much software becomes out of date by the time it is implemented because the implementation is based on current hardware and subsequent to its limitations.

In a distributed network, it would be important to centralize software maintenance and supply back-up procedures. Spectroscopists would need to be trained to use the system. In addition to manuals, video tape and optical disks could be used to help meet these training requirements. It might be possible to implement an expert system with a natural language interface to form an active help facility rather than a traditional passive facility (see [13] for an expert system to assist users of the UNIX operating system). This expert system would be a centralized network resource to answer questions for which the user had insufficient knowledge to issue the right help command. It would not be a replacement for a help facility.

The remainder of this section will describe the current Kodak sample-management system and the proposed spectroscopy network. The sample-management system, SOFTLOG, has been used by three spectroscopy groups at Kodak for more than a year. Its most important task is to inform spectroscopists about related analyses performed at the same or other spectroscopy laboratories. It also facilitates communication between spectroscopists when they arrive at inconsistent interpretations for spectral data on the same sample. The ability to cross-reference analyses on samples is providing more information, which is useful in determining the reference quality of spectral data. With this ability, SOFTLOG is becoming a key to establish reference spectral databases on chemicals of interest to the company.

It will also become an interface to the reference system and analysis software. The structural and spectral components of the SOFTLOG database are required to implement automated queries of the spectral data manager (SDM). For example, it is expected that the system will inform users automatically about relevant model compounds in the software system. The user would not need to perform interactive structural searches of the SDM to obtain this kind of information. It would also function as the interface to expert-system routines.

When a record is created, the computer assigns a submission date and sample-identification number. The user enters various text-fields that identify the sample and can optionally add remarks and the chemical structure. After a SOFTLOG record is created with SUBMIT, it can be retrieved by any user. The system immediately updates the SOFTLOG database to include the record.

After the interpretation of the spectral data is complete, the UPDATE command is used to enter the results, analyses performed, the interpreter's initials, and related information into the record for the sample. The structure and remark fields can be modified. The system assigns a reporting date.

The sample database can be queried by various text-fields, the complete structure, or a substructure. The CROSS_REFERENCE command will, given a sample-identification number, cross-reference it to other records with the same chemist, structure, or notebook number. It also checks the SDM system for the same structure and, if it finds it, will return the reference number and spectral data available for the structure.

SOFTLOG automatically sends user messages relevant to an analysis when records are created with SUBMIT or modified with UPDATE. At submission time, it searches the reference spectral database by structure and, if a match is found, the reference system number and kinds of spectral data on the sample are reported. It also searches the SOFTLOG database by structure and returns the sample-identification numbers and interpretation results for samples with the same structure. At update time, SOFTLOG searches its database for 'inconsistent' interpretations for the same sample. The user adding the interpretation result will immediately receive a message, and both groups will get a similar message in their mailboxes.

Reports can be generated on the basis of the submission and reporting dates. A list can be generated of samples that have been submitted but not yet updated with interpretation results.

The sample-management software serves as the application interface for the proposed spectroscopy network. The long-distance network would include several local-area networks in the continental United States and Europe (Fig. 1.1). Long-distance communications would be implemented through a central network dispatcher.

A large local-area network in the proposed spectroscopy network is shown in Fig. 1.2. This network would reside within a building or complex of buildings. The most important computer is the 'structure-elucidation host' processor. This computer would run SOFTLOG, the SDM, and most or all of the programs for computer analysis of spectral data. It is the workhorse of the local-area network. All other computers are its slaves. The 'data collection' processor's main function is to communicate with spectrometers or other processors dedicated to the off-line work-up of spectral data. It would off-load the time-consuming task of asynchronous communication with spectrometers. It would also reformat the data to the standard format used by the network software.

A structure-elucidation host may be dedicated to one large analytical facility (the bottom host in Fig. 1.2 with directly attached terminals), or it may be a general-purpose host serving several small facilities. The user terminals for this latter host would be connected to the network rather than directly to the host. Chemists served by a spectroscopy laboratory could

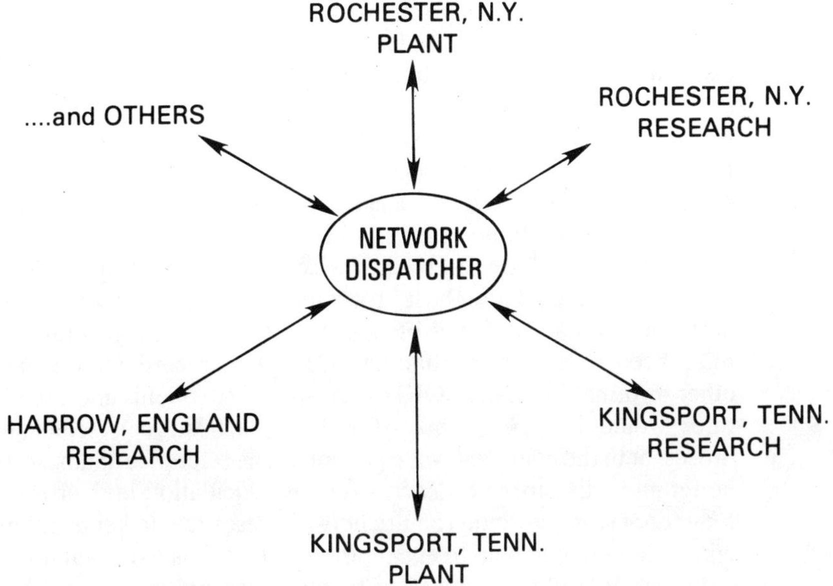

Fig. 1.1 — Local-area networks connected to the dispatcher.

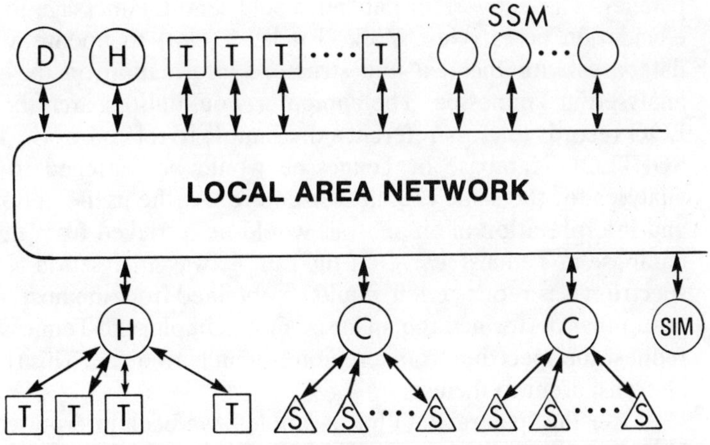

Fig. 1.2 — Local-area network.

determine the status of a problem or examine data relevant to their sample, via the general-purpose host. Heavy terminal traffic within the large analytical facility would not put a load on the network.

The 'substructure search machine' (SSM) is a specialized parallel processor to off-load from the structure-elucidation host the time-consuming task of substructure search (see Section 1.5). Expert-system software may need to be implemented on specialized hardware; this is represented by the spectral interpretation machine in Fig. 1.2.

Spectral data acquired by a data-collection processor would be sent to the structure-elucidation host processor for the spectroscopy groups by the host. These data, an archive of most or all spectral data generated, would be referenced to the corresponding SOFTLOG record for the sample. All other information in the SOFTLOG system, text-fields and chemical structure, would be redundantly stored on each structure-elucidation host processor in the company -wide network. The reference database would also be redundantly stored on each structure-elucidation host processor. Such redundant storage would require network resources to keep multiple copies current, but would help to ensure the self-sufficiency of local hosts, and the redundancy could also be used to maximize up-time. Local hosts could continue to operate even when the network or other hosts were down. Users could also continue to examine routinely generated spectral data residing on any active host if the terminal had a separate redundant connection to that host. A user in an interactive network could also use an alternative host when the normal host computer was down. Any operating host disconnected from the network would still provide access to expert systems (except those running on the SIM), access to the reference database, and the ability to log samples and inquire about related analyses.

For example, when a laboratory in Tennessee received a sample, a SOFTLOG record would be created containing the text-fields (e.g. submitting chemist, notebook number, date) and the chemical structure. The computer would immediately send this information to the network dispatcher. The network dispatcher would send the message to all structure-elucidation hosts (New York, England, etc.) to update all SOFTLOG databases with the text and structure information on the sample being analysed in Tennessee. The computer would also search the local SOFTLOG records to cross-reference the sample to related work. Thus the local SOFTLOG database in Tennessee would be searched to locate other analyses for the same chemical structure. At the user's option, the source and interpretation of an analysis would be retrieved from the SOFTLOG database in Tennessee even if the sample was analysed in New York. If a spectrum was requested, it would be obtained from the host supporting the group that performed the analysis. For example, the Tennessee site would request the spectrum from a remote site in New York. This retrieval would be transparent to the user.

After the spectral data for a sample have been interpreted, the SOFTLOG record would be updated to include the interpretation result and other text-fields. This information would be sent to all structure-elucidation hosts in the company-wide network. The computer would then automatically check for other analyses of the same sample. The user would be informed immediately about inconsistent interpretations.

1.5 HANDLING CHEMICAL STRUCTURES

An important problem for computer-assisted structure elucidation is the use and representation of chemical structures. The chemical structure is required to cross-reference records by full structure, search by substructure, and retrieve similar structures. Substructure search is an important step in extracting structure–spectrum correlations from the reference database. A common substructure procedure would allow the sample-management system to retrieve similar structures automatically from the reference database.

In contrast to the representation of spectroscopic knowledge, there is a wealth of research on codifying chemical structures. Many subproblems have been solved, but some remain. Inorganic, organometallic, and tautomeric structures do not yet have chemically meaningful structural representations. This is especially important for computer-assisted structure elucidation, for which interpretive procedures must be based on meaningful correlations between structure and spectrum. Representing tautomeric structures with 'normalized' tautomer bonds that do not represent reality, as Chemical Abstracts has done [14], is not a satisfactory solution.

Another problem is the task of finding substructures that are common to some of the structures in a set, but not necessarily all. Varkony *et al.* [15] have implemented a procedure to find substructures common to the entire set of structures. This latter task is computationally demanding but not nearly as difficult as the first. The Varkony approach is also applicable to the first task, but it would be extremely time-consuming. This problem may not be solved successfully until parallel processors become available.

Problems that have been solved, but with limitations, are structure entry and structure display. The entry of chemical structures, perhaps the most time-consuming step in using chemistry-related software, must be efficient; users in spectroscopy laboratories will be entering structures to the computer daily. It is also desirable to have a routine to display structures directly from the connection table.

To improve the efficiency of entering chemical structures, we have implemented a new program, CHEMwriter, which has many advantages over existing programs. This program has powerful and user-friendly features that far surpass the traditional basic command set found in most structure-entry programs. The program has been in use for several months at Kodak. Some users have reported that they can enter many structures with CHEMwriter faster than they can draw them on paper.

The CHEMwriter program allows chemical structures to be entered in a natural, intuitive, and rapid manner. CHEMwriter is a menu-driven computer graphics program. The primary display is shown in Fig. 1.3. As a recovery feature, the UNDO command in the menu area on the left allows each structure-entry step to be undone. The REDO command allows

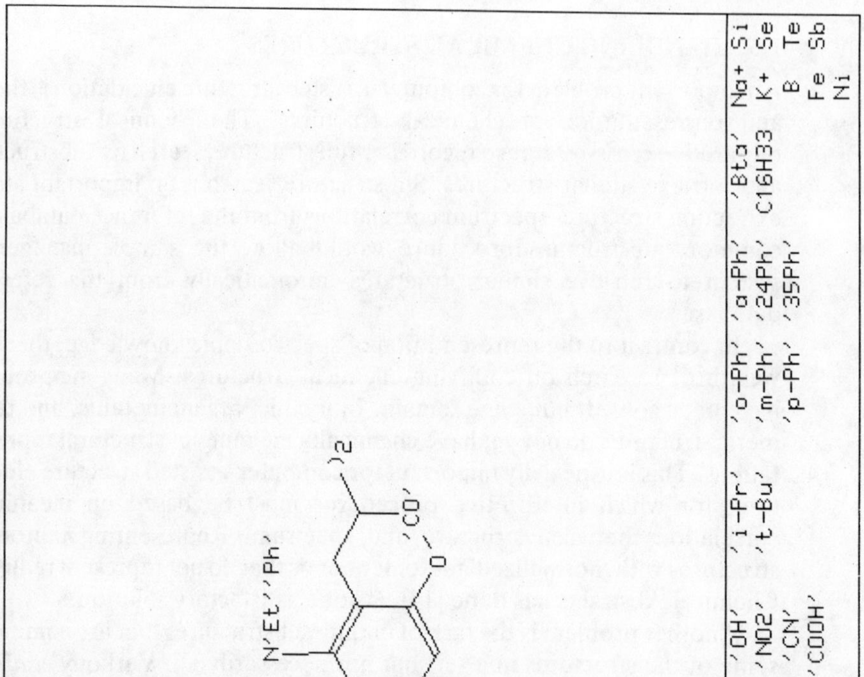

Fig. 1.3 — Structure entry.

operations that have been undone to be redone. If it is wished to use a structure from the previous session, perhaps as a starting point for the current structure, an initial access of REDO or UNDO will fetch it. Each user has the option of repositioning menu commands and symbols to tailor the program to his needs.

One of the more powerful facilities is the use of chemical symbols, e.g. the CH_3OOC in Fig. 1.3 to represent carbomethoxy. The SUBSTITUENTS, INSERT, and REPLACE commands provide the user a great amount of flexibility in enetering symbol strings. The strings that can be interpreted by CHEMwriter are most often the ones used by chemists, but can also include some that are outside normal chemical conventions. The following are strings that can be interpreted by the program. $CH_3CH_2CH_2CH_3$, $CH_3(CH_2)_3CH_3$, C_5H_{12}, $CH_3C_3H_6CH_3$, and $CH_3C_4H_9$ all represent n-pentane. $CH_3CH(NO_2)CH_3$, $CH_3(NO_2)CHCH_3$, and CHHH(NOO)CHCHHH all represent 2-nitropropane. $(CH_3)_2$ is ethane. $((CH_3)_2CH)_2$ is 2,3-dimethylbutane. C_6F_5COOH is pentafluorobenzoic acid. C_6H_{12} is cyclohexane. $CH_3CH(COO^-)CH_3$ is isopropylcarboxylate. PF_6^- is a hexafluorophosphate anion. $HOCH_2CHOHCH_2OH$ is glycerine. If the user is in doubt of CHEMwriter's interpretation, he can access the REDRAW command twice, and CHEMwriter will interpret the structure and display it as a conventional stick diagram. By accessing UNDO the user can then return to the structure he entered.

An extremely useful feature is the ability to define and use 'superatoms', a structural fragment with up to six attachments, that is referenced by name. Superatoms, the strings set apart by apostrophes in the lower-right menu of Fig. 1.3, can also be used in symbol strings; e.g. superatoms are used in the ethylphenylamino group in Fig. 1.3. CHEMwriter includes many template facilities to initiate structure entry from a starting structure or connect templates to an existing structure.

Another powerful and unique feature of CHEMwriter is its ability to interpret parenthetical expressions. In the structure in Fig. 1.3, the parenthetical expression is used to represent a dimer. This structure can be interpreted and redisplayed with two accesses of the REDRAW menu item. The resulting structure is shown in Fig. 1.4. This step requires a routine to display the chemical structure directly from the connection table. An approach to this problem that does not require a template dictionary of ring systems has been published [16]. We have recently extended this program to include the display of structures with stereochemistry.

Substructure search is a demanding task that should ideally be off-loaded from a general-purpose processor to special-purpose processors. These special-purpose parallel processors would implement the search in parallel. The Chemical Abstracts Service has divided a large database among several minicomputers [17]. Each minicomputer implements substructure search in a traditional manner but only for a subset of the database. Wipke and Rogers have simulated a parallel implementation of the backtracking step of substructure search [18]. The 'substructure search machine' (SSM in Fig. 1.2) is a special-purpose parallel processor that would off-load the task from

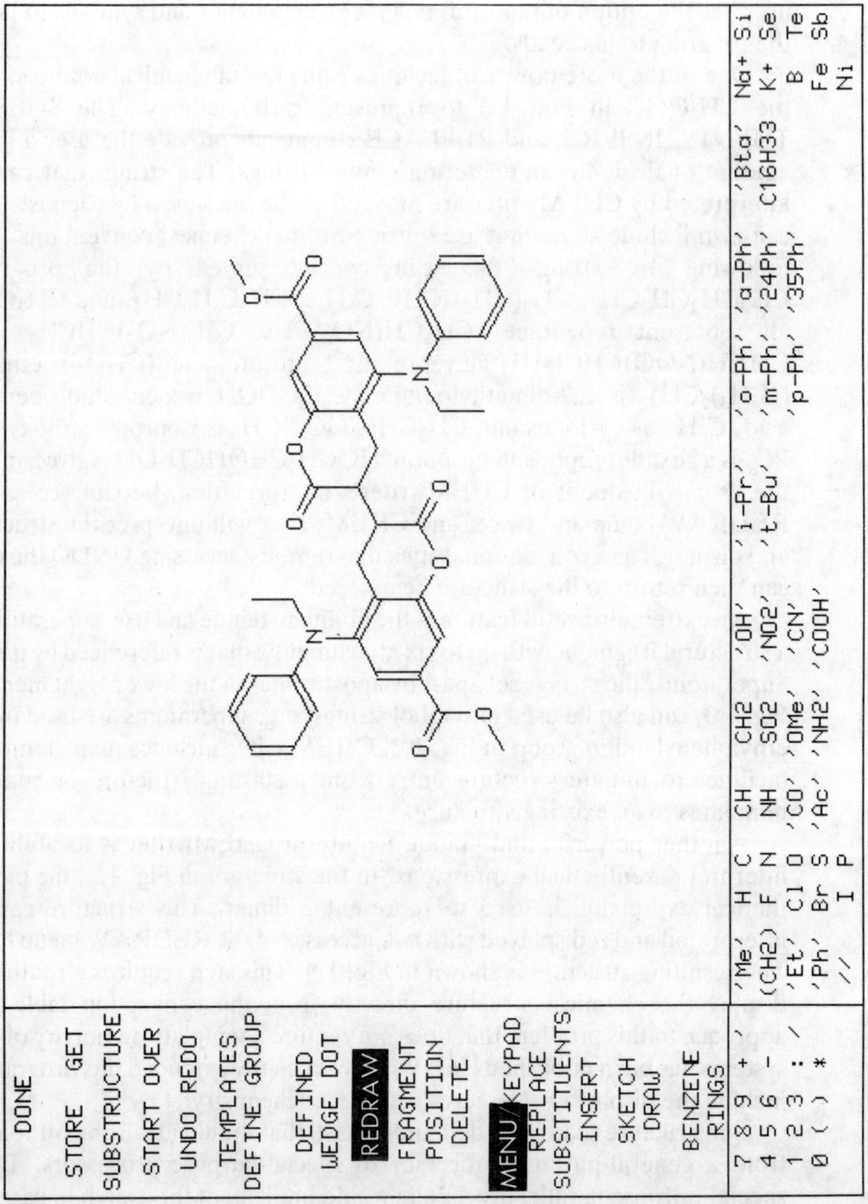

Fig. 1.4 — Structure display.

the structure-elucidation host in the proposed spectroscopy network. The implementation is similar to Chemical Abstracts Service's implementation. Microcomputers dedicated to the process would each search a subset of the entire structure file. In other words, the parallelism is with respect to the database rather than to the search algorithm as in Wipke and Rogers's implementation. In addition, the structure file would be stored in the RAM memory of the micros to eliminate time-consuming disk accesses. A traditional substructure search facility would still be implemented on the structure-elucidation host system to ensure local self-sufficiency. The user initiating a substructure search request would transparently initiate a request to use the SSM hardware; if it was not available, the search would be implemented on the host. Additional microcomputers could be added to improve response time by reducing the size of the subsets of the database that each microcomputer would search.

1.6 SUMMARY

The intent of this chapter was to evaluate the current status of computer-assisted structure elucidation. Suggestions were made where appropriate. The spectral databases that have been created are plagued with problems. It is hoped that future database developers will pay more attention to quality than quantity. It is generally more time-consuming to correct errors than to make the original entry. New databases should include the entire spectrum and the connection-table-like representation for the chemical structure. The database must represent diverse structure types. At the minimum, the database must be structurally relevant to the company's business.

The computer representation of spectroscopic knowledge must be far more sophisticated than the current correlation-table-like data structures in order to deal with the ambiguity inherent in the structure-elucidation process; however, it is suggested that perhaps in some cases the ambiguity is more apparent than real. Expert systems must fully exploit all the available information. They do not need to operate in the same way as a spectroscopist. People and computers each have inherent advantages. The computer has better recall of information than a spectroscopist has. It also has a better ability to handle a very large number of details at the same time, but fails, often miserably, in its ability to make the best use of the information. The chemist, with his current superior problem-solving ability, would most likely outperform the computer when given the same information, correlations, and raw data. It may be possible to impart to a computer some problem-solving ability by giving it access to enough pieces of information (far more than a person could handle) for it to resolve the apparently ambiguous problem. For example, the computer could make use of correlations that contain substantial probabilistic details, and these correlations could be derived automatically from a database during the computer's analysis of the problem, in such a way that they change as conclusions are reached. In other words, the correlation for a sulphonamide would dynamically change if it was known that a nitro group was unlikely to be present (both groups have a band near 1350 cm^{-1}). It is reasonable to expect that the computer will have a superior ability to solve many problems when it has substantially more information than the chemist has or could assimilate.

The importance of integrating sample-management, reference-database management, and expert-system software is emphasized. The practical application of computer technology in spectroscopy laboratories requires this kind of integration. Spectroscopy laboratories should be networked to facilitate the exchange of software and spectral data throughout a large organization.

The handling of chemical structures is a fundamental problem, but much is known. Programs should be more accommodating to the chemist. The chemical-symbol string parser in the CHEMwriter program is a good example. The representation of tautomers and various other structures needs further development. Procedures for the detection of substructures common to a subset of a given structure set are needed.

These problems are not insurmountable, but they are challenging. It will be interesting to see how the accomplishments of the last two decades of research in computer-assisted structure elucidation compare with the state of the art after two more decades have elapsed. Many researchers in artificial intelligence believe that the computers of the future will have problem-solving mechanisms that are superior to those of people. Perhaps the overzealous current claim of a program that "surpasses all humans at its task and, as a consequence, has caused a redefinition of the roles of humans and machines in chemical research" [2] will then be history. My guess is that the current gap between the problem-solving mechanism of the chemist and that of the computer will narrow; but the greatest improvement in the computer's problem-solving ability will come from increasing the amount of information available to the computer. The computer will play a complementary role rather than outperform the chemist at all structure-elucidation tasks.

REFERENCES

[1] R. K. Lindsay, B. G. Buchanan, E. A. Feigenbaum and J. Lederberg, *Applications of Artificial Intelligence for Organic Chemistry — The DENDRAL Project*; McGraw-Hill, New York, 1980.

[2] F. Hayes-Roth, D. A. Waterman and D. B. Lenat, *Building Expert Systems*, p. 9. Addison Wesley, London, 1983.

[3] M. E. Munk, C. A. Shelley, H. B. Woodruff and M. O. Trulson, *Z. Anal. Chem.*, 1982, **313**, 473.

[4] S. Sasaki and H. Abe, in *Computer Applications in Chemistry*, S. R. Heller and R. Potezone (eds.), pp. 185–206. Elsevier, New York, 1983.

[5] H. B. Woodruff and G. M. Smith, *Anal. Chem.*, 1980, **52**, 2321.

[6] Information System Karlsruhe, c/o Fachinformationszentrum, P.O. Box 2465, D-7500 Karlsruhe, Federal Republic of Germany.

[7] Nicolet Instrument Corporation, 5225 Verona Road, Madison, WI 53711.

[8] National Bureau of Standards, U.S. Department of Commerce, Washington, DC 20234.
[9] Fein-Marquart Associates Inc., 7215 York Road, Baltimore, MD 21212.
[10] C. A. Shelley and M. E. Munk, *Anal. Chem.*, 1982, **54**, 516.
[11] T. D. Salatin and W. L. Jorgensen, *J. Org. Chem.*, 1980, **45**, 2043.
[12] M. O. Trulson and M. E. Munk, *Anal. Chem.*, 1983, **55**, 2137.
[13] R. Wilensky, *AI Magazine*, 1984, Spring, 29.
[14] J. Mockus and R. E. Stobaugh, *J. Chem. Inf. Comput. Sci.*, 1980, **20**, 18.
[15] T. H. Varkony, Y. Shiloach and D. H. Smith, *J. Chem. Inf. Comput. Sci.*, 1979, **19**, 104.
[16] C. A. Shelley, *J. Chem. Inf. Comput. Sci.*, 1983, **23**, 61.
[17] N. A. Farmer and M. P. O'Hara, *Database*, 1980, **3**, 10.
[18] W. T. Wipke and D. Rogers, *J. Chem. Inf. Comput. Sci.*, 1984, **24**, 255.

2

The DARC Philosophy of Knowledge Information Processing Systems: Evolution of Chemical Database-Management Problems

Jacques-Emile Dubois and **Yves Sobel**
Association pour la Recherche et la Developpement en Informatique Chimique, 25, rue Jussieu, 75005, Paris, France and Institut de Topologie et de Dynamique des Systèmes de l'Université Paris 7, associé au CNRS, 1, rue Guy de la Brosse, 75005, Paris, France

2.1 INTRODUCTION

In chemistry, the problem of data-handling in spectroscopy is dealt with by documentary search, either of exact or neighbouring spectral data in banks or by computer-assisted calculation of these data, provided appropriate laws or empirical rules (expert systems) are available.

When the problem is stated in this way, it appears very simple, as long as the perception level of the data is low and the volume of data is not great. However, problems arise as soon as attempts are made to answer questions which are neither precisely defined nor 'frozen' in access time. In the retrieval of specific information from large masses of data, the difficulties are the same as those encounterd by an editor attempting to cover a subject in both depth and breadth, to serve the generalist in need of first-hand information and the professional looking for more precise data or for data sources.

In fact, a data item is never well enough described and is rarely sufficiently well located in context to satisfy the most searching queries. Thanks to informatics, we can improve those documentary organizations which were rejected because they slowed up research too much. This can be done by imposing a technical localization on files, without considering the real space of the data. At first, as with all new methods, the speed of these improved procedures seems advantageous. Nonetheless, great care must be taken, since the size of the computer tools to be set up is inextricably linked to the fineness and detail of the basic data, to the power of the data-management system, to the compromises of the query system and to the flexibility of the end-user query languages.

Subsequently, as the limitations of the first generation of informatic solutions were revealed, more systematic solutions were organized. The database management systems (DBMS) were proposed, as a second generation of tools fitted for different applications. These seemed promising because they offered more general solutions for simple systems, different classifications for objects not linked to each other, such as inventories, civic status, etc. However, they do not solve the problem of data description itself. In some instances, the real description of objects shows the poorer achievement of these standard DBMS. It is therefore advisable to reconsider, with an eye to complementarity, the problems of conceptual description of objects and of their handling in DBMS. In this context, let us note that chemistry, like other highly structured sciences, is capable of managing the localization of structural data in an appropriate space. This problem cannot be approached with proper rigour through systematic nomenclature that is too text-oriented, but needs a richer structural nomenclature with a rigour which will not suffer from compromises linked to manual use. Freed from these constraints of time, access and difficulty in handling complex and multiform descriptions, the potential developer of a chemical database and, even more, of a future knowledge bank, must return to taxonomy, grammar and the synthesis of object-describing languages. His objective must be to achieve a complex description, able to contain derived forms of canonical description which can be generated by programs.

However, the usual descriptions of objects are often reductionist in nature, i.e. they are based on a description of defined isolated parts of objects, whereas, in our opinion, it is essential to proceed towards a holistic description which takes into account the whole of the object, its location and its complexity, accessible by local ordering.

In this chapter we shall evoke the general principles basic to the conception of a factual data bank which would be open to gradual evolution, easy to update and capable of being used as the logistic tool of a spectroscopic knowledge bank. In the first part, we shall set forth these aspects; in the second, we shall look at the subsystems of current chemical DBMS with structures which are highly evolutionary. We shall also approach the problem of creative data, although this will take us slightly beyond the framework of this chapter. In the final part, we shall evoke the kinds of problems posed by creating several very varied spectroscopic banks. Should certain subsystems be integrated? Should they be federated, thus allowing them a good deal of autonomy? The answers to these questions have evolved together with firmware and the arrival of powerful microcomputers. Our discussion will be modified by this recent technical evolution of computer hardware.

2.2 TRENDS IN CHEMICAL DBMS

The evolution of factual data banks in chemistry and, in particular, inorganic spectroscopy, runs in two principal streams.

2.2.1 Evolution of DBMS: information engineering

First, database management systems (DBMS) have been making great strides in dealing with complex data. This is essential because chemical structures and their associated spectra involve far more complex data than those usually handled by general DBMS [1–3].

Figure 2.1 illustrates some problems arising in trying to manage such

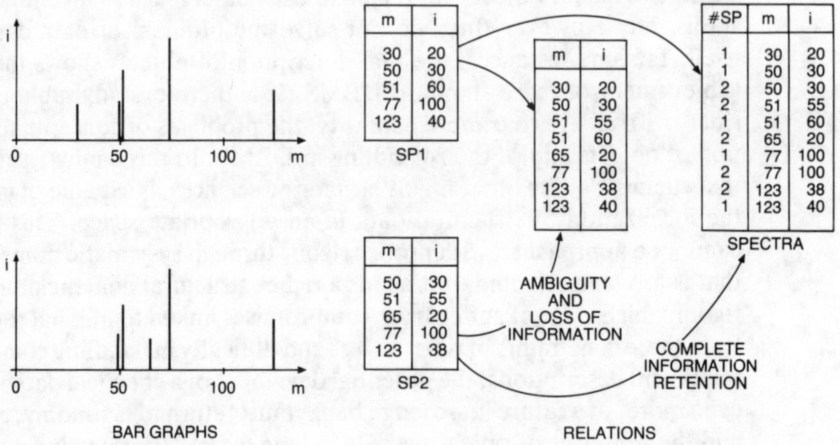

Fig. 2.1 — Relational DBMS. Two mass spectra SP1 and SP2 of nitrobenzene can be combined into one record by a simple merging (middle) or by retention of complete information (right).

information by a relational DBMS. Table 2.1 shows the adaptations necessary for dealing with some specific points of spectral information. This evolution has been gradually transforming DBMS into true decision-aiding systems (Figs. 2.2, 2.3).

Ideally, they are capable of interacting with the user in a language close to his own language (Fig. 2.4).

The complexity of the data handled is more and more controlled by their intrinsic nature as well as by the degree of precision with which the specialist in the field has assessed them. The proportion of available information which he models and represents effectively depends on this precision, which in turn is less and less limited by technical considerations. Sophisticated systems for handling chemical information, such as DARC [4–7] or DENDRAL [8], have in fact played a pioneering and decisive role in the general evolution of knowledge engineering tools.

2.2.2 Improved informatic transformation of chemical information

The second stream involves just that gradual clarification in the chemist's conception of structural and spectral data: their nature, their link with experimental phenomena, their use. In the beginning, this conception was

Table 2.1 — Adaptions necessary for dealing with some specific types of spectral information: (a) for spectra represented in the form of peak abscissa/peak height tables; (b) for mass spectra; (c) for ^{13}C NMR spectra

```
(a) for two spectra represented by relations SP1(x,h), SP2(x,h)
        where x is peak abscissa
        and   h is peak height:

SP2 (=)  SP1 <==> CARD(SP1 U SP2) = CARD(SP1 EQUIJOIN SP2 OVER x,h)
SP2 (<=) SP1 <==> CARD(   SP2   ) = CARD(SP1 EQUIJOIN SP2 OVER x,h)
```

```
(b) for two mass spectra represented by relations MS1(m,i), MS2(m,i)
        where m is mass/charge ratio (peak abscissa)
        and   i is relative abundance (peak height):

MS2 (=/MS/10%)  MS1 <==> CARD(MS1 U MS2)
                       = CARD(MS1 EQUIJOIN MS2 OVER m
                              WHERE MS1.i-10% < MS2.i < MS1.i+10%)
MS2 (<=/MS/10%) MS1 <==> CARD(   MS2   )
                       = CARD(MS1 EQUIJOIN MS2 OVER m
                              WHERE MS1.i-10% < MS2.i < MS1.i+10%)
```

```
(c) for two 13C NMR spectra represented by
        relations CNMR1(delta,mult), CNMR2(delta,mult)
        where delta is chemical shift (peak abscissa)
        and   mult is multiplicity:

CNMR2 (=/CNMR/1ppm)  CNMR1 <==> CARD(CNMR1 U CNMR2)
                              = CARD(CNMR1 EQUIJOIN CNMR2 OVER mult
                                WHERE CNMR1.delta-1ppm < CNMR2.delta
                                AND   CNMR2.delta < CNMR1.delta+1ppm)
CNMR2 (<=/CNMR/1ppm) CNMR1 <==> CARD(   CNMR2   )
                              = CARD(CNMR1 EQUIJOIN CNMR2 OVER mult
                                WHERE CNMR1.delta-1ppm < CNMR2.delta
                                AND   CNMR2.delta < CNMR1.delta+1ppm)
```

limited by its narrow relationship with each experimental field and therefore reflected but poorly all the available information concerning each structure. Another weakness was the relative poverty of the available mathematical modelling tools with which to display the real complexity of the data. Indeed, both the informatic tools and the tools used in searching for relationships between data, often badly mutilated the available information. This conception was based on procedures of data analysis and informatic handling of information which were only rudimentary in form. In the DARC system, rather than remain subject to these limitations, we chose from the start to improve the tools for mathematical modelling [9,10], relation searching [11,12], and informatic handling of information whenever this seemed necessary or desirable. We followed the example of those pioneers of structural chemistry whose role was essential in the development of graph theroy, primarily because they did not possess an appropriate mathematical model which would enable them to represent adequately their conception of experimental reality. The need for such an approach became very clear later on, as the processes which mutilated available information came into conflict with the borders of limited fields of applicability. At times, it was possible to push back those borders by extensions and generalizations. Now, however, we see clearly that this could only lead to limited progress. A method with no *a priori* mutilation can only be envisaged within the framework of a system capable of adapting the precision of its modelling to that of the experimental data [11.12]. The DARC system took on this difficult challenge at a time when the necessary tools were not yet shaped. At the crossroads of progress in knowledge engineering tools and of regression in *a priori* mutilation of chemical information, this decision proved most fruitful.

2.3 SPOTLIGHT ON RECENT RAPIDLY EVOLVING SECTORS OF DBMS

2.3.1 Specific information *vs.* generic rules

Apart from the handling of specific data, i.e. immediate images of experimental results stocked in factual data banks, the rules establishing connections between structural and spectral data (Fig. 2.2) stem from different origins: scientific theories, expert knowledge, empirical laws. They appear in various forms. A mathematical relationship links scalar or vectorial characteristics of the structure with analogous characteristics of the spectrum. These rule banks interact vigorously with the factual data banks in different fields. Factual data bank data are controlled through regularities [11,12] recorded in the rule banks. In turn, the reliability of the rules is judged [11,12] by comparing their predictions with the specific correspondences stored in the factual data banks (Fig. 2.2). Finally, given the quantity of dormant data stockpiled in factual data banks, it seems clear that the future lies in using such data in order to compile interactive rule banks.

2.3.2 Knowledge information processing systems

Indeed, such dormant data, though potentially important, may be incompletely exploited because of the limitations of certain expert advice or because of scientific hindrances. The Knowledge Information Processing System (KIPS) of the future [13–15] must be able to rely on intelligent procedures, at different stages of creation and consultation, in order to call up the strategic sets of existing data needed to answer given queries. The KIPS must also be provided with the built-in capacity to evaluate both their potential and their weakness concerning a given target problem. To fulfil these various requirements, we are now developing appropriate mechanisms [7]. These can be summed up as follows.

1. To Wake Up Stored Data so as to produce creative data and linked meta-rules (WUSD software).
2. To Spot Missing Key Data (SMKD software).
3. To instigate an External Search for production of certain Key Data (ESKD software).

In this way we hope to build an original general Knowledge Autoproduction Generator (KAG), which will be optimized for different structural and associated data sets.

From its inception, the DARC system aimed at constituting various factual data bases [16,17]. Its originality resided in the double objective it set for these. In the first place, it naturally aimed at supplying the user with data stocked more or less interactively. In the second place, it aimed at supplying a corpus with specific organization rules [18]. These were to make it possible, in turn, to generate the rule bases which current expert systems rely on [11,12,19,20]. These results are achieved by a careful and in-depth formalization of factual bases and by creating the necessary rule generators.

2.3.3 Multilevel relationship between structures and ^{13}C NMR spectra

Carbon-13 NMR adds a further correspondence between atoms and assigned peaks to the global relationship between structures and spectra [1] (Fig. 2.2a). It supplies a supplementary relationship between components of the test compound and components of the measurement results. Thus we have to distinguish the implied relationship between the substructures composed of given atoms, and the subspectra containing the corresponding peaks. This relationship is quite complex (Fig. 2.3). Between structures and spectra we have a one-to-many relation, i.e. for each structure we have several spectra. However, we suppose here that for each spectrum we have a single associated structure. Between structures and substructures we have a many-to-one relation, i.e. several substructures are extractable from a given structure, and a given substructure is usually found in numerous structures. As the relation between spectra and subspectra is analogous, the relationship between substructures and subspectra is also 'many-to-many'.

The position of a substructure inside a structure is memorized by using atom numbers. Two kinds of information can be distinguished: the substructure and the numbering information. If a given substructure can come from two different structures the numbering will generally be different. The correspondence established is that between the substructure (with its numbering) and a subspectrum.

We have observed [21] that carbon-focused environments in a substructure can be limited to give a partial match with approximately constant subspectra. Such Environments are Limited, Concentric and Ordered within the framework of their DARC organization and so are called ELCOs.

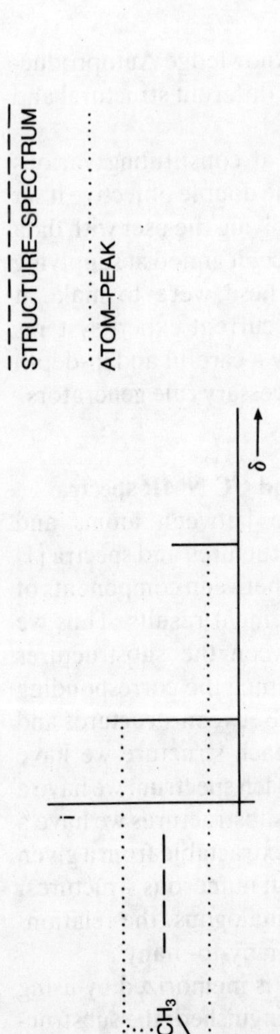

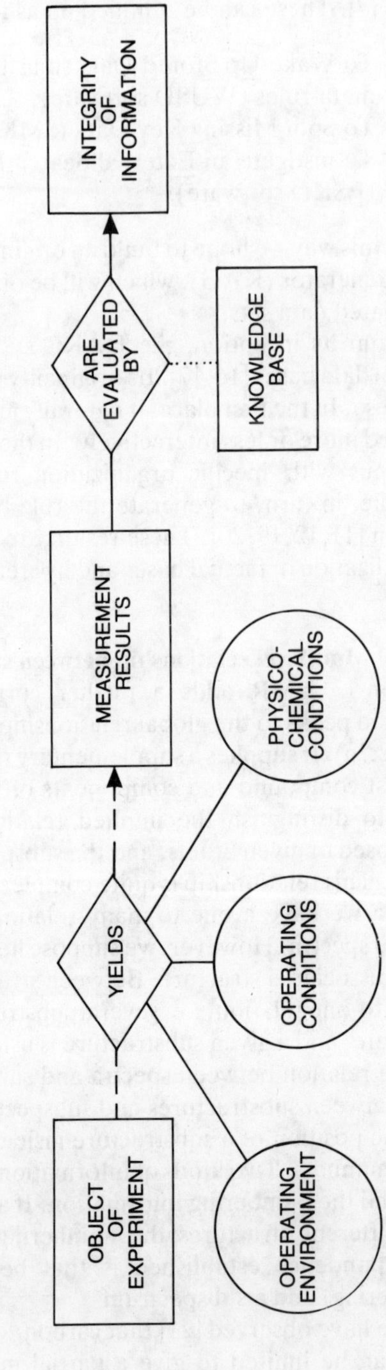

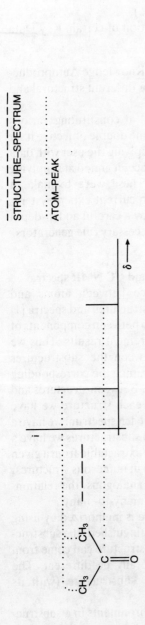

Fig. 2.2 — Simple and complex relationships in a scientific data bank. (a) To a global relationship between structures and ^{13}C NMR spectra (dashed arrow) a correspondence between atoms and assigned peaks is added. (b) The future of the data banks lies in using dormant data stockpiled in factual data banks. This can be achieved only by linking all attributes (circles), relationships (diamonds), and entities (boxes) into interactive rule banks.

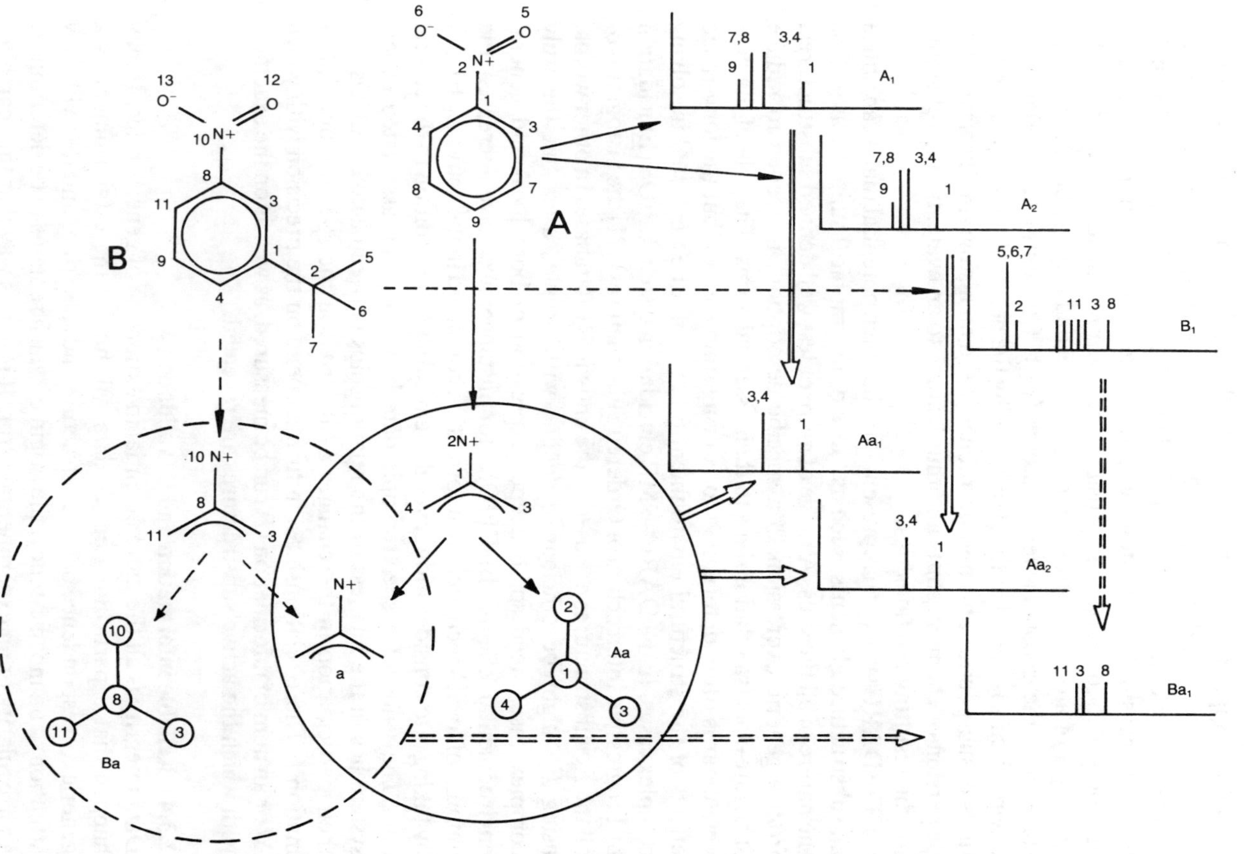

Fig. 2.3 — Multilevel many-to-many relationships between structured data. Two structures A and B are related to three ^{13}C NMR spectra A_1, A_2, and B_1, respectively. Accordingly, the common substructure a, described by different atom numberings Aa and Bb, is related to three subspectra Aa_1, Aa_2, and Ba_1, respectively.

The problem is to find the appropriate border limiting the active environment [4–6,11,12] of each ^{13}C nucleus considered as a focus. It can be solved with good approximation by systematically testing concentric (or equidistant) borders around the ^{13}C focus. The first layer of bonds attached to the focus constitutes an environment (called type E_a) which is usually too small; the chemical shifts of ^{13}C atoms with the same E_a but in different structures are too widely dispersed. It is usually necessary to include in addition the first layer of atoms (environment E_A), the second layer of bonds (E_b), and sometimes the second layer of atoms (E_B). Concentric development of environments is halted at the stage yielding the best assignment of substructures to subspectra. This optimization is based on histograms displaying the dispersion of chemical shifts and thus leading to an evaluation of reliability for the resulting relationships.

The DARC structural representation has such potential that it can utilize all substructure elements, such as those of its graphical support, as well as the nature of all the sites. A range of more or less well defined substructures, from a generic expression to a specific description, is needed to reduce structure–spectra relationships to their essential terms. The role of the next neighbour is often determined for solving simple cases, but the long-range effects of the structural environment (ε) must not be neglected in solving complex cases. In the DARC–NMR elucidation system EPIOS (Elucidation by Progressive Intersection of Ordered Substructures) [21] the histograms of all the E_b substructures are used in the knowledge database. In other words, using E_b might be efficient in dealing with simple cases, but the truly complex cases need some deeper expression of both local and general environmental effects. In EPIOS, for instance, we have increased the amount of local spectroscopic information contained in the active E_b ELCO by taking into consideration several chemical shifts in addition to the central one. The value of a spectroscopic data bank or of an associated expert system lies in the fineness of the relationships between active ELCOs and their participation in the changes ΔI incurred in the spectroscopic information I. These relationships, in turn, depend on the precision with which ΔI or an item of information (I) can be measured, as well as on the exactness with which the active substructures are revealed.

2.3.4 Reliable information and its validation

Data integrity is all the more essential in extraction of generic rules. It may happen that a particular item of data will hinder the establishment of a generic correspondence between structure and spectrum, and this will draw attention to an inconsistency, the origin of which remains to be determined: an irregularity or an experimental error. It is in this way that the search for generic rules intervenes in the validation process (Fig. 2.2). However, if such an inconsistency exists but escapes detection, the rule will be based on false premises. The error will then be propagated throughout the data predicted by means of this rule, and the result may be poorly simulated spectra or poorly elucidated structures.

It is therefore, vital to detect and correct errors as far as possible: this is an important part of data acquisition [17]. The ideal would be to avoid the principal causes of error from the start, but this is as yet unrealistic, as there are too many links in the information chain.

All data banks are essentially limited in reliability by the indexing stage. Each stage, publication, transcription onto indexing sheets and spectra acquisition, carries the risk of error due to manual handling, and these operations are long and expensive in wages. A direct connection [16] between GC/MS and data banks allows shortcuts which eliminate the many error-producing stages involved in manual indexing.

That portion of the indexing which is not wholly automated — the structural information and certain experimental conditions — is also more reliable and more complete because it is implemented on the spot by the spectrometer operator. For example, in the CIS bank, the experimental conditions are often absent or incomplete, because they were not indexed immediately on taking the spectrum.

Furthermore, the possibility of interrogating the data bank on the same site as the spectrometer, with direct connection between the mass-spectrometer and data-bank computers is not merely practical and fast, but also means that the whole experimental spectrum will be available for use, and this is of major significance in identifying the components of a mixture that is unresolved by chromatography.

2.3.5 Interaction with the user in his own language

We are dealing here with input, interaction and output mechanisms that regulate man/machine relations or, in this case, the dialogue between the chemist and the computer (Fig. 2.4). The DARC system was based from the start on this dialogue taking place in natural chemical language, i.e. through chemical formulas, global entities or substructures [17,18]. The DBMS must contain structures and substructures, and we had to decide [7] whether it would be preferable to store all the formulas and fragments at the input stage or to invent an input cycle which would encode the image and reconstitute it each time on request.

The GRAPHEDIT system which we adopted indeed reconstitutes the image by means of the storage code and provides a legible display based on atom connectivity. This merger of powerful graph facilities with our data-handling systems is essential and is also coherent with our decision to give priority to structure-drawing over the systematic name, which is only associated with the structure. This, very early on, led the DARC system to implement interactive systems on different graphic materials (black/white or colour), (e.g. the Evans and Sutherland Multiple Picture System graphic station or the various Tektronix displays).

We have been able to provide graphic assistance to the input of structural data by data blocks with adequate software or step-by-step input with our home-made 'topocodeur' [22] machine, which provides fast input thanks to a special chemical keyboard and a matrix network serving as an electronic drawing board. Flexibility and compatibility of access to different visual terminals and printing devices have been attained.

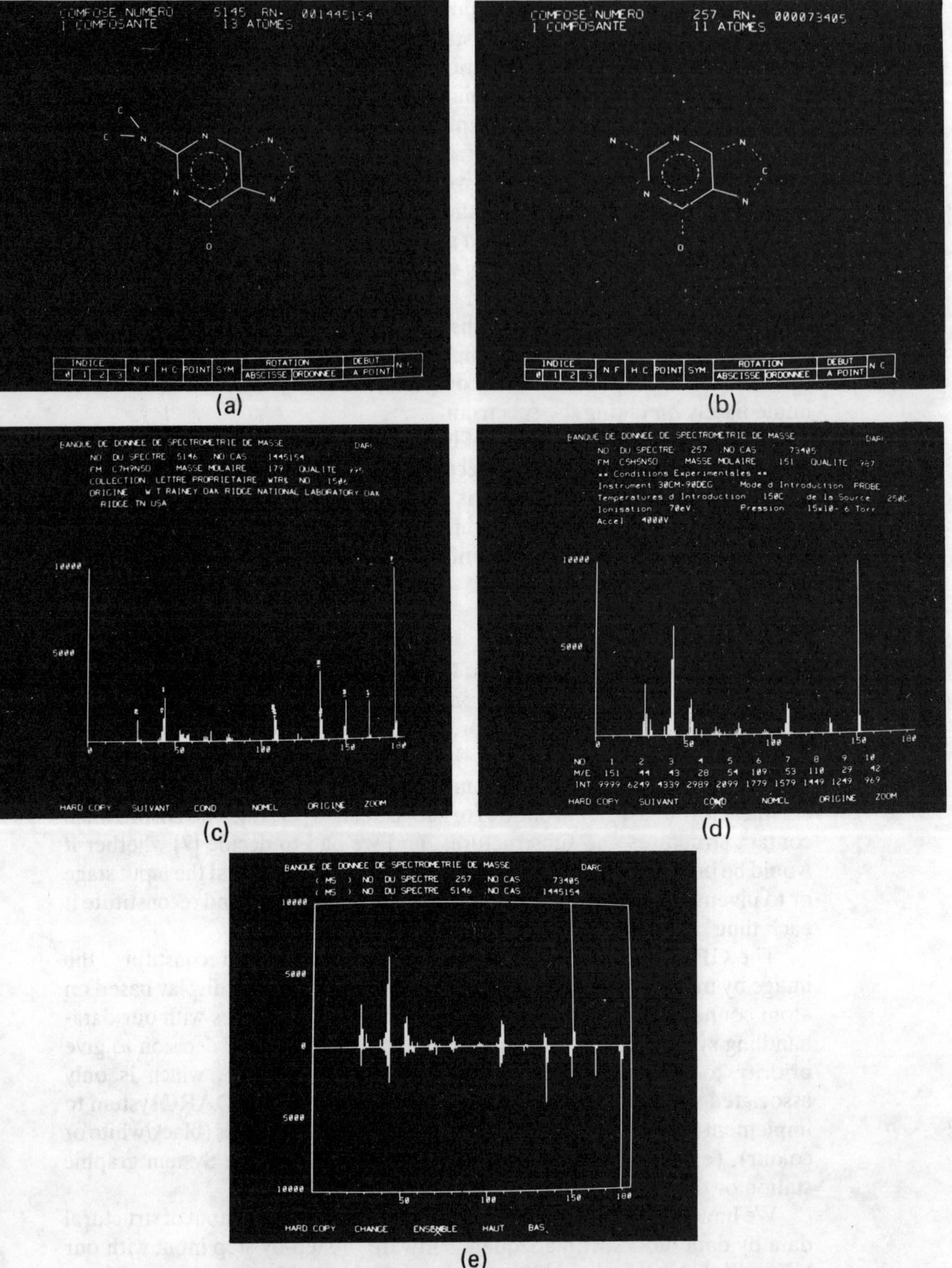

Fig. 2.4 — Data display in DARC by using GRAPHEDIT is employed for chemical structures (a), substructures (b), their spectra (c) and (d), or for handling data esential for the problem in question (e) [in this case a comparison of the two mass spectra (c) and (d)].

2.3.6 Defined and fuzzy situations

Flexibility is primarily a function of the topological tools of specific and generic structures. In the DARC syntax, some generic structures appear as a result of the special step-by-step descriptors. Each site is described stepwise: first generically, then specifically with regard to its character. Thus, introducing a chlorine atom into a substructure corresponds to three steps which engender two generic substructures (locating the future Cl site and specifiying its bond values) and to one explicit or specific substructure (definition of the Cl). Besides this generic aspect of graph construction and thus of the associated descriptors, other more generic expressions of basic graphs exist. We must also note the possibilities available to the user for specifying a query either in a very generic and thus general way, or with restrictions included, e.g. a list of atoms, e.g. $-C^*\{C,O,S,N,...\}$ (which means that the atoms C,O,S,N etc. can be attached to atom C*), located at a specific position of the query graph. Some consider this type of limitation to be an approach defining a precise fuzziness for a single, possible site. Others see it as the classical procedure used in the Markush formulas to specify a subset of formulas referred to in a patent. In other words, the user has access to the ordered DARC substructures, structures, and fuzzy or generic entities or sets of entities. Through these, he can interact with systems having internal concepts based on these structural items and their connections with various forms of located spectral information.

We have shown that the adjustment of a substructure (SS) to an information item (*I*) for the purpose of obtaining an efficient SS/*I* couple is both *information-oriented* and *precision-oriented.* Difficulties arise because a data information bank contains scientifically verifiable information based on expert rules *and* a very important mass of purely experimental and non-correlated information. Defining the SS/*I* relation is, therefore, most delicate. This situation justifies such varied approaches as that of critical substructures or clusters contained in spectra, or even that of the global study of non-deconvoluted spectra [23] so as to take advantage of the database wealth. SS identification tools and creative algorithms for candidate structures based on them require the active descriptors SS/*I* or SS/ΔI to be combined intelligently.

2.4 ISOLATED, INTEGRATED OR FEDERATED SPECTROSCOPIC DATA BANKS

Once the requirements to be fulfilled by a spectroscopic data bank have been recorded, it remains to determine its relations with other chemical data banks, spectroscopic or otherwise. A completely integrated solution using a single structural data base seems utopian and not particularly useful in the light of previous experience (CIS [24], DARC/PLURIDATA, KISIK [25]). Indeed the structural categories for which two types of spectra are available rarely overlap. The structural characteristics to be retained in the data bank can also differ from one spectroscopic method to another. In any event, the experimental conditions will differ, as well as the generic structural characteristics involved in the correspondence rules (Fig. 2.3 and Table 2.1).

The experience gained in using one spectroscopic method is seldom widely applicable to another, since the two kinds of spectral information obtained are not identically linked to the structural context. This means that though economic and structural reasons exist for unifying spectroscopy banks in simple documentation, in reality a search for points of intersection is useful only for transferring a problem from one technique to another.

At the other extreme, it would be a pity to consider that each bank should be organized in total independence of all the others. Clearly, the tools for handling one structural database apply to all the others even if the way in which they are used differs slightly. However, interaction between different chemical data banks, whether spectroscopic or not, involves many other aspects. The optimal organization of a set of chemical data banks is thus probably a *federated organization*, which does not have the unwieldiness of an integrated system, but allows for using synergy of information, and optimizing tool conception and profitability.

The advantage of federated data banks lies in the possibility they furnish for communication in ordinary language. This feature allows data transfer on any desired level of precision, and means that at any given moment an integrated subset can be extracted. For the user, federation renders the set of banks user-friendly, since the end-user language and the up-dating procedures are similar and follow the same syntax. Programming, clarification and maintenance are optimized, since modules can be used as they are, adapted from others by simple parametric changes, or generated from general meta-modules. On a more fundamental level, which explains all these properties, a common logic can be implemented from common general principles.

In addition to the synergy which stems from the similarities in federated banks, far more complex interactions can be implemented between modules which do not belong to the same field. This is how the DARC/PARIS [7] system for generating reaction networks simulates mass spectra by using a fragmentation-rule base, established by means of the spectrometric bank.

2.5 FEDERATED DATA INFORMATION BANKS

Federated knowledge engineering tools using coherent languages going beyond the borders of spectroscopy are particularly essential in mass spectrometry. The apparent originality and complexity of mass spectrometry in comparison with classical absorption spectroscopy (NMR, infrared, ultraviolet) stem from the fact that the comparison can only be made in terms of experimental results (the spectra) and their ordinary use (elucidation). However, mass spectrometry is closer in character to chemical characterization procedures (characteristic reactions, preparation of derivatives) and this explains its sensitivity to experimental conditions as well as its relatively poor reproducibility. In fact, the study of fragmentation reactions in the reactor constituted by the spectrometer constitutes an important branch of this subject. Therefore a generator of reaction networks, relying on a knowledge base comprising generic fragmentation, must be capable of interacting with a mass spectrometry bank in order to validate the simulation and structural elucidation. A project called MASOPSYS employs the DARC/PARIS generator in this way [7].

Elucidation work calling upon the synergy of spectroscopic methods will rely more and more on complementary strategies where knowledge banks are concerned, and on global identification strategies.

The organization of future elucidation KIPS will be at best of a federal type but considerable care has to be taken to achieve real working KIPS going beyond elementary elucidation or routine structural determination. Solving the problems of higher complexity in elucidating the DARC philosophy requires (1) increase in the precision of the substructure/artificial intelligence packages, (2) improving the strategies for embedding them in the appropriate representation spaces defined by structure and property relationships, and (3) combining different approaches dealing with structure generation and spectra generation [23,26].

2.6 CONCLUSIONS

Throughout this chapter we have stressed the growing importance of artificial intelligence procedures in spectoscopic data banks. In ordinary use, they make for rapid and user-friendly access. We have also drawn attention to the strong interaction needed between intelligent data banks and knowledge banks. This interaction must rely on a common logic allowing for validation of data and also for the shaping of rules to be included in the knowledge.

A true Knowledge Autoproduction Generator (KAG) should even stimulate the experimentation necessary when key data are lacking for production, clarification or validation of meta-rules. However, the goals and tasks of data banks and expert systems imply a clear-cut division in their methods of procedure, if confusion is to be avoided in their global and local managements and their constant updating. Indeed, both systems possess the adaptability, but also the fragility, of true living organisms.

Their orientations and tasks separate them, but their necessary interaction forces them to maintain intelligent federated relations and also implies that their evolution is concerted.

The considerations presented here encountered the difficulties met in the cognitive sciences and in artificial intelligence. As both hardware and software progress so rapidly, it is difficult to draw definitive conclusions as to what should be done in this field of spectroscopic DBMS, where tomorrow the user might have available on his bench the tools that formerly were centralized and thus remote from him.

Nonetheless, whatever the future achievements in the field of KIPS or in knowledge engineering, it is our belief that chemistry, and spectroscopy in particular, represents an excellent, if not the best, testing ground for evaluation of new methodologies or organization in DBMS and in artificial intelligence.

RFEFERENCES

[1] Y. Sobel, I. Dagane, M. Carabedian and J. E. Dubois, *Specific Features of Scientific Data Banks*, in *Role of Data in Scientific Progress*, P. S. Glaeser (ed.), Elsevier, Amsterdam, 1985.

[2] C. J. Date, *An Introduction to Database Systems*, 3rd Ed., Addison Wesley, Reading, Mass., 1981.

[3] P. P. Chen, *ACM Trans. Data Base Systems*, 1976, **1**, 9.

[4] J. E. Dubois, *J. Chem. Doc.*, 1973, **13**, 1.

[5] J. E. Dubois, *Ordered Chromatic Graph and Limited Environment Concept,* in *The Chemical Applications of Graph Theory*, A. T. Balaban, Academic Press, London, 1976.

[6] J. E. Dubois, *Isr. J. Chem.*, 1975, **14**, 17.

[7] J. E. Dubois and Y. Sobel, *J. Chem. Inf. Comput. Sci.*, 1985, **25,** 326.

[8] R. K. Lindsay, B. G. Buchanan, E. A. Feigenbaum and J. Lederberg, *Applications of Artifical Intelligence for Organic Chemistry: the DENDRAL Project*, McGraw-Hill, New York, 1980.

[9] J. E. Dubois, D. Laurent, A. Panaye and Y. Sobel, *Compt. Rend.*, 1975, **281C**, 687.

[10] G. Sicouri, Y. Sobel, R. Picchiottino and J. E. Dubois, *Compt. Rend.*, 1984, Série II, **299**, 523.

[11] J. E. Dubois, C. Mercier and Y. Sobel, *Compt. Rend.*, 1979, **289C**, 89.

[12] J. E. Dubois, C. Mercier and Y. Sobel, *Compt. Rend.*, 1981, Série II, **292**, 783.

[13] J. E. Dubois, *DARC Creative Data to Meet the Challenge of the Fifth Generation in Chemistry*, International Conference on Information and Knowledge (ICIK) 1984, Tokyo, Japan.

[14] G. Sicouri, Y. Sobel, R. Picchiottino and J. E. Dubois, in *Role of Data in Scientific Progress*, P. S. Glaeser (ed.) pp. 373–380. Elsevier, Amsterdam, 1985.

[15] E. Feigenbaum and P. M. McCorduck, *The Fifth Generation*, Addison Wesley, Reading, Mass., 1983.

[16] Y. Inoue, J. P. Lemaire and Y. Sobel, *GC–MS News*, 1981, **9**, 30

[17] R. Picchiottino, G. Georgoulis, G. Sicouri, A. Panaye and J. E. Dubois, *J. Chem. Inf. Comput. Sci.*, 1984, **24**, 241.

[18] R. Attias, *J. Chem. Inf. Comput. Sci.*, 1983, **23**, 102.

[19] R. Picchiottino, G. Sicouri and J. E. Dubois, in *Data for Science and Technology*, P. S. Glaeser (ed.), pp. 229–334. CODATA, North-Holland, 1983.

[20] R. Picchiottino, G. Sicouri and J. E. Dubois, *DARC-SYNOPSYS Expert System. Production Rules in Organic Chemistry and Application to Synthesis Design,* in *Computer Science and Data Bank*, Z. Hippe and J. E. Dubois (eds.) Polish Academy of Sciences, Warsaw, 1984.

[21] J. E. Dubois, M. Carabedian and I. Dagane, *Anal. Chim. Acta*, 1984, **158**, 217.
[22] J. E. Dubois and J. A. Miller, *Appareil pour le codage et la visualisation simultanée d'un graphe,* ANVAR Patent, 1974.
[23] M. Razinger, J. Zupan, M. Penca and B. Barlič, *J. Chem. Inf. Comput. Sci.*, 1980, **20**, 158.
[24] S. R. Heller, *J. Chem. Inf. Comput. Sci.*, 1980, **20**, 204.
[25] J. Zupan, M. Penca, M. Razinger, B. Barlič and D. Hadži, *Anal. Chim. Acta*, 1980, **122**, 103.
[26] J. E. Dubois, unpublished work.

3

Hierarchical ordering of spectral databases

Jure Zupan and **Marjana Novič**
"Boris Kidrič" Institute of Chemistry, Ljubljana, Yugoslavia

3.1 INTRODUCTION

The use of computerized spectrometers that can be linked to laboratory or main-frame computers, and thus the possibility of generating and maintaining libraries of many thousands of spectra has become reality in many scientific and industrial laboratories throughout the world. Although researchers are vitally interested in such libraries, the most common use of the recorded spectra is still comparison, referencing, search for similar spectra, etc. It is clear that the retrieval of the best match or the identity from the spectral library is a very important task, that should be achievable in any chemical information system of this kind. However, we feel that the retrieval is perhaps overemphasized in comparison with the information that could be obtained from a spectral library as a whole, i.e. any library of several thousand spectra will contain much more information than is needed to give the best match to a sample spectrum and this can be extracted if proper methods and algorithms are employed.

It must be said that the usual organization of computer storage for spectroscopic data (inverted and sequential files [1, 2]) allows little room for anything else than the retrieval and evaluation of reference spectra. Thus, the basic concept of storing and organization of data files has to be changed in order to achieve better information output.

In the present work the idea of hierarchical organization of databases to achieve hierarchical clustering of spectra of chemical compounds having similar or identical structural features is suggested and discussed. There are quite a number of problems to be solved before a large number of spectra can be routinely updated into an existing hierarchical tree. Our intention is to make evident the most important problems and to suggest some solutions. Besides the basic concept — how to generate a hierarchical tree from a large number of spectra and use it as a retrieval system — the main problem which will be discussed is the proper representation of data. There is no single best solution for all environments and for all spectroscopic methods. For example, a representation that is adequate for infrared spectra may not be good enough for mass spectra, or *vice versa.* Additionally, it is necessary to take into account the computer system (micro, mini, main-frame, operating systems, etc.) with which such a collection should be implemented.

Another important aspect, after the hierarchical tree has been generated, is the extraction of accumulated information about the similarity between the chemical structures of which the spectra are joined in clusters. The hierarchical organization allows us to conduct the object of enquiry (spectrum) through the tree from vertex to vertex. The assignment of vertices (i.e. identification of which properties, in terms of chemical structurs or at least fragments, are held in common) is a difficult and time-consuming task because the vertices on the lower levels represent a large number of spectra. From our experience the assignment cannot be done automatically simply by considering the structures involved, and a good deal of spectroscopic knowledge about spectra–structure correlations must be taken into account as well.

Although the formation of a hierarchically organized database is very time-consuming, our results [3–7] show that the information gained is worth the effort.

3.2 HIERARCHICAL ORGANIZATION

Let us consider the organization of 13 data items, marked with capital letters as in Fig. 3.1. The data (A, B, ... M) are linked in a hierarchical manner: on the first level there are three groups of 5, 6 and 2 objects, respectively, while on lower levels these 3 groups are subdivided into smaller groups until each object forms an individual 'group'. Each vertex in the hierarchical tree represents a cluster of objects that can be reached from this vertex. In other words, a vertex is an 'object' that in some way represents all objects in the cluster. It can be interpreted as an 'average' or 'main' object of the entire cluster, and may or may not be a member of a cluster.

In hierarchical ordering of clusters (average objects) the retrieval and updating of objects are done in very similar manner. The new objects for the

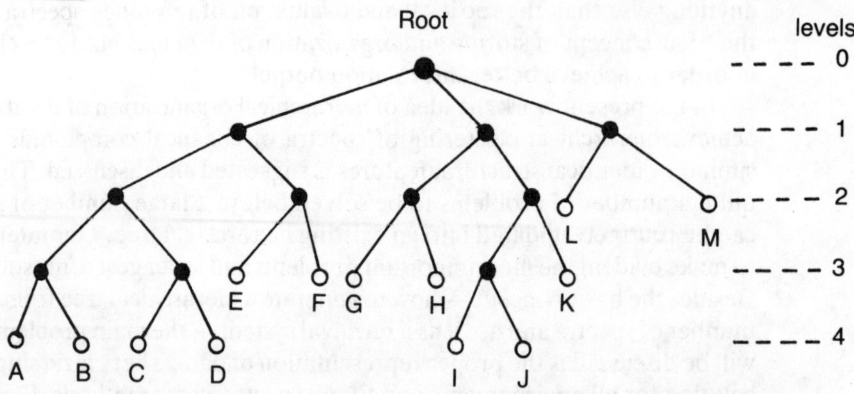

Fig. 3.1 — Hierarchical tree of 13 objects (marked with capital letters A...M). On the first level there are three clusters: linking 6 (A,B,C,D,E, and F), 5 (G,H,I,J, and K), and 2 objects (L and M), respectively. Each cluster represents all objects that can be reached from it.

updating, or the query objects for the search, enter the tree at the root and then traverse the tree towards the leaves. At each vertex on the path all possible continuations are considered. By use of an evaluation function (usually based on distances) the path to the closest or most similar descendant is chosen. The procedure is repeated until a vertex without descendants (a leaf) is encountered. In updating, the vertices on the path taken by the new object have to be modified because the new object becomes a member of a cluster (sub-tree) after passing a given vertex. The amount by which the vertex is modified depends on the number of objects it represents and the position of the new object relative to the position of this particular vertex (average object). Note again that vertices are represented in the same measurement space as the objects and are therefore treated as objects. At the end of the tree the new object forms a small cluster of two objects: the leaf to which it is linked and itself.

In retrieval the path of the query object at each vertex is guided by the same evaluation function as in updating. The only differences are that the vertices encountered are not changed and that the query is not permanently stored in the tree.

From this short description of a database organized in a hierarchical manner it can be seen that there are two outstandingly useful features.

First, the average retrieval time for any object from a well balanced hierarchical tree is logarithmically proportional to the number of objects in the tree (Fig. 3.2), the logarithmic base depending on the degree of branching (e.g. base 2 for a binary tree). This logarithmic dependence of the retrieval time on the size of the database is clearly a very convenient property, especially when the database starts to grow.

Secondly, on the way through the tree the properties of the query object can be predicted on the basis of the properties of the vertices encountered.

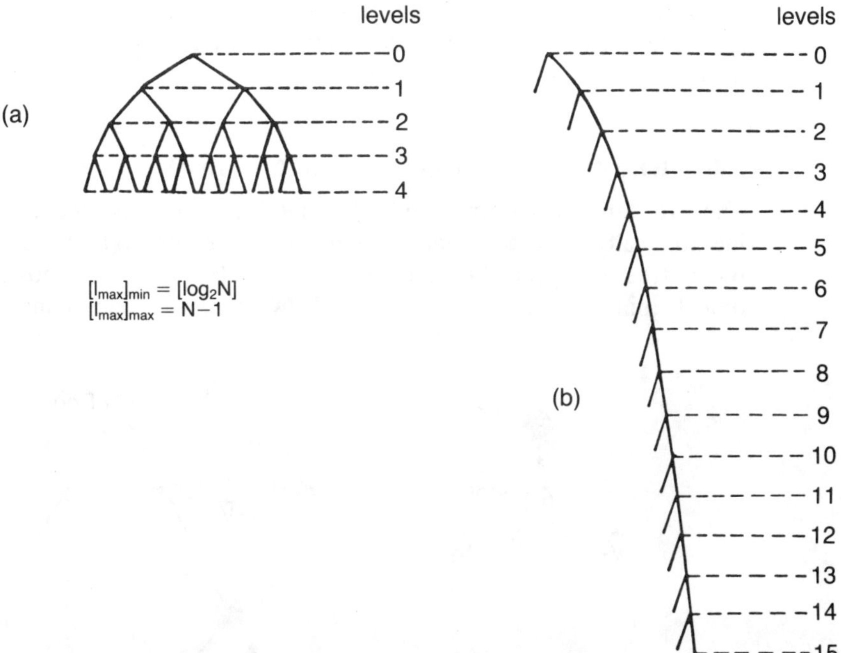

Fig. 3.2 — A perfectly balanced (a) and an extremely chained (b) tree. The shortest maximal path $[l_{max}]_{min}$ that exists in binary hierarchical trees containing N objects can be found only in the perfectly balanced trees. On the other hand, it is easy to see that the longest maximal path in the trees of N objects is $N-1$ levels long.

Because a vertex represents a cluster of objects having one or more properties in common, these properties can be associated with the cluster as a whole. Hence the linkage of the query object with the particular cluster indicates with high probability that it has the property(ies) assigned to that cluster. It is important to note that we say "indicates with a high probability" rather than "it has". The reason for such care is that the objects in some clusters (notably the smaller ones) may have some properties in common purely by chance and not as a result of their position in the measurement space. For example, if a few compounds represented by their infrared spectra are linked in a cluster, they may exhibit the same or very similar properties even though these cannot be directly related to their vibrational spectra. We shall discuss the assignments of clusters later on in more detail.

It should be clear by now that if the clusters are adequately assigned, much valuable information could be obtained by knowing the path taken by the query object through the hierarchically organized database.

Some problems in connection with the generation of a hierarchical organization now have to be considered: (a) how hierarchical organization of a larger database can be accomplished; (b) whether a hierarchical ordering can be generated for infrared, ^{13}C NMR, and mass spectra databases; (c) how the spectral data should be represented for hierarchical ordering; (d) how to find and assign clusters exhibiting some relevant structural features in the generated hierarchical tree. These questions will be dealt with in the following sections.

3.3 THE 3-DISTANCE CLUSTERING METHOD

The 3-distance clustering method (3-DCM) [8–11] for generation of a hierarchically ordered database is a procedure for updating an existing binary tree. The procedure starts with the smallest binary tree possible: two objects joined in a cluster (Fig. 3.3a). New objects are added one by one at

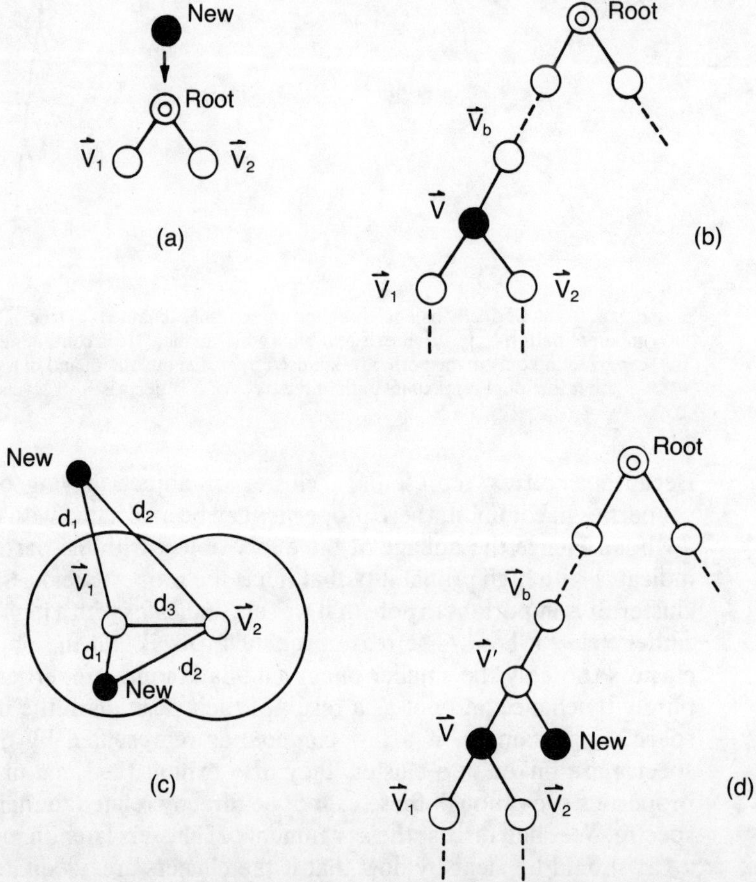

Fig. 3.3 — The generation of the hierarchical tree. The smallest possible cluster of two objects (a) is a 'seed' for the generation which continues with the addition of new objects at the root. At each vertex $\vec{V}$ three distances, d_1, d_2, and d_3 are calculated (b and c). if d_3 is the minimal distance, a new vertex $\vec{V}'$ is formed between vertices $\vec{V}$ and $\vec{V}_b$ (d), otherwise the new object continues its traverse towards $\vec{V}_1$ or $\vec{V}_2$.

the root and guided through the tree to find the most suitable position for them in it. In the preceding section we discussed the updating procedure which implicitly assumes that the new objects *always* traverse the entire tree from the root to the leaf.

In the 3-DCM, however, the situation is quite different. The evaluation function, on the basis of which the direction towards the new vertex is chosen, allows an additional possibility, namely, to stop the transit of the new object and to 'bud' a new final branch in the middle of the tree (Fig. 3.3d).

The evaluation function is based on the comparison of three distances calculated at each vertex; hence the name 3-distance clustering method. At each vertex $\vec{V}$ the following distances:

$$d_1=d(\vec{X}, \vec{V}_1), \tag{3.1}$$
$$d_2=d(\vec{X}, \vec{V}_2), \tag{3.2}$$
$$d_3=d(\vec{X}_1, \vec{V}_2), \tag{3.3}$$

are calculated and compared. The smallest of the three distances:

$$d_{\min}=\min(d_1, d_2, d_3) \tag{3.4}$$

decides the direction of the path of the new object $\vec{X}$. $\vec{V}_1$ and $\vec{V}_2$ are the descendants of the vertex $\vec{V}$ (Fig. 3b). If either d_1 or d_2 is the minimal distance, the object $\vec{X}$ continues its movement towards $\vec{V}_1$ or $\vec{V}_2$, respectively. The minimal distance being equal to d_3 indicates that $\vec{X}$ is an outlier (Fig. 3.3c). This last case is essential to the operation of the 3–DCM and deserves special consideration. If $\vec{X}$ is an outlier, it cannot join $\vec{V}_1$ or $\vec{V}_2$ or $\vec{V}$ ($\vec{V}$ represents both $\vec{V}_1$ and $\vec{V}_2$) because $\vec{V}_1$ is more similar to $\vec{V}_2$ (d_3 is the smallest distance!) than $\vec{X}$ is to either of them. The only solution is for the new object $\vec{X}$ to bud a new branch above the vertex $\vec{V}$, thus avoiding all the unacceptable links (Fig. 3.3d).

In the generation of a hierarchical tree the calculation of distances is the most frequently used procedure and requires a short and simple algorithm. Throughout this work the Manhattan (or city-block) distance [12]:

$$d(\vec{X}_i,\vec{X}_j) = \sum_k |(x_{ik} - x_{jk})| \tag{3.5}$$

is used, where k refers to the components of the representation vector.

By application of this evaluation function in the updating procedure a hierarchical tree can be built from any already existing hierarchical tree provided that the starting tree consists of at least two objects.

Unfortunately, not all procedures for generating hierarchical trees (e.g. that shown in Fig. 3.4, which we will call procedure P1) provide trees with 100% retrievability of the component objects. The reason for the failure is the 'overlap' effect caused by the shift of the average vectors (cluster representations) when new objects are added. An object located in a

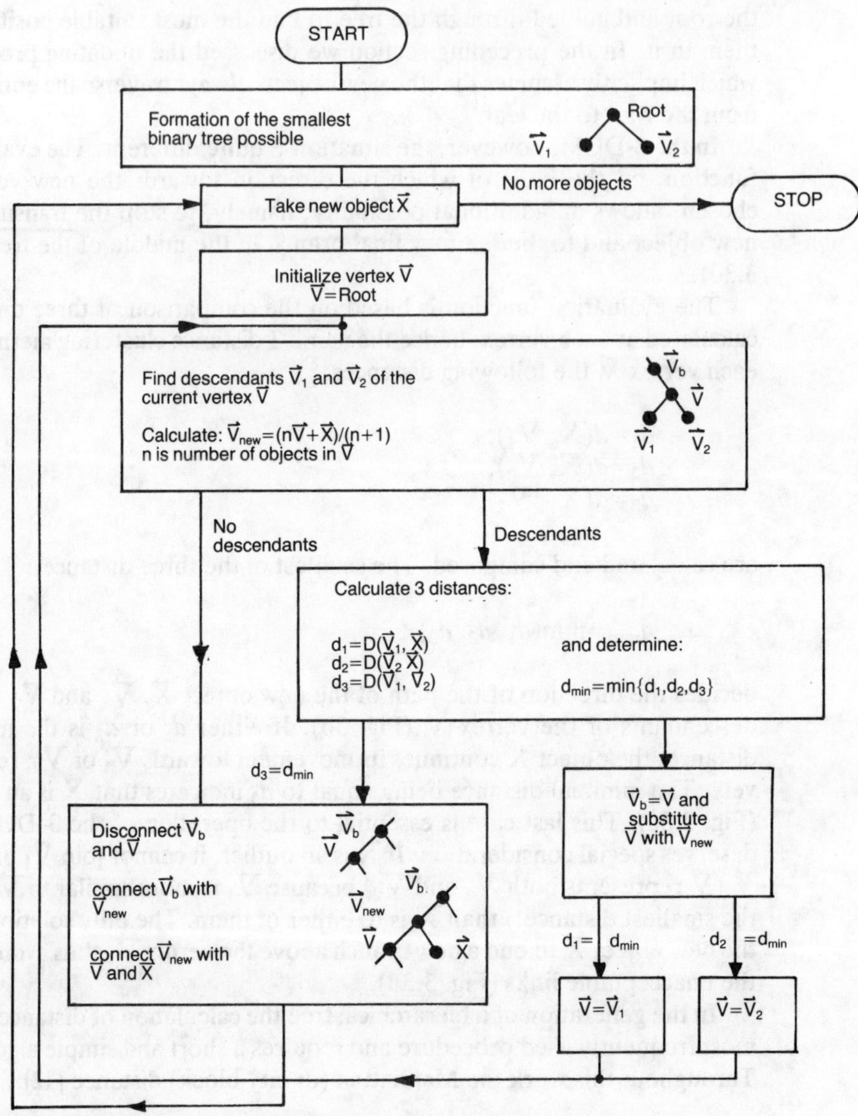

Fig. 3.4 — The 3-DCM algorithm (P1) for the generation of hierarchical trees.

particular cluster might later on become inaccessible owing to the shift of the representation of this cluster towards another cluster which was initially much more distant. Both clusters might even overlap. Thus in the search for the object in question, at some level both descendant cluster representations might be much closer to each other than they were when the object was introduced in updating the tree. Hence, the search path branches off from the proper direction or is even stopped before the end of the tree is reached.

To ensure 100% retrievability from the hierarchically organized database, additional relocations of objects are mandatory [9,10]. Figure 3.5 shows one of the possible solutions for including procedure P1 in an iterative algorithm (P2) which should eventually lead to 100% retrievability. The iterative procedure (P2) seriously reduces the economy of the hierarchical tree generation, but once the tree has been generated the efficiency of the retrievals, similarity searches, and predictions about queries more than pays for the time lost during the generation.

3.4 REPRESENTATION OF DIFFERENT TYPES OF SPECTRA

The choice of a proper spectral representation is by far the most critical part of the entire tree-generating procedure. To emphasize this, the goals of a good representation are listed below. The representation of spectra should:

(a) contain as much as possible relevant information on the structures of the recorded compounds in order to enable meaningful clustering of spectra with respect to chemical structure;
(b) be short enough to ensure economical handling of the large numbers of spectra necessary for generation of the hierarchical tree;
(c) enable the coding of a group of spectra with the same attributes as an individual spectrum, i.e. the representation for a group should be formed by the same set of rules as for the individual spectrum, or in other words the cluster representations in the hierarchical tree should be represented in exactly the same manner as the spectra;
(d) enable the retrieval of spectra and the prediction of the structural features of compounds not already having their spectra clustered in the hierarchical tree.

It is clear that the way the specta should be represented strongly depends on the type of spectroscopy: infrared, mass, ^{13}C NMR, and so on. In this section three examples for coding three different kind of spectra (infrared, mass, and ^{13}C NMR) will be worked out in detail. We do not intend to imply that any of the three representations described is the best possible, but rather to show the variety of possibilities that should be considered if a new system is under development. Interested readers are welcome to try their own ways and ideas for representing the spectra.

3.4.1 Representation of infrared spectra

Infrared specta are usually obtained directly from the spectrometer as a set of approximately 4000 measurements at equidistant wavenumber intervals of about 1 cm^{-1} in the region from 4000 to 200 cm^{-1} (depending on the type of spectrometer or the interest of the experimentalist). Obviously, a measurement space of several thousand dimensions is rather inconvenient and not economical for fast, on-line handling of thousands of spectra. Therefore, a highly compressed representation that still contains a large proportion of the initial information is needed.

It has been shown [13,14] that first a linear reduction of the number of

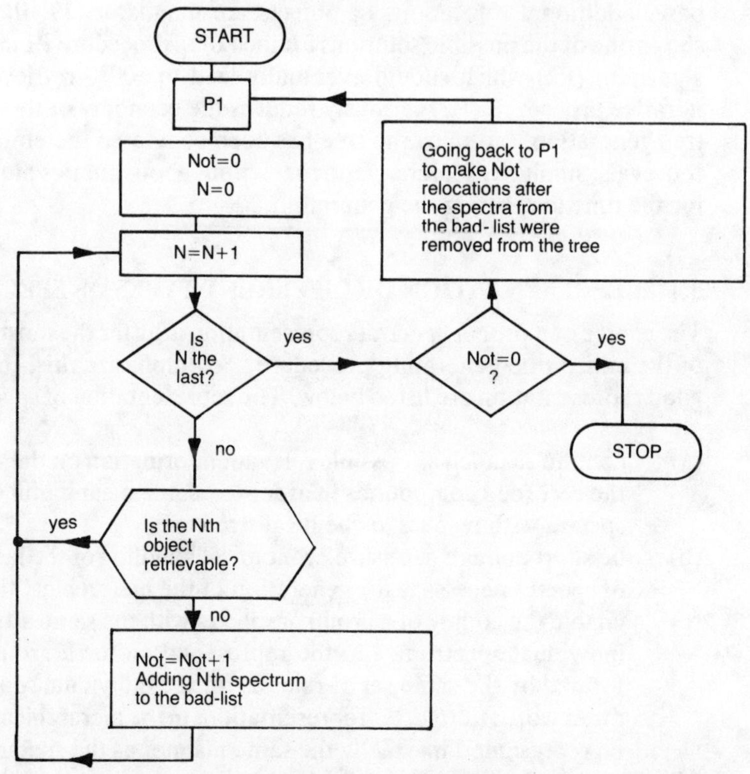

Fig. 3.5 — Algorithm P2 for the iterative relocation of objects to achieve 100% recall. The P1 algorithm is used for the relocation of the inaccessible objects detected during one pass.

points and then further reduction of the space dimensions by omitting the high-order Fourier coefficients of the Fourier transform of the linearly reduced spectrum leads to an acceptable 160–200-dimensional representation of an infrared spectrum. The scheme for such two-step reduction is shown in Fig. 3.6.

The advantage of the representation that employs a reduced set of Fourier coefficients is the possibility of reconstructing the orginal spectra. As we shall see later on, this is not the case with the representations of ^{13}C NMR and mass spectra. The quality of reproduction of the infrared spectrum strongly depends on the percentage of the original Fourier coefficients taken into account for the reproduction. Once removed, the information can never be recovered. Of course, if the original spectra are still saved in some random-access file on a mass storage medium and linked with the short representations by identification numbers, the full infrared curves can be retrieved from disk. Unfortunately, not all of us are rich enough to have 200-Mbyte disks at hand for permanent on-line retrieval of

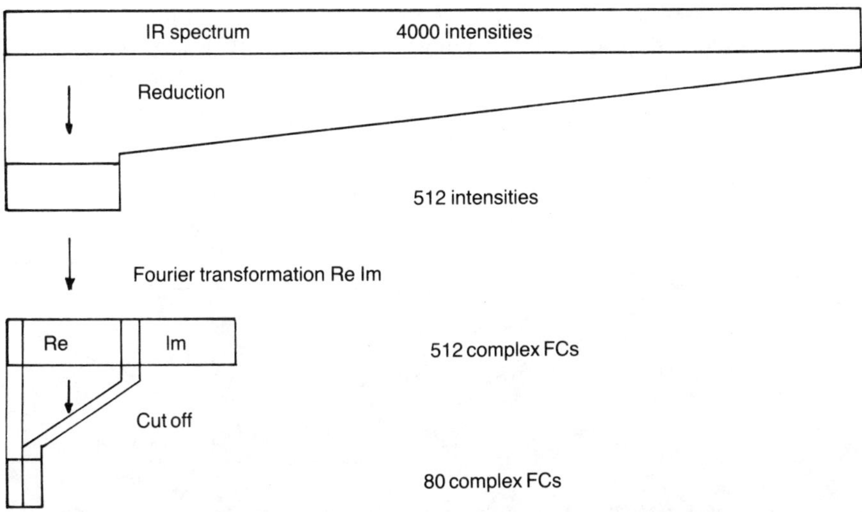

Fig. 3.6 — Reduction of the dimensionality of infrared spectra by linear reduction and Fourier transform. In the present example 80 complex (160 real) numbers were used as the representation of infrared spectra.

the original spectra. Usually, this most valuable information is stored somewhere on magnetic tapes, to be inspected and consulted very seldom.

For the examples here, the infrared spectra were taken from our information system KISIK [15] and represented by 512 equidistant points. Next, the Fourier transformation was performed on the 512 points and 512 complex (1024 real numbers) Fourier coefficients (FCs) were obtained. Finally, from the set of 512 complex FCs only 80 low-order FCs (160 real numbers) were taken for representation of the infrared spectra. For larger hierarchical trees such a short representation would not be acceptable, but here, for the sake of simplicity, it is quite adequate, as can be seen from the resulting tree.

3.4.2 Representation of ^{13}C NMR spectra

Chemical shifts for ^{13}C NMR spectra are usually given in ppm units relative to the chemical shift of TMS (tetramethylsilane) and are, with few exceptions, distributed in the region from −20 to 250 ppm. Because the positions of the signals are more informative than their intensities, the ^{13}C NMR spectra are often encoded into approximately 2700 bits (ones and zeros for the presence or absence, respectively, of signals within 0.1-ppm intervals). If lesser accuracy of the shift positions is acceptable, 270 intensities could serve as the representation of the spectrum divided into 1-ppm intervals. The problem inherent in the representation of the ^{13}C NMR spectra with equidistant intervals is irregular grouping of the shifts in all regions. This has led to the idea of non-equidistant interval representation. However, all the spectra ought to be represented in the same manner, i.e. coded into the same interval-boundary scheme. Recently, a simplex optimization [16–18] combined with principal component analysis [19–21] was employed in order to obtain an optimized choice of intervals [6, 7] for ^{13}C NMR representation. The 20-dimensional representation obtained, together with the interval limits (in ppm) is shown in Fig. 3.7.

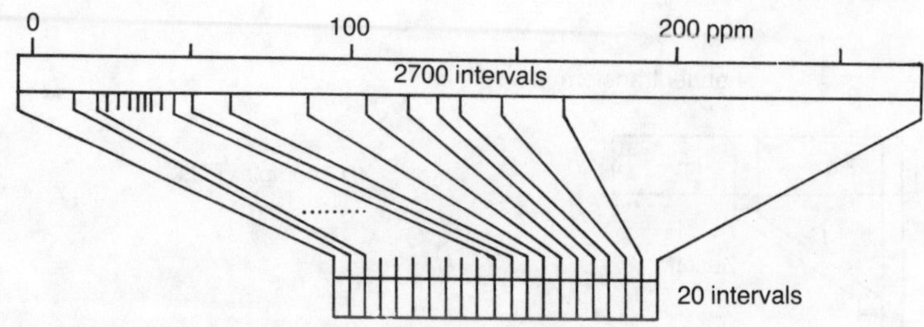

Fig. 3.7 — Reduction of ^{13}C NMR spectra, using 20 optimized intervals. The interval boundaries obtained are 14.5, 21.2, 24.1, 28.2, 31.3, 33.9, 36.0, 38.6, 40.9, 44.9, 51.2, 63.3, 87.5, 106, 118, 127, 134, 147, 166, and higher (ppm relative to TMS), respectively.

Although extremely short, the representation has produced, in a database of 2200 different ^{13}C NMR spectra, only 400 duplicates or triplicates and has enabled the generation of a hierarchical tree of 2000 spectra. Remarkably, all the spectra (duplicates included) were retrievable from the tree in an average of only 14.7 comparisons. Owing to the fact that all identical spectra (duplicates, triplicates, etc.) were clustered together the identification of an experimental spectrum on the basis of full spectra was extremely easy.

For larger data banks, in spite of the efficiency just demonstrated, a larger (higher-dimensional) representation is desirable in order to avoid the unnecessary handling of duplicates which could, for larger collections, considerably diminish the prediction ability of the tree and increase the processing time.

The ^{13}C NMR spectra for the present examples were taken from the ASU collection [22] and coded into the described 20-dimensional representation.

3.4.3 Representation of mass spectra

Low-resolution mass spectra differ in many respects from infrared and ^{13}C NMR spectra. They are not continuous and can easily be regarded as discrete frequency distributions of molecular fragments in 1-m/z intervals, ranging from 1 to, in general, slightly more than the value corresponding to the molecular-weight peak. The intensity (abundance) in a given interval is practically independent of the intensities in the neighbouring intervals, which makes mass spectra very convenient for vector representation. However, with increasing molecular weight the length (dimensionality) of the representation increases. As a consequence, all mass spectra considered for a hierarchically organized database should have a representation that would fit even the largest molecule, but such a waste of computer space and handling time is not justified. In order to avoid this situation the autocorrelation function is introduced to transform the standard linear *m/z* representation of mass spectra into a shorter one. The autocorrelation function $A(l)$ of a mass spectrum $\vec{M}$ $(m_1, m_2, \dots m_i, \dots)$ can be written in a discrete form:

$$A(l) = \sum_i m_i \cdot m_{i+l} \text{ for } l = 0,1,2\dots \tag{3.6}$$

with summation over the entire spectral range. For better comparison the autocorrelation terms are normalized as shown:

$$A'(l) = A(l)/A(0) \tag{3.7}$$

Figure 3.8 shows the mass spectrum of methyloxirane [23] and its 38 autocorrelation terms $[A(l), l = 0\text{–}37]$ obtained by using Eq. (3.6).

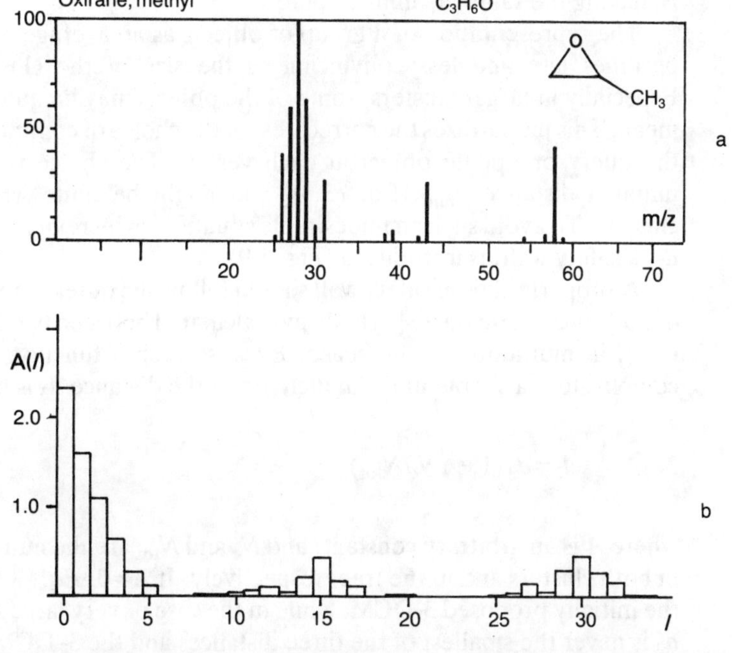

Fig. 3.8 — Mass spectrum of methyloxirane (a) and 38 autocorrelation terms (b). The maximal distance (in *m/z* units) between two peaks in the mass spectrum is 34, which causes larger $A(l)=0$ for $l>34$. Note the difference $\Delta l=15$ in the autocorrelation spectrum, which corresponds to the CH_3 ($m/z=15$) group.

The mass spectra for the present example were taken from the EPA/NIH collection [23]. They were represented by the first 80 autocorrelation terms calculated by using Eq. (3.7).

3.4.4 Representation of a group of objects

The representation of a cluster $\vec{V}_i$ in which a group of "similar" objects $\vec{X}_k$ is linked, was calculated in all the present examples as a mean representation of these objects:

$$\vec{V}_i = \left(\sum_{k1} x_{k1}, \sum_{2k} x_{k2}, \ldots \sum_{k} x_{kj} \right) \Big/ N_i \tag{3.8}$$

where N_i is the number of objects in the cluster $\vec{V}_i$ and x_{kj} is the jth component of the kth object $\vec{X}_k$ linked in the cluster $\vec{V}_i$.

When an object $\vec{X}$ has to be removed from the tree (see iteration procedure P2, Section 3.3) the representation of the new cluster $\vec{V}'_i$ was calculated from the old one $\vec{V}_i$ as follows:

$$\vec{V}'_i = (N_i \vec{V}_i - \vec{X})/(N_i - 1) \tag{3.9}$$

N_i having the same meaning as before.

The representation of a group of objects as an average or mean object becomes less and less convincing as the size of the cluster increases. Especially in larger clusters, some of the objects may lie quite far from the mean. This jeopardizes the correctness of the choice of continuation path for the query or update object at each vertex. The choice is based on the minimal distance $d_{\min}$ [Eq. (3.4)] and might be quite wrong for large clusters. To avoid such an undesirable situation an increment of the distance d_3, a safety wall, is introduced (Fig. 3.9).

A properly chosen safety wall should follow the outer shape and position of both clusters involved [d_3 is always calculated between two clusters—Eq. (3.3)] in multidimensional space. Because such a function would be too complicated, a simple uniform increase of the distance d_3 is used:

$$d'_3 = d_3(1 + AN_c/N_{\text{tot}}) \tag{3.10}$$

where A is an arbitrary constant, and N_c and N_{tot} are the number of objects in both clusters and in the tree, respectively. If $A=0$, Eq. (3.10) reduces to the initially proposed 3-DCM, while in the case of very large A the distance d'_3 is never the smallest of the three distances and the 3–DCM becomes the two-distance update method. The 3-DCM has a tendency to develop long chains, while the two-distance method allows linking of rather dissimilar objects. By varying the constant A, a compromise can be achieved, minimizing both undesirable properties [5]. Equation (3.10) was derived empirically by using the following reasoning: first, the equation should reflect the size of both clusters and secondly it should be as simple as possible to minimize

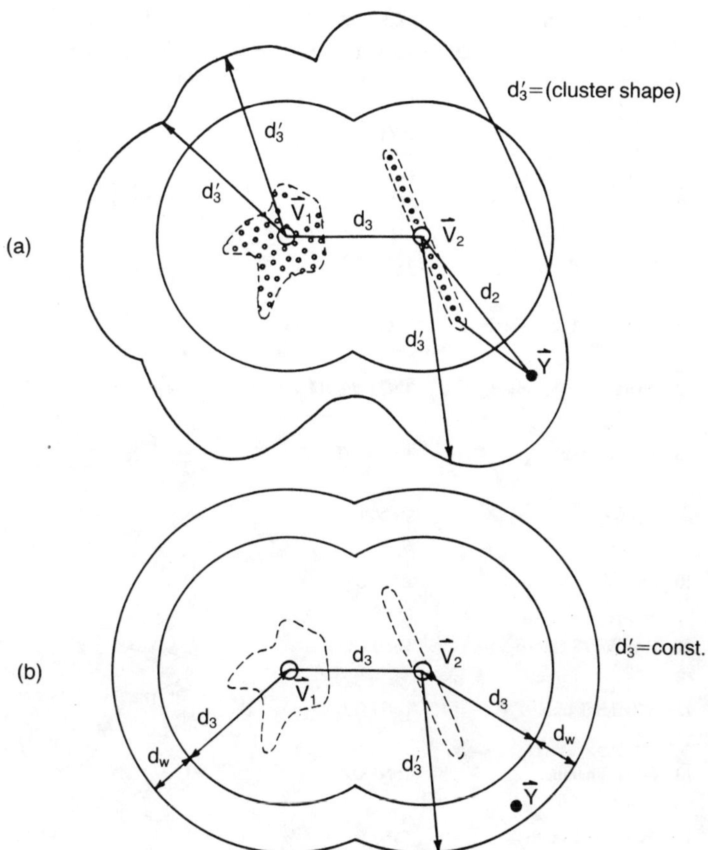

Fig. 3.9 — The concept of the safety wall. A properly chosen safety wall should follow the shape and position of both clusters ($\vec{V}_1$ and $\vec{V}_2$) in multidimensional space (a). Because such a function would be too complicated, a simple uniform increase d_w in the safety wall is introduced (b).

additional computation time. It is by no means the only or the best one. Users could try some other approaches.

3.5 HIERARCHICAL TREES

For the *same* set of compounds, by use of the algorithm outlined in Section 3.3 three different hierarchical trees were generated. For each of the first 20 organic compounds, the structures of which are shown in Table 3.1, the infrared, ^{13}C NMR, and mass spectra were represented as described in the preceding section, enabling the generation of three hierarchical trees based on completely different representation of the *same* set of objects. As expected, the structural properties associated with the cluster generated were related to the spectroscopic technique used for the representation.

Table 3.1 — Structures of 23 compounds used for hierarchical clustering and the prediction of structural fragments in the examples described

No.	Chemical name	WLN	Structure
1	Propane, 1,2-dibromo-	EY1+1E	$Br–CH(CH_3)–CH_2–Br$
2	1-Propene, 1-bromo-	E1U2–T	$Br–CH{=}CH–CH_3$
3	1-Propene, 3-chloro-	G2U1	$Cl–CH_2–CH{=}CH_2$
4	Propane, 1,2-dichloro-	GY1+1G	$Cl–CH(CH_3)–CH_2–Cl$
5	Oxirane, methyl-	T3OTJ B1	
6	Oxirane, (bromomethyl)-	T3OTJ B1E	
7	Oxirane, (chloromethyl)-	T3OTH B1G	
8	1,3-Dioxolane	T5O COTJ	
9	Oxetane	T4OTJ	
10	Phenol, 2-amino-	ZR BQ	
11	Pyridine, 3-chloro-	T6NJ CG	
12	2-Pyridinamine	T6NJ BZ	
13	4-Pyridinamine	T6NJ DZ	
14	Pyridine, 2-methyl-	T6NJ B1	
15	Pyridine, 4-ethyl-	T6NJ D2	
16	Pyridine, 2-ethyl-	T6NJ B2	
17	L-Serine	QVYZ1Q	$HO–C(=O)–CH(NH_2)–CH_2–OH$
18	L-Threonine	QY1+YZVQ	$HO–C(=O)–CH(NH_2)–CH(CH_3)–OH$
19	L-Leucine	QVYZ1Y1+1	$HO–C(=O)–CH(NH_2)–CH_2–CH(CH_3)_2$
20	L-Lysine	Z4YZVQ	$HO–C(=O)–CH(NH_2)–(CH_2)_4–NH_2$
21	1,3,5-Trioxane	T6O CO EOTJ	
22	Benzenamine	ZR	
23	L-Valine	QVYZY1+1	$HO–C(=O)–CH(NH_2)–CH(CH_3)_2$

The hierarchical trees (Fig. 3.10) were generated by the 3–DCM procedure with the same expressions for the calculation of the distances [Eq. 3.5)], the representations [Eqs. (3.8) and (3.9)], and the safety walls [Eq. (3.10)] in all cases. The only parameter that was changed was the represen-

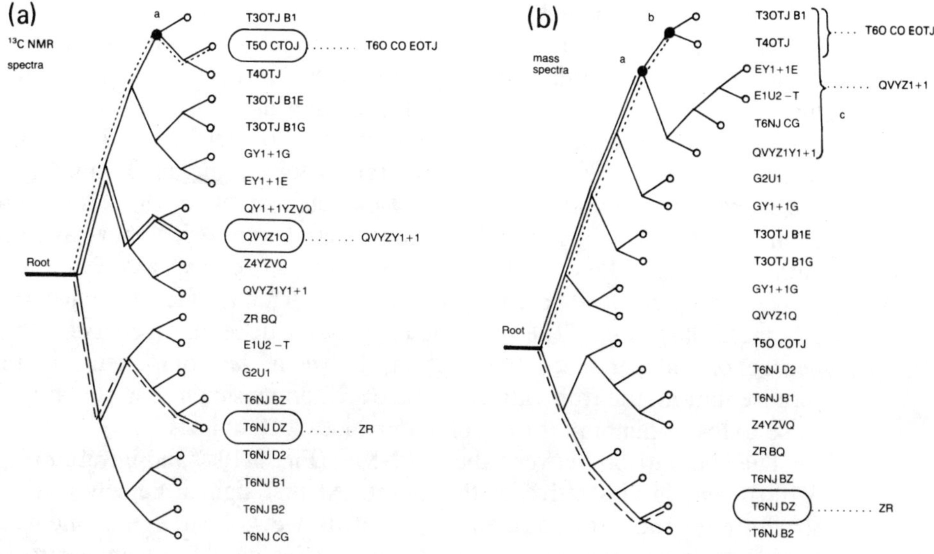

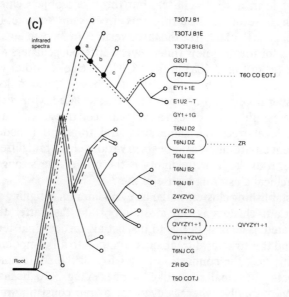

Fig. 3.10 — Hierarchical trees of ^{13}C NMR (a), mass (b) and infrared spectra (c) generated by using the 3-DCM algorithm and the described representations of spectra. In the trees the retrieval paths for each test search are shown. The search starts at the root and ends either at the leaf or stops at some cluster [as in the mass spectra trees], according to procedure P1.

tation of the object. The relevant parameters for building the hierarchical trees are given in Table 3.2.

Although the generated trees (Fig. 3.10) are very small they already exhibit features generally found in larger trees. Here, we shall discuss only the most important one, the clustering. Clustering in the trees is strongly dependent on the choice of representation of the objects. First, the average path length in the tree increases if the ratio between the dimensionality of the representation and the number of objects increases, which is evident from the ^{13}C NMR, mass, and infrared spectral trees, which have average paths 4.4, 4.9, and 6.6 levels long, respectively. A danger associated with this feature is that too short a representation will not lead to good clustering schemes in large trees. The length actually usable depends, of course, on the degree of independence (correlation) between the components in the representation, but from our experience a 20-dimensional representation is close to the minimum for trees of about 2000–3000 objects.

The comparison between the ^{13}C NMR (Fig. 3.10a) and infrared (Fig. 3.10b) trees is illustrative of this point. At first sight a heavily chained structure for the infrared tree is apparent. In view of earlier statements in favour of well balanced trees, such long chains would not appear to be desirable. It seems rather strange that compounds such as methyloxirane, oxetane, and 1,3-dioxolane (compounds 5, 8, 9 in Table 3.1), for example, do not form a single cluster, but three one-object clusters on the main branch. In terms of clustering, this effect is undesirable, but with regard to further growth of the tree the three vertices (a, b, c, in Fig. 3.10c) allow more choices for forming new (maybe very different) clusters than does only one vertex (a, in Fig. 3.10a) in the ^{13}C NMR tree. In other words: chains give more freedom for budding new branches in the middle of the tree. The incoming objects do not need to be associated with certain properties as early as would be the case in a well balanced tree. As a consequence, in large hierarchical trees the same structural fragment (bonded, of course, in different environments) appears in various clusters at different positions and different levels. This flexibility is the one of the strongest advantages of hierarchical clustering by use of the 3-DCM.

Establishing clusters in the tree and later on assigning structural features to certain clusters is the most important task after the tree has been generated. The first step is to inspect all vertices (cluster representations) and find the structural fragments common to all compounds in the clusters. For this task the connection tables for all the compounds in the tree are mandatory. In small trees, like the ones in Fig. 3.10 the inspection can easily be done visually, whereas even for a tree consisting of only a thousand objects there will be 998 clusters to be checked, with 500 compounds per cluster, which is an extremely time-consuming operation even for a computer. On levels close to the root (i.e. very large clusters) there will be a number of clusters which have no structural feature common to all the constituent compounds, but to find them it is necessary to check *all* the clusters in the tree.

After the first step has been accomplished, the fragments or structural

Table 3.2 — Parameters for the generation of hierarchical trees

Spectroscopy	Type of representation	Dimension of the reprsentation	Safety wall, *A*
^{13}C NMR	Optimized intervals	20	5
Mass	Autocorrelation	80	5
Infrared	Fourier transform	160	5

features found have to be correlated with the chosen representation. It may happen that compounds linked in a cluster have some of the structural fragments in common only by chance and not because of spectral similarities. For example, the fragment OH–, even if found in all compounds of a cluster in the ^{13}C NMR tree, should not be assigned as a 'common property' to the cluster, because the hydroxy group does not contribute signals to the ^{13}C NMR spectra. For trees based on infrared spectra, however, the hydroxy group is a very significant structural feature and should be assigned to clusters whenever possible. Less-than-careful consideration of every assignment may result in an overinterpretation, e.g. a structural feature larger or more specific than warranted. The assignments in the 20-object trees generated on the basis of very reduced representations are not realistic and are therefore omitted. Such small trees may be regarded only as 'seeds' for larger ones and are discussed here only for the sake of clarity and demonstration of the method.

The 3-DCM does not call for any fixed or prerequired hierachy of structural fragments, no matter what type of spectroscopy is used for the representation. Hierarchies form during the generation process itself, depending only on the structure of the data set, representation of objects, and sequence of updating objects (spectra). The actual hierarchy, (the number, or position of clusters) which exists after the tree is generated reflects all these parameters. What really matters is that in retrieval, i.e. *after* the tree has been generated, objects having similar structures strongly tend to be associated.

The term 'similarity' of structures, even if replaced by the term 'distance', is very complex in a chemical (not mathematical) sense and changes even during the clustering process, with growth of the clusters or the entire database. Structures that seem 'similar' in a group of, let us say, ten compounds, may no longer necessarily appear 'similar' when ten new compounds are added.

3.6 RETRIEVAL AND PREDICTION BY USING HIERARCHICAL TREES

Retrieval from the hierarchical tree obtained by the 3-DCM is straightforward. Because the 3-DCM procedure requires all objects in the tree to be retrievable, any spectrum in the final tree is guaranted to be correctly retrieved in a number of comparisons proportional to $\log_2(N)$ if the tree is at least moderately balanced. The importance of this property increases with the increasing number of spectra in the tree. For trees containing a few thousand spectra the average retrieval paths are around 15 levels long [7]. Such short retrieval paths reduces computer time by a factor of at least 100, compared to sequential search. Additionally, the hierarchical organization enables correct retrieval for very similar spectra [5,7] and good predictions about the structures of compounds for which spectra are *not* stored in the tree.

It should be mentioned that hierarchical trees obtained by standard clustering methods [21,24,25] such as single and complete linkage, the Ward method etc., *do not* allow retrieval. If a new object is to be added to such a tree the entire clustering procedure has to be repeated. The consequence of this, even if a tree of only 1000 objects is considered, is evident. To establish the position of the query object in the tree obtained by using standard methods, the entire clustering procedure, the analysis, and the assignation of clusters on the path of the query object, from the root to the place of the query object in the tree, should be made again *for each retrieval.* In a hierarchical tree generated by the 3-DCM, however, only $\log_2(N)$ comparisons are necessary to accomplish the same task. The logarithmic dependence of comparisons on the number of objects in the tree clearly results in the method outperforming the 'retrieval' offered by the standard clustering methods, for which the generation time is not even linearly dependent on the number of objects, let alone the time necessary for the analysis of vertices and for the assignments.

To show the ability and efficiency, as well as some limitations, of the hierarchically organized database, three searches through trees of ^{13}C NMR, mass, and infrared spectra have been worked out in detail. The "unknowns" for each retrieval were the same compounds, represented by the corresponding spectra. The chemical structures of the query objects are given in Table 3.1 (Nos. 21–23). The retrieval paths taken by these objects in traversing the three trees are shown in Fig. 3.10.

The first example, 1,3,5-trioxane (No. 21), has made its way to very similar compounds, namely 1,3-dioxolane, oxetane, and a cluster of oxetane and methyloxirane, in the trees of ^{13}NMR, infrared, and mass spectra, respectively. The search path in the tree of mass spectra shows that the search was terminated before the leaf was reached. The 80-dimensional spectrum of 1,3,5-trioxane arrived at vertex b but did not join any of its constituent spectra. The distance between the oxetane and methyloxirane spectra was smaller than the distances between 1,3,5-trioxane and the two constituents.

It is interesting to see that benzenamine (aniline) (No. 22) is linked to 4-pyridinamine in all three searches, and not to 2-aminophenol. Apparently, higher topological symmetry prevails over chemical 'similarity'.

In the last example in the trees of ^{13}C NMR and infrared spectra, L-valine (No. 23) joined L-serine and L-leucine (two very similar compounds), rspectively, while in the tree of mass spectra it stopped at vertex a for the same reason as 1,3,5-trioxetane stopped at vertex b. The explanation for the poorer prediction performance of the mass spectra tree might be the choice of representation. It should be kept in mind that the autocorrelation function completely neglects the absolute values of peak positions, which are, of course, very important for structure elecidation from mass spectra. Possibly, from a combination of both the autocorrelation terms and the absolute positions of the *m/z* peaks, better representation could be obtained. On the other hand, it is hard to conclude on the basis of only tree searches that the chosen representation is not useful. Final judgement of the value of the representation could be reached after a much larger tree has been generated, its clustering ability checked, and prediction ability tested with a large number of searches.

Hence, the intention of the examples given here (different representations, hierarchical trees of 20 objects, and three searches in each tree) is less to show 'how-to-do-it' than to promote the idea that spectal databases can be hierarchically organized and utilized.

Summarizing, the examples above demonstrate the ability of the 3-DCM to generate hierarchical trees based on different representations. Furthermore, these hierarchical trees enable not only 100% accurate recall of all their component objects in a number of comparisons that is logarithmically proportional to the number of objects, but also reliable predictions about structural fragments on the basis of spectra which are not stored in the trees.

3.7 CONCLUSIONS

It is hoped that the advantages of hierarchically organized databases in general and the use of 3-DCM in particular have been convincingly shown. There are other possibilities for using hierarchically organized databases, that are not discussed here, partly owing to lack of space and partly to the limited scope of the chapter. Very important among the advantages are the so-called 'feed-back search' [26] and sequential linking of many hierarchical trees [5], which both enhance the prediction ability if the spectra of the compounds sought are very unlikely to be found in the database. Next, there is the ease of on-line linking with spectrometers, especially infrared instruments, because no peak-finding software with a preselected noise level is required. The use of a hierarchically organized database in speech and image recognition should also be mentioned. There are other fields of applications and readers are encouraged to explore beyond the spectroscopic applications.

It is equally important to know the shortcomings and limitations of the method. As said before, the method is very computer-time and computer-space intensive where preprocessing of spectra, generation of trees, and analysis and assignments of vertices are concerned. In our opinion, however, the quality of the answers retrieved, the information gained by using the 3-DCM retrievals and predictions, and the economy of the searches, outweigh the initial 'investment' costs. One of the limiting factors for the growth of hierarchical trees is the iterative checking (procedure P2) if 100%

recall is still to be available. To avoid the resulting increase in computer-time needed, a partial solution is to generate and link many small trees sequentially instead of building one giant tree [26]. A more serious aspect is the propagation of errors inherent in all hierarchically ordered data sets. If only one spectrum or its representation is wrong or even slightly erroneous, the influence of the error will be spread through vertex representations ('average spectra') through half of the tree. It is true that in a cluster of, let us say, a hundred or a thousand spectra one wrong spectrum will not considerably change the average spectrum, but closer to the leaves, in the smaller clusters, the error is much more apparent. There is only one remedy to this plague: constant and thorough checking of the spectra that are already in the tree and double checking of the spectra selected for updating.

The fundamental problem scientists encounter if trying to improve the information system is very similar to its counterpart in materials science: the more sophisticated the procedure and better the properties of the final product, the better and purer must be the starting material.

REFERENCES

[1] J. Zupan, *Anal. Chim. Acta,* 1978, **103,** 273.
[2] J. Zupan, *Z. Anal. Chem.,* 1982, **313,** 446.
[3] J. Zupan, *Anal. Chim. Acta,* 1982, **139,** 143.
[4] J. Zupan and M. E. Munk, *Vestn. Slov. Kem. Drus.,* 1983, **30,** 61.
[5] J. Zupan and M. E. Munk, *Anal. Chem.,* 1985, **57,** 1609.
[6] M. Novič, *Ph. D. Thesis,* University of Ljubljana, 1985.
[7] M. Novič and J. Zupan, *Anal. Chim. Acta,* 1985, **177,** 23.
[8] J. Zupan, *Anal. Chim. Acta,* 1980, **122,** 337.
[9] M. F. Delaney, *Anal. Chem.,* 1981, **53,** 2356.
[10] J. Zupan, *Clustering of Large Data Sets,* Wiley, Chichester, 1982.
[11] J. Zupan, *Proc. Intern. Conf. General Systems Research — Hierarchy Theory as a Special Topic,* New York, May 1984, Vol. 2, pp. 633–640.
[12] K. Varmuza, *Pattern Recognition in Chemistry,* p. 25. Springer-Verlag, Berlin, 1980.
[13] M. Janežič and J. Zupan, *Z. Anal. Chem.,* 1982, **444,** 311.
[14] M. Novič and J. Zupan, *Anal. Chim. Acta,* 1983, **151,** 419.
[15] J. Zupan, M. Penca, M. Razinger, B. Barlič and D. Hadži, *Anal. Chim. Acta,* 1980, **122,** 103.
[16] K. Varmuza, *Pattern Recognition in Chemistry,* pp. 48–53. Springer-Verlag, Berlin, 1980.
[17] D. E. Long, *Anal. Chim. Acta,* 1969, **46,** 193.
[18] S. N. Deming and L. R. Parker, Jr., *CRC Crit. Rev. Anal. Chem.,* 1978, **7,** 187.
[19] H. Abe, S. Kumazawa, T. Taji and S. I. Sasaki, *Biomed. Mass Spectrom.,* 1976, **3,** 151.
[20] H. Margenau and G. M. Murphy, *The Mathematics of Physics and Chemistry,* Van Nostrand, Princeton, 1956.
[21] D. L. Massart and L. Kaufman, *The Interpretation of Analytical*

Chemical Data by the Use of Cluster Analysis, pp. 40–65. Wiley, New York, 1983.

[22] Arizona State University, Department of Chemistry, Collection of ^{13}C NMR Spectra; see for example H. B. Woodruff, C. R. Snelling, Jr., C. A. Shelley and M. E. Munk, *Anal. Chem.*, 1977, **49,** 2075.

[23] S. R. Heller and G. W. A. Milne, *EPA/NIH Mass Spectral Data Base,* Vols. 1–4, Suppls. 1, 2, U.S. Department of Commerce, NBS, NSRDS — NBS 63, 1978.

[24] P. H. A. Sneath and R. R. Sokal, *Numerical Taxonomy,* pp. 118–247. Freeman, San Franciso, 1973.

[25] B. Everitt, *Cluster Analysis,* Heinman, London, 1977.

[26] J. Zupan and M. E. Munk, *The Feed-back Search in a Hierarchically Organized Data Set,* VIIth International Conference on Computers in Chemical Research and Education, Garmisch-Partenkirchen, June 1985.

4

Infrared databases — their use, structure and implementation on a microcomputer system

Heinrich Somberg
Bruker Analytische Meßtechnik GmbH, Wikingerstraße 13, D–7500 Karlsruhe 21, FRG

4.1 INTRODUCTION

This chapter describes the structure of an infrared database and the necessary software, both implemented on a microcomputer which is part of a Fourier Transform Infrared Spectrometer [1]. Although this system is to some degree tailored to the built-in process computer with a computer word length of 24 bits, it is in principle adaptable to one of the numerous personal computers now available. The chapter is primarily aimed at chemists or programmers who have to deal with the problem of verifying a database for documentation or identification. The chemist does not have to be an experienced programmer but the chapter should be useful to him if he has to give assistance to a professional programmer. On the other hand it should also help the programmer to get some inside information about spectroscopic problems. Therefore some general ideas and basic considerations are discussed which may seem trivial to the more experienced reader but can be quite important in the first — the planning phase — of such a project.

4.1.1 General considerations

Nowadays, when all of us are deluged by 'information', databases on computer systems have become an indispensable tool for scientists. This is especially the case for chemistry and spectroscopy. Originally, all this information was (and still is) compiled in journals and books [2–4]. Reduction of the long rows of books, journals etc., to a more handy format by using microfiches [5] or microfilms [6] is without doubt quite useful but does not alter the problem of retrieving specific information. (To be fair to the 'printed' information, however, I must state here that this problem can also arise with computer-supported systems.)

Thus we really have some kind of 'natural' necessity to store data of all kinds in computer systems. The personal computer or a computer terminal on a desk in an office or laboratory is becoming as normal as a row of books on a book shelf.

Since there seems to be no doubt about the necessity to feed data into a computer we have to decide three important questions:

— which data are to be stored?
— in which form should they be saved?
— what kind of computer system is to be chosen?

4.1.2 Which data are to be stored?

Which data are needed and therefore stored in the computer memory certainly depends on the individual needs of the user of these data. Information is stored not for its own sake but to serve a purpose — to help the user to solve certain problems.

Because of this, the data stored should always be problem-oriented and, because even a definite application area can be split into lots of different problems, should be as complete as possible for a specific field of work. This is self-evident but does not always seem to be so to a data bank supplier.

4.1.3 In which form should data be saved?

The question of the form (or format) in which the data should be stored again seems trivial at first sight if we fulfil the requirement for completeness. We should save the original data without any reduction or manipulation.

In practice, however, this is nearly impossible. On the one hand each computer system has a limited storage capacity (hardware limitation) and on the other a computer program has to be able to process these data in a highly functional manner but within a reasonable time (software limitation).

These are the main reasons why a reduction of information is necessary, but it should affect the information content as little as possible.

4.1.4 What kind of computer system should be used for a database?

The last remaining general question is: where should the data be placed?

Some years ago this question was easy to answer: in a big central computer system. Even today there is a tendency to give the same answer, and it is no doubt still true with respect to large data collections. The best example is the Chemical Abstracts database [7] with more than 6.5 million literature citations stored. Also, the ever increasing amount of new data can only be handled by a strict centralization, but this centralization itself causes new problems in the usability of such databanks.

To access and work with such data the user has to make a connection by telephone line or data networks. In other words he couples his input terminal by telephone or modem directly to the central computer — he is 'on-line'. As long as this is done by only a few users no problems will arise since all such computers work with 'multi-user' operating systems. These operating systems allocate each user a certain amount of time, a 'time slice', in such a way that he does not realize that the computer is not working for him alone. On the other hand it is obvious that these 'time slices' become smaller if there is an increase in the number of users who access the computer at the same time. The gaps between these time slices will also become longer and longer, resulting in sometimes drastically increased response times. This situation is comparable to the daily 'rush hours' in a city and the problem of preventing these is nearly the same as with computers.

The costs for the user can also be for or against centralization. The effective costs are split into those for access to the system and those for the connection lines. In many cases both depend on the connection time and not on the effective computer or calculation time. Frequent use can thus become quite expensive.

These and some other reasons have caused a change in mind in favour of decentralization, which has become possible because of the rapid development of mini- and microcomputers and the corresponding drop in their price.

It often happens that two extremes meet in a compromise after some time. In the case of our problem this 'compromise' (although it is no compromise but a real advantage) lies in coupling those small systems to the big central one (Fig. 4.1). This computer network, which can be much more

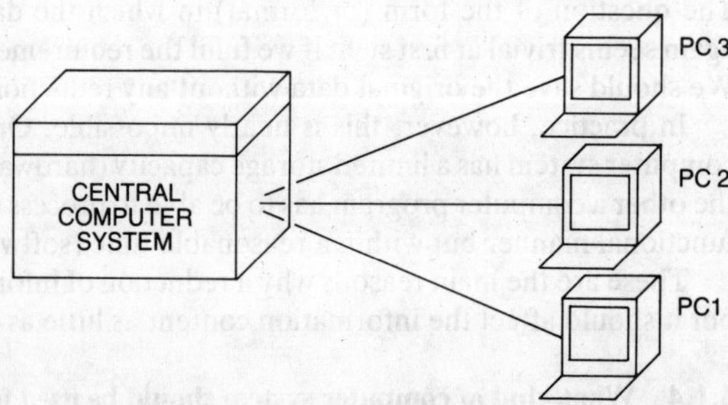

Fig. 4.1 — A simple computer network with three personal computers connected to a central computer system (star-shaped coupling).

complex than in the example above, results in job-sharing in such a way that simple problems can be solved immediately in the smaller systems, thus relieving the central system, which is then available for tasks which are too big for the smaller systems.

How do the databases fit into this network concept? We can also have some kind of job sharing with data banks if they are complementary. Large and more generalized data compilations have to be kept in the big systems, while smaller and more specific libraries of data are stored in the small computers. The 'everyday' routine problems can be solved by use of the bases in the smaller systems (sometimes referred to as 'in-house' databases), which should be tailored for the purpose, and seldom occurring questions are left to be answered by the large 'on-line' collections.

As stated in the introduction this deals only with the databases in such small systems.

4.2 INFRARED DATABASES

4.2.1 Theory of infrared spectroscopy

It is not the aim of this chapter to go into the details of infrared spectroscopy, which are well known and often enough published [8,9], but the inexperienced non-chemist reader should be made aware of at least the basics of this method, which will now be given in a brief and simple way.

Chemical compounds consist of molecules, i.e. of groups of atoms connected by chemical bonds. In a simple model these atoms can be represented as balls of different size and weight. The chemical bonds are not rigid, but flexible, and can be represented by spiral springs of different length and strength. Building such a model, we immediately recognize that it can easily be stimulated to vibrate, and that the frequencies of the vibrations will depend on the masses of the balls and strengths of the springs.

In our model we can excite these vibrations by mechanical pulses (pushing the balls with the fingers). In the case of molecules this excitation is done by electromagnetic waves in the infrared region, the range of thermal radiation, but only certain definite frequencies can stimulate the vibration of a particular group by energy absorption. If a beam of infrared radiation is passed through a sample, several frequencies will be more or less absorbed, in inducing vibrations of the molecules. Since the frequencies absorbed are dependent on the atom-masses and the bond strengths between the atoms, we have a direct relation between the structure of a molecule and the frequencies absorbed. In reality this relation is not so simple as it may appear and is not so easy to interpret. Several different modes of vibration can exist for a group of atoms, overtones or combinations can occur, some of the vibrations are not excited by infrared radiation, interactions between molecules can change the bond strengths, and many other complications can arise, which we need not discuss here.

4.2.2 Application of infrared spectroscopy

Use of the infrared technique for basic research is not the subject of this chapter. Therefore we concentrate on its use as a tool for characterization and identification of compounds.

What we get as a result of an infrared measurement is the infrared (IR) spectrum, a curve showing the relation between the infrared frequencies and the change in the radiation intensity when the radiation is passed through a sample (Fig. 4.2).

In earlier times the complexity of IR-spectra limited the use of this technique to some degree. This was especially so for routine work, since experienced chemists were (and still are) needed for analysis of the spectra.

To identify a chemical compound by its infrared spectrum two different basic approaches can be made: interpretation and comparison.

4.2.3 Infrared spectrum interpretation

Spectrum interpretation is a method which is based on the correlation between certain absorption bands (regions where the infrared radiation is absorbed by the sample) and certain groups of atoms, the functional groups, within a molecule. To simplify matters we can treat a functional group within a molecule as if it is isolated. A chemist confronted with an IR-spectrum first tries to determine which functional groups are in the molecule by consulting tables in which absorption bands are assigned to functional groups [10,11]. This can be quite difficult in some cases since the absorption ranges for different groups can overlap. In the second step these functional groups have to be combined to yield a sensible structure.

The whole process is a complicated procedure which sometimes results in wrong decisions.

4.2.4 Comparison of spectra

The visual comparison of spectra seems to be a feasible way to identify a compound or at least to find a similar spectrum which may be hoped to belong to a similar compound (whatever 'similar' means). The problem is that the comparison of a measured spectrum with spectra compiled in one or more books can become a gamble. It is a time-consuming task and because of the different sizes, formats and scales of the reprints of spectra [6,12,13], can also become quite a difficult job.

As long as the number of laboratory infrared spectra examined is low, use of the two methods can be justified. With the development of computerized grating spectrometers and Fourier transform spectrometers, for which a computer system is an essential part of the equipment, the throughout of measured samples has rapidly increased. The bottleneck of spectrum evaluation becomes more and more obvious and necessitates the assistance of computers.

4.2.5 Computerized comparison of spectra

Attempts were made to simplify the manual comparison of spectra and hence the identification of compounds long before the 'computer age' in infrared spectroscopy. All these methods worked with a drastic reduction of an infrared spectrum by coding rules. The most widely used system was the SpecFinder® [14], developed by Sadtler. The coding procedure records only the strongest absorption band within certain frequency intervals (26 in SpecFinder®) thus reducing a complete spectrum to a set of a maximum of 26 numbers. A second condition defines an intensity limit, bands below that limit not being taken into account at all. These codes are then sorted

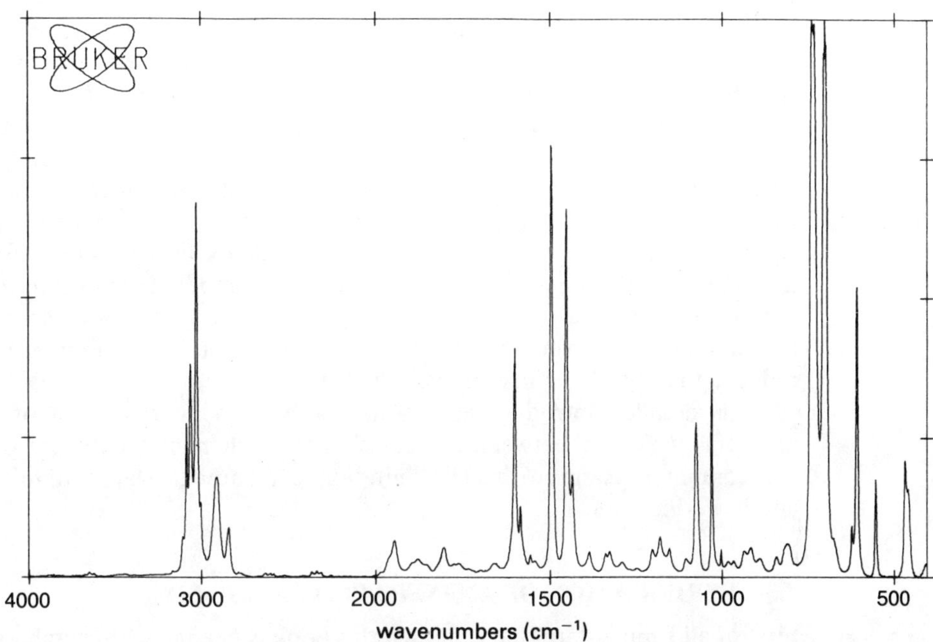

Fig. 4.2 — Infrared absorption spectrum of diphenylmethane, representation of wave numbers *vs.* amount of energy absorbed (low *y*-value≡high energy, high *y*-value≡low energy).

hierarchically, first according to the strongest band of the complete spectrum, then within these groups according to the number of bands occurring in the spectral regions from 2000 to 400 cm^{-1}. The spectrum of an unknown compound has to be coded by the same rules and only the resulting codes have to be manually compared, which is easy owing to the hierarchical order of the stored codes.

The amount of information lost in this coding scheme, and errors made during coding, sometimes caused unsatisfactory results to be obtained.

All such coding algorithms had the disadvantage that some really important information was lost forever. With the establishment of computers the way was opened for better and more efficient search algorithms but this did not alter the necessity of data reduction, because of the limited storage capacity. So, for example, transfer of the manual SpecFinder® algorithm to computers could not increase the reliability of the system but only the speed of a search through a database of SpecFinder® codes, which in my opinion was the wrong approach.

Two main search methods were then developed for smaller computer systems coupled with infrared spectrometers. In the first, a quite simple algorithm compiles peak tables, where the locations of the absorption bands of a spectrum are listed. A comparison of the peak table of the measured spectrum with corresponding tables stored in the database then finds the database entries for which most bands coincide with the bands of the unknown [15]. The second method is based on a subtraction algorithm which calculates the sum of all point by point differences between the measured spectrum and the library spectra [16]. Both these and also some other methods [17] have the same disadvantage, that the information contained in a spectrum has to be reduced to such an extent that important information can be lost. The peak tables for the peak by peak comparison normally contain the frequency of only those bands which are beyond a predefined threshold. For the point by point subtraction the number of points stored for a spectrum must be reduced drastically, which causes a loss of spectral resolution. A spectrum which normally consists of 3600 points is then reduced to only 225 points, or even further.

This detailed introduction was necessary to point out some of the problems which lie between the decision to implement a database on a minicomputer system (with all its limitations compared to a large computer) and its verification.

4.3 VERIFICATION OF AN INFRARED DATABASE

First of all I must state that although this book is dealing with 'databases', those databases cannot be discussed without mention of the tool needed to access and manipulate the data — the corresponding software program. Both data collection and software build an inseparable unit and influence each other. The internal organization and structure of a database is defined by the program, while the latter must fulfil all the requirements connected with the data in the collection. Therefore we are also forced (as in the previous section) to give some basic information, in this case on the software connected to a database.

4.3.1 General structure of an infrared database

As already mentioned, a database is always problem-oriented. In our example the overall 'problem' is chemistry, and within this infrared spectroscopy. The centre of interest is in both cases the chemical compound from which an infrared spectrum can be recorded. In this manner we have a natural classification of the information which we intend to store in the database; first the information about the chemical compound itself, which is independent of the spectroscopic method used, and secondly the information concerning the infrared or other type of spectrum. The first class includes the general properties of a chemical compound. As this can provide a basis for all compound-oriented chemical data collections, this class provides a linkage between databases for different spectroscopic libraries. The second set of information consists only of application- or spectroscopy-specific data, and includes the infrared spectrum itself. For the purpose of this database, which — besides documentation — is identification of compounds, all this information should be searchable and should reflect the 'chemical knowledge' a chemist can include in a search.

Another more or less natural division of databases is created by the different fields of work of the users of such a system. A chemist dealing with polymer chemistry is in general not very interested in a pharmaceutical collection, for example. Thus splitting a large database into smaller sets allows the user to use together his individual data collections. The redundancy between some of those sets (e.g. solvents can be quite important in a polymer library) which is caused by this separation can be tolerated.

At this stage we should be able to define what information is to be stored in a spectroscopic database.

General compound information
- — alphanumeric information
- — chemical structure

Spectrally relevant information
- — alphanumeric information
- — infrared spectrum
- — information derived from the spectrum

By alphanumeric information we mean everything which can be printed as text or numbers, for example the compound name or molecular weight. The chemical structure is of such importance that we will discuss it under a separate heading. The infrared spectrum should be saved as completely as possible but this makes it necessary to have an additional set of information derived from the spectrum because a spectrum search, whatever algorithm is used, with the complete spectrum will take far too much time. In the following we will discuss all these items in more detail.

4.3.2 Spectrally relevant data

The essential information is certainly the infrared spectrum, which relates the absorption of infrared radiation to the frequency of the radiation. Several different representations and formats exist. The spectrum can be presented in terms of transmission or absorption (we use the latter in our system). The ordinate is given in absorbance units,† and the abcissa is not in frequency or wavelength units but in reciprocal wavelength (so-called wavenumber) units (cm^{-1}).

The representation of such a spectrum can either be analogue, a curve on a sheet of paper, or digital, a 'curve' in the memory of a computer system. Since an analogue spectrum can only be processed by an analogue machine (like the human brain) it has to be converted into digital format for use within a computer. Digital in this context means that a curve must be represented by discrete data-point pairs, the wavenumber and the corresponding absorbance. To reduce the space needed for storing such spectra, the wavenumber intervals between neighbouring points are kept constant so that besides the intensity information only the wavenumbers of the first and last spectrum point and the number of points have to be stored.

† The absorbance is the logarithm of the ratio of the incident radiation power to the transmitted radiation power, and hence is related to absorption.

The wavenumber of an individual point can then be calculated quite easily as:

$$\nu_{(n)} = \left(\frac{FLP - FFP}{NPT - 1}\right)n + FFP$$

where ν = wavenumber; n = point number (starting with 0 for first point); FFP = wavenumber of first point; FLP = wavenumber of last point; NPT = number of points.

Some other terms which will be used later should also be explained here.

The spectral resolution of a spectrum is to be understood as the minimum distance (in wavenumber units) permissible between two absorption bands if they are to be distinguishable as two bands. We will use sometimes this definition in a slightly different manner, as the 'digital' resolution, which means the point distance between two neighbouring spectrum points. These definitions should not be mixed up. The standard infrared range runs from 4000 to 400 cm^{-1}, the first spectrum point having the higher wavenumber.

4.3.3 The spectrum-search database

The spectrum search is the most extensively used part of our system. I will not explain the search method here but focus on the main problem, the data reduction. This reduction is necessary only to enhance the speed of the search and not to save storage space. There are several methods for reducing a spectrum, two of which (reduction to a band-location table and decrease of digital and spectral resolution) have already been said to be too drastic. We can find a better solution by treating a spectrum as a set of independent but sometimes overlapping functions. The analysis of such functions shows that they have mainly Lorentzian characteristics. Besides the location of a Lorentzian function on the abscissa, only two other parameters, the height (intensity) and width are needed to describe such a band completely. Thus we have the possibility of reducing a spectrum to a set of three parameters for each band, which for an average spectrum of 30 absorption bands means a set of 90 numbers. Using only these parameters, we can rebuild a spectrum with excellent quality and without loss of spectral resolution. Figure 4.3 shows two examples of such reconstructed spectra in comparison with the originals. The similarity is so high, that even a visual comparison is possible without any restrictions.

Nevertheless, we have already intimated the need for the complete, original spectrum. The search algorithm we use even allows the analysis of mixtures which, in a first approximation, can be regarded as having a spectrum which is the sum of the spectra of all the components. Thus we subtract the spectrum of one component and use the resulting difference spectrum for further analysis.

By this method mixtures of three or more components have already been

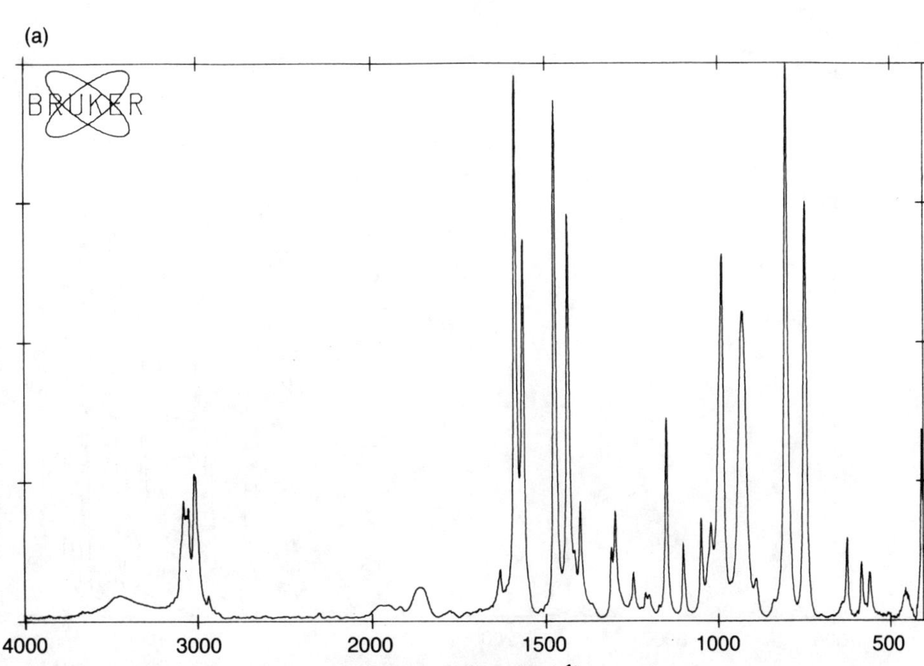

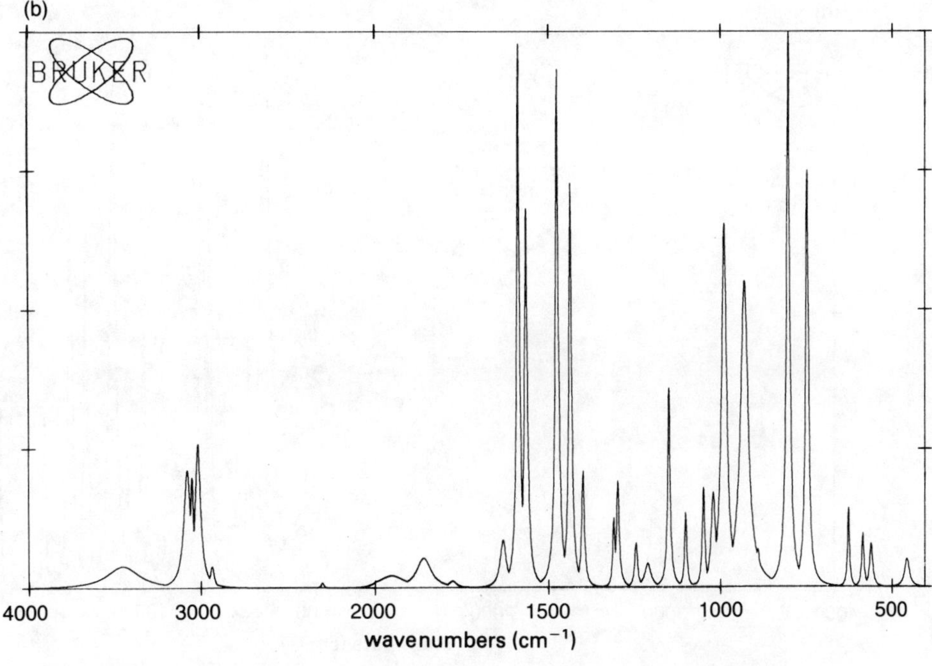

Fig. 4.3A — Original measured absorbance spectra of 2-vinylpyridine (a) and 1,4-butanesultone (c) compared to the reconstructed spectra (b) and (d), respectively. The reconstructed curves were calculated from peak tables of 32 absorption bands derived from the originals (a) and (c). Calculation by using Lorentzian functions.

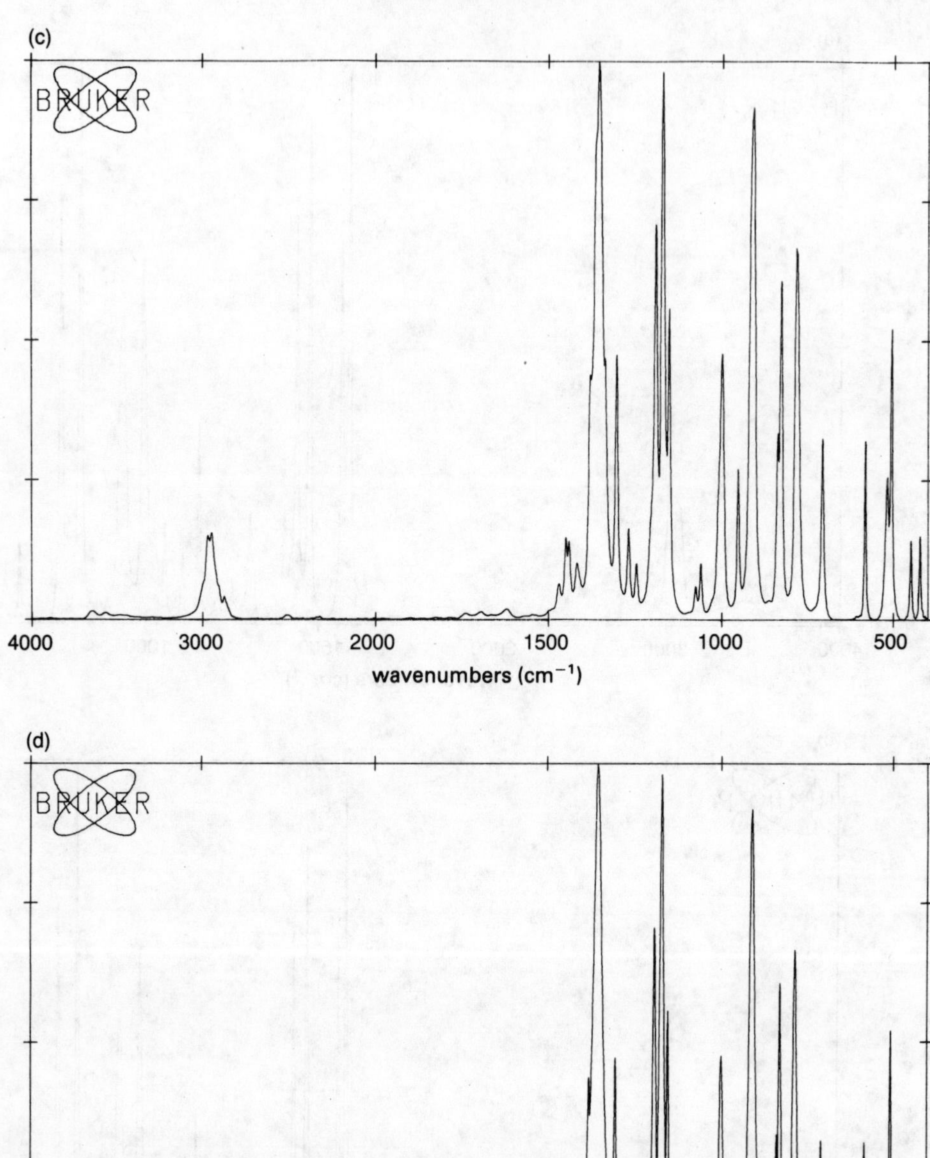

Fig. 4.3B — Original measured absorbance spectra of 2-vinylpyridine (a) and 1,4-butanesultone (c) compared to the reconstructed spectra (b) and (d), respectively. The reconstructed curves were calculated from peak tables of 32 absorption bands derived from the originals (a) and (c). Calculation by using Lorentzian functions.

successfully analysed. For this subtraction, however, the quality of a reconstructed spectrum is not sufficient, since the absorption bands can only be approximated by Lorentzian functions. This disadvantage is easy to see in Fig. 4.4, where the reconstructed spectrum is subtracted from the original. A further problem is that the band height is a function of the concentration of the corresponding compound, so analysis of mixtures is possible only when there is adequate resolution of specific bands.

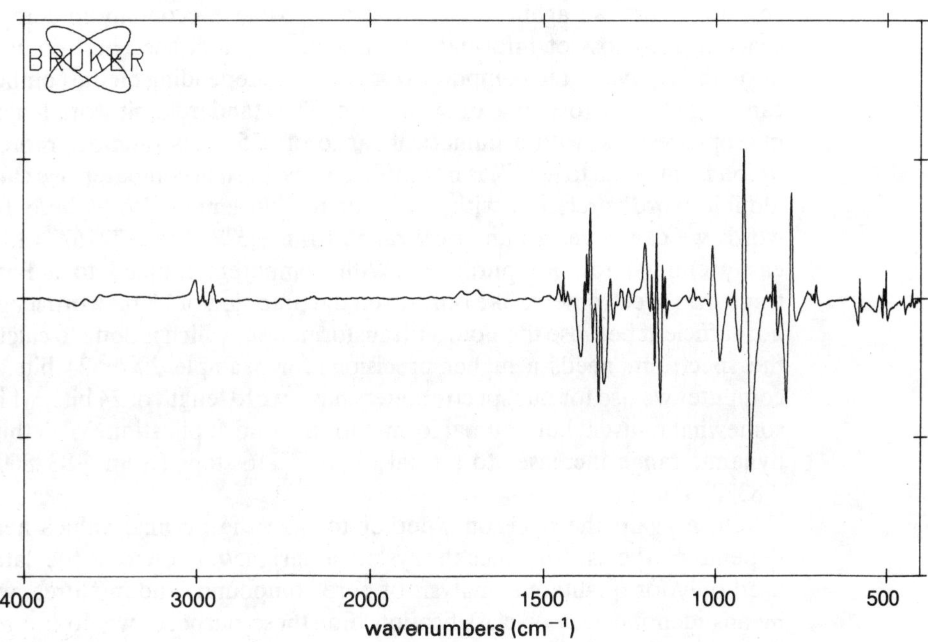

Fig. 4.4 — The result of the subtraction of the reconstructed spectrum (Fig. 4.3d) from the original one (Fig. 4.3c). The differences are mainly due to the asymmetrical absorption bands of the original spectrum.

4.3.4 The complete spectrum

The spectral resolution with which the complete spectrum should be recorded mainly depends on the field of work. It may range from 16 cm^{-1} down to 0.003 cm^{-1}. For standard applications a resolution of 2 cm^{-1} is normally chosen. For storage in a library the selected digital resolution need not necessarily be the same as the resolution of the measurement. For routine work a digital resolution of 4 cm^{-1} has been proposed as sufficient. Particularly in the range between 2000 cm^{-1} and 400 cm^{-1}, the so-called fingerprint region, no lower resolution should be used, whereas in the range from 4000 cm^{-1} to 2000 cm^{-1} a lower resolution of 8 cm^{-1} satisfies most requirements because here the information density is much lower. Despite this, the user of the system must be able to define the resolution which is optimal for his purpose. In addition he should be allowed to choose between 'compressed' wavenumber scaling with, as mentioned above, different resolutions in the two different wavenumber regions, or the linear format with equal point-distances over the full range. The 'compressed' format has the advantages that storage space is saved and that chemists are used to looking at spectra in that format.

Besides the resolution, the intensity information must be taken into account. Here we again have to carefully balance economy in computer space against loss of information. In a data system spectrum points are normally equivalent to computer words which, depending on the computer, can range from 8 to 32 bits or even more. The standard 8-bit word length of microprocessors, with a numerical range of 255 steps (number representation from −128 to +127) is not sufficient. With such computers we can use 'double word' precision with words of double length. With these 16-bit words we can cover a numerical range from −32768 to +32767, which is easily enough for our purposes. With computers coupled to a Fourier transform spectrometer like ours, even the precision of 16-bit word length is not sufficient because the Fourier transformation, which is done to calculate the spectrum, needs a higher precision, for example 20 or 24 bits. The computer we use for our spectrometers has a word length of 24 bits, which is somewhat unusual but optimal format for the said application. With this the dynamic range increases to a total of 16777216 steps (from −8388608 to +8388607).

Once again the decision whether to take the original values heavily depends on the use for which the system is designed. In our case the data are used only for qualitative analysis of pure compounds and mixtures, which means identification or classification. For these purposes we do not really need the full 24-bit precision, so we can reduce that range. The most obvious (and simple) reduction is to pack two data points instead of one into a computer word. The resulting 12-bit range is as sufficient for the above-mentioned analysis, including spectrum subtraction, as it is for the spectrum representation on a display screen or plotter. The range allows 4095 steps in intensity and halves the space needed. Thanks to the philosophy of the system the user still has the option of avoiding this reduction and can take the original (24-bit) data points if he also intends to do some quantitative work with the data.

4.3.5 Compound-specific information

That part of the database which refers to the chemical compound on its own should characterize the compound unequivocally, which means that theoretically it should contain all 'natural' properties such as molecular weight, melting point etc. and all 'given' properties such as compound name, Chemical Abstracts registry number [4] etc.

A glance at compilations such as 'Beilstein' [3], where such properties are collected, as well as common experience, shows that the literature values for a given property sometimes vary over quite a wide range. This forces a decision between taking everything (with the hope that at least one of the pieces of information is correct) or nothing. For documentation of a pure compound it is undoubtedly essential to put all available facts into the database, but when we are dealing with a spectroscopic data bank we should renounce this approach and concentrate on selecting reliable characteristic facts. Because of this and the still existing limitations of mini- or micro-computer systems it is necessary to limit the compound-relevant information to the most important data. If comprehensive information is required, it has to be taken from one of the large compound-oriented data collections, which of course requires a unique and unmistakable cross-link to these libraries.

The use of the compound name for this purpose has always been and still is a problem, even after the attempts to come to an international unique naming convention such as IUPAC nomenclature [18]. The alternative of registering more than one name for a single compound, though sometimes used, gives no guarantee that all possibilities are recorded, increases the space needed and (though this is often forgotten) increases the probability of making simple typing errors in the data input. This last is the worst case in name-search, since the computer is not able to recognize such errors and the incorrectly entered compound can never be found by name.

An excellent solution is to use the Chemical Abstracts registry number (CAS-number) which is given to each newly published compound. Besides the fact that this registration is not error-free either, the main disadvantage is that the registry number is a simple index number, and just as the page-number in a book can give no hint to what is written on that page, the CAS-number not only does not indicate any properties of the compound, it does not even indicate its name. The only international, unique, immediately understandable and nearly faultless information about a chemical compound is its structural formula. This is so important that we devote a separate section to the structure.

It is self-evident that besides the compound name and the CAS-number the fundamental information of the molecular formula and molecular weight (for pure compounds) should be included. Less important but also desirable are the melting and boiling point, whereas (in my opinion) density, refractive index or chemical properties are unnecessary. Summing up, the minimum information set should include:

— compound name
— CAS-registry number
— molecular formula
— molecular weight
— melting point
— boiling point
— chemical structure

4.3.6 Spectrally specific information

By spectrally specific information I mean everything which influences the characteristics and appearance of an infrared spectrum. Primarily this means the measurement technique (e.g. transmission, diffuse reflectance) and the preparation technique (e.g. solution, KBr-pellet). The spectral results can differ so much from method to method that it is good policy to create separate collections for different methods, for instance a library of compounds measured in the gas-phase. Another important parameter, already pointed out, is the spectral resolution. Here, we should try not to intermix spectra with different resolutions in one collection, or if we do must clearly say so.

The purity of the measured sample also certainly affects the spectrum. Normally we assume that only pure samples are measured, but technical products or sometimes mixtures also have the right to exist in a database, and must then be clearly marked. Other measurement conditions such as concentration in a matrix such as KBr which does not itself give rise to absorptions, or such as temperature etc. which influence the spectrum only a little or not at all, can be excluded from the data collection.

4.3.7 Disposition of the compound-information set

Commercially offered databases (prepared and distributed, as in our case, by an instrument manufacturer) have predefined sets of information which can certainly differ for the various collections. The following computer print-outs show two examples of information sets from different libraries.

Example 1

```
COMPOUND NAME
                          : BIS-4-HYDROXYPHENYL-SULFONE
MOLECULAR FORMULA : C12.H10.O4.S1
MOLECULAR WEIGHT  : 250.28
MELTING POINT     : 243
CAS-NUMBER        : 80-09-1
SAMPLE TECHNIQUE  : KBR-PELLET
REFERENCE         : MERCK 803258
```

Example 2

```
COMPOUND NAME     : NEOCRYL B810
SAMPLE TECHNIQUE  : CAST FILM FROM THF ON KBR
MANUFACTURER      : POLYVINYL CHEMIE
COMMENT           : ACRYLIC RESIN;
                    NON CROSSLINKING
```

These sets are selected from one larger set designed for an industrial laboratory:

COMPOUND NAME	REGISTRY NUMBER
MOLECULAR FORMULA	SPECTRUM NUMBER
MOLECULAR WEIGHT	ANALYSIS NUMBER
MELTING POINT	CHARGE NUMBER
BOILING POINT	CUSTOMER
CAS NUMBER	DEMANDER
SAMPLE TECHNIQUE	RELEASED
SAMPLE QUANTITY	COMMENT
COMMERCIAL NAME	WISWESSER LINE NOTATION
MANUFACTURER	CHEMICAL CLASS CODE
REFERENCE	SADTLER ID NUMBER
	SADTLER MICROFICHE NUMBER

Sometimes, however, the user requires a totally different composition of information items, beginning with the wish to have the information titles in his native language. Therefore the system must have enough flexibility for the user to create his own set of information tailored to his own requirements.

Finally we must state that the main problem still is the decision whether to include a specific kind of information or not. In case of doubt it is recommendable to include this formation.

4.4 THE CHEMICAL STRUCTURE

The important role of a chemical structure formula has already been mentioned. Any remaining doubts can clearly be removed by the examples in Fig. 4.5. If a chemist is confronted with such a lengthy or complicated name he has to transform this name into a structural formula either in his head or on a sheet of paper. So why not give him the structure immediately? Currently the structural formula is the only internationally standardized description of a chemical compound, because it is based on the periodic table and its element symbols, which are also used world-wide. Besides that, structures are very simple to read and understand, although, not surprisingly, their representation can differ (Fig. 4.6).

Nevertheless, all these pictures can clearly be identified. These arguments are so conclusive that it is really surprising to find that only a few databases include the chemical structures. The problem lies in the difficulty of string structures and working with them in a computer system [19,20], though so far this has been established only for large computers.

The first attempts at coding were made in the 'precomputer age' and used linear codes resulting from coding rules. These coding rules assign a part of a structure an alphanumeric code. A very simple example will demonstrate the basic principle. The structure of ethyl benzoate can be written

O
||
C–O–C–C

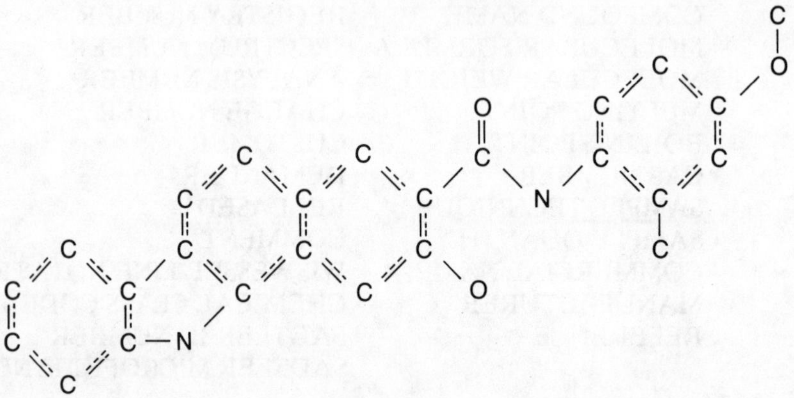

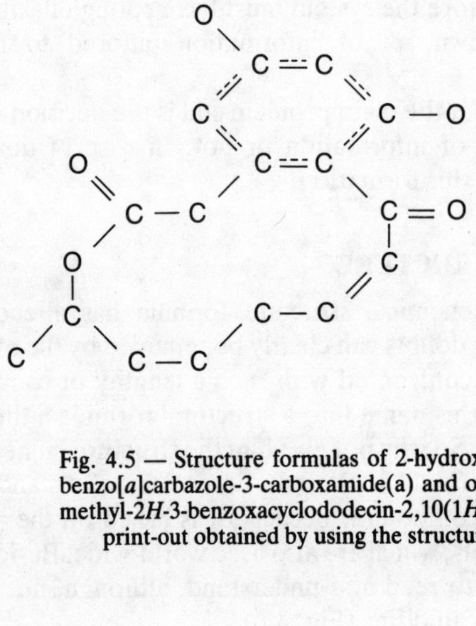

Fig. 4.5 — Structure formulas of 2-hydroxy-*N*-(4-methoxy-2-methylphenyl)-11*H*-benzo[*a*]carbazole-3-carboxamide(a) and of 4,5,6,7-tetrahydro-11,13-dihydroxy-4-methyl-2*H*-3-benzoxacyclododecin-2,10(1*H*)-dione (b) in the form of a computer print-out obtained by using the structure program of the BIRSY®-system.

and represented by the linear code ABC, generated by using the coding rules

A=monosubstituted benzene
B=carboxylic ester
C=ethyl

Examples of codes like this are the Wiswesser Line Notation [21] or the decimal code used by Hummel [22] for the classification of polymers.

The advantage of these linear codes is that they can be compared very easily and quite quickly either by eye or with a computer program.

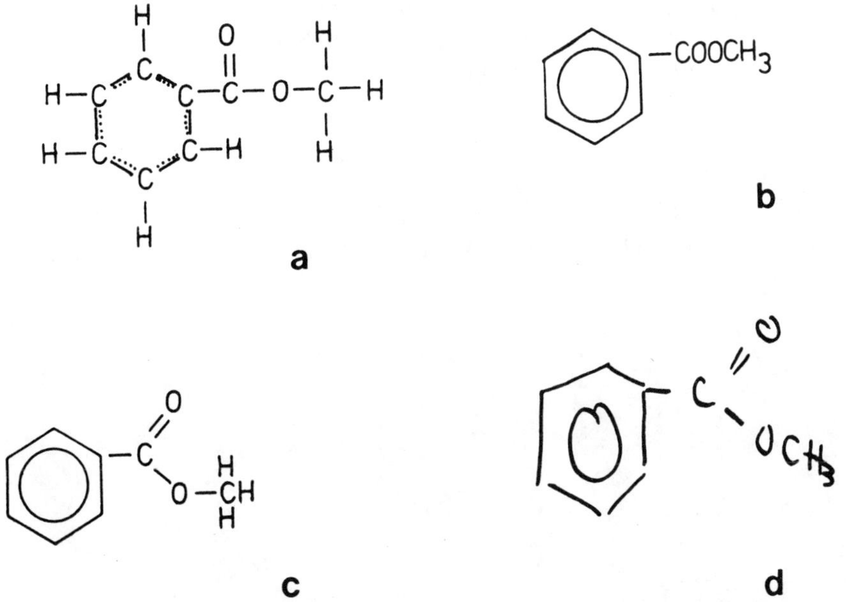

Fig. 4.6 — Four different representations of the same structure of the methyl ester of benzoic acid. Complete structure formula with all carbon and hydrogen atoms (a); simplified structure formula with a ring symbol for benzene and a linear formulation of the ester group (b); structure formula using the ring symbol for benzene and a complete representation of the ester group (c); and a hand-drawn structure formula using the ring symbol and a complete representation of the ester group (d).

The disadvantage is that a chemist needs long tables to decipher a code to get back to the structure again and that he also needs these tables to code a structure. Furthermore, this coding–decoding procedure is quite difficult to implement on a computer.

One of the main problems with structures is again the excellent performance of the human brain, which in contrast to the 'digital thinking' computer is able to recognize and process analogue patterns and images. Although the development of image-analysing computers is making progress in big leaps, the processing of structure images is still in the future.

Hence we have to assist the yes/no or 1/0 working computers in doing this job. The complete task can be split into three different parts:

— input of structure formula into the computer
— storage of structure inside the computer
— output of the structure as a graph

4.4.1 Input of chemical structures

The silliest way to feed a structure into a computer would be to do it in exactly the format which is used inside the computer. In practice we have to do it via the standard communication device between the operator and the computer, the keyboard. The most frequently used method requires a mnemonic command language which builds a structure in steps. The fictitious example in Fig. 4.7 shows how this can be done:

BENZ	—	builds a benzene ring, the atoms of which are numbered from 1 to 6
2 CARBOX	—	appends at atom 2 a carboxylic group
9 ETHYL	—	adds an ethyl group at atom number 9.

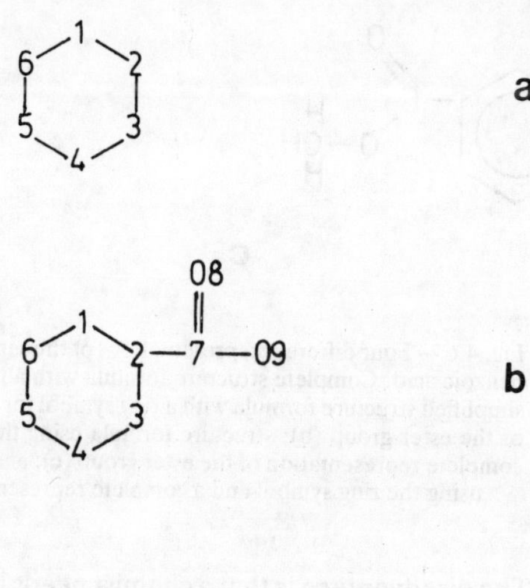

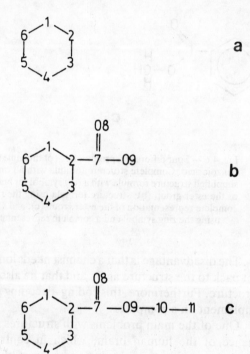

Fig. 4.7 — At the first step of structure generation, a 6-membered ring, atoms numbered from 1 to 6, is formed (a); at the second step, a carboxylic group, atoms numbered from 7 to 9, is appended at atom 2 (b); at the third step, an ethyl group, atoms numbered 10 and 11, is appended at atom 9 (c).

This is a simple and fast method if enough structure elements are predefined, but a new 'language' has to be learnt, which is quickly forgotten if it is not permanently used.

If the computer is equipped with a graphic video terminal as an input and output medium a structure can be generated interactively directly on the screen. The only thing we need are keys which allow the movement of a cursor (an arrow for example) on this screen. Only four keys, for moving up, down, left and right on a lattice-like squared paper, each square being a possible position of an atom or bond between two atoms, are necessary.

The whole input procedure to be learnt is reduced to the movement of the cursor from square to square and — at the desired position — typing either an element symbol or one of the bond symbols. Because we are using a standard typewriter style keyboard we must take easily-remembered standard characters to indicate the types of bonds:

.	single bond
=	double bond
%	triple bond
+	aromatic bond
<	co-ordinate bond

The procedure may be somewhat slower than the use of the command language but is much easier to learn and facilitates the input by permanent control of the complete structure image. The whole input can be speeded up if predefined structure fragments can be recalled, and the generated structures can be added to this fragment library.

4.4.2 Structure storage

The international format in which a structure is stored need not be known or accessed by the operator. He can simply use it like a black box, but for the interested reader I will describe the storage.

The heart of nearly all the systems used is the connection or connectivity table, a list of all subsequently numbered elements of a structure, with their nearest neighbours and the bond type between them. Table 4.1 shows an example of the connection table for the acetone structure:

```
    O          4
    ‖          ‖
C—C—C      1—2—3
```

The redundancies (e.g. atom no. 1 is connected to atom no. 2, atom no. 2 is connected to atom no. 1) can be removed before storage. Although it is simple to generate a connection table from a structure the reverse procedure is much more complicated [23] and sometimes results in structure images which are correct but look quite strange for a chemist. To get an exact copy of the input image we also have to store the co-ordinates of each element. Since we use a limited number of possible element positions (in our case a 32×32 matrix with 1024 positions) we have to register only one number for an element position.

To store such an extended connection table most efficiently we use a

Table 4.1 — Connection table for the acetone structure given above; hydrogen is not represented since it can be added very simply

Atom No.	Element	Connected with	Bond
1	C	2	single
2	C	1	single
		3	single
		4	double
3	C	2	single
4	O	2	double

linear format, the so-called topological vector (TOVE) [24]. The simplest way to explain this is again by means of a short example (Table 4.2).

We use the following codes (the coding is automatically done by the computer):

carbon : 14
oxygen : 16
single bond : not coded
double bond : 21
matrix field : 01–09

The resulting (fictitious) TOVE is

14 04 02 14 05 03 04 21 14 06 16 02

Explanation of the code:

14 04	carbon no. 1 in position 4
02	is connected to element 2 by single bond
14 05	carbon no. 2 in position 5
03	is connected to element 3 by single bond
04 21	and to element 4 by double bond
14 06	carbon no. 3 is in position 6
16 02	oxygen no. 4 is in position 2

It is as easy to go back from TOVE to image as to convert from image to TOVE via the connection table.

However, these efforts would be hardly worthwhile if only a nice picture is the result, and would also be in contradiction to the requirement that everything which is stored should be searchable.

Table 4.2 — The extended connection table, without redundancy, for acetone; the base matrix is assumed to be a 3×3 matrix

Atom No.	Element	Matrix field	Connection with	Bond
1	C	4	2	single
2	C	5	3	single
			4	double
3	C	6		
4	O	2		

The TOVE is searchable in principle, but only if the query structure is an identical copy of the stored one, even to the position of each element in the matrix.

We therefore have to create a second code to fulfil the following requirements:

— the whole or any part of a structure can be searched;
— the search must be independent of the orientation and absolute position of the structure within the co-ordinate system.

The code we use for searching is an extension of the well documented HOSE-code (hierarchically ordered spherical description of environment) [5,25] which is described in brief below.

For each atom of a structure a linear code, the 'environment code' EVIC, is constructed which describes the surroundings of this atom. This is similar to a connection table, where the connections to a central atom are listed. Let us look for example at methyl acetate, Fig. 4.8, for which we create five different connection tables, each with a different central atom. For greater clarity we use a graphic representation of the connections. An arrow in the drawing represents 'is connected with'.

To store this relation in a computer we have to convert this representation into a linear code again, for the present in a symbolic way. We have to use new symbols as separators between the so-called 'spheres' (the circles in the structures in Fig. 4.8 which separate the nearest, next but one and so on, neighbours of the central atom) and between atoms which are in the same sphere but connected to different atoms (the trees). We use an oblique stroke (/) as sphere separator and a comma (,) as tree separator.

The five resulting codes are:

(1) C/–C/=O–O/–C,/
(2) C/–C=O–O/,,–C/
(3) O/–C–C/–C=O,/
(4) C/–O/–C/–C=O/
(5) O/=C/–C–O/,–C/

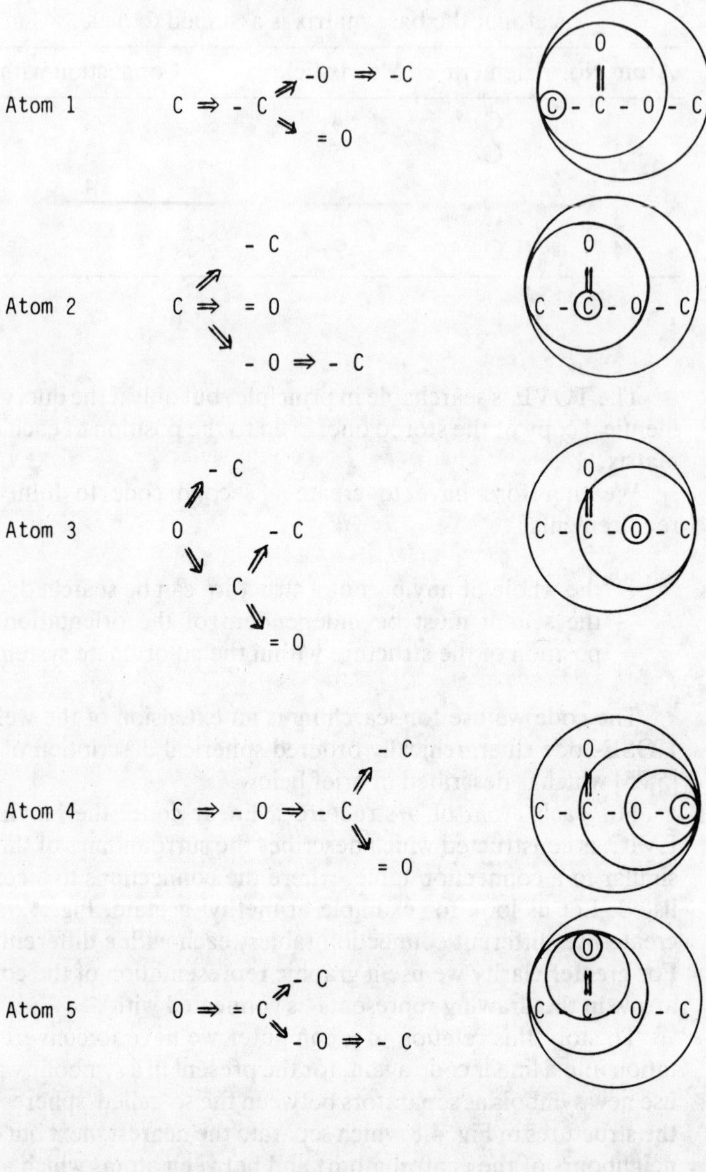

Fig. 4.8 — Structure formula of the methyl ester of acetic acid and the paths for the generation of five connection tables, each starting with a different central atom. The circles represent the different 'spheres', each sphere containing atoms with the same degree of 'neighbourhood' (first, second, ... neighbours).

The problem with such linear codes is that the sequence within the code can be interchanged, as the reader will realize on trying to relate these codes to Fig. 4.8. A computer does not like this very much because it is then unable to compare these codes in a simple way. Therefore we have to use some rules which define the sequence by setting priorities. If, for example, the central atom is connected to one carbon atom by a single bond and to another by a double bond, and the rule says that the double-bonded carbon atom has the higher priority, then the code must have the sequence =C−C. If two (or more) next neighbours are the same (which also means equal priority) then the sequence is defined by the priority of their bond partners. The higher the symmetry around the central atom the further we have to follow the bond trees to fix the priority. Only if we have complete symmetry will all these considerations become unimportant, because we will then get identical codes for each tree. To save space on the storage disk the symbols used above [C,(/), (,) etc.] are represented as binary numbers.

It is obvious that the length and quantity of these codes will rapidly increase with larger structures and an enormous amount of redundancy exists, since each of these codes represents the complete structure. On the other hand we need all these codes to be able to search parts of a structure. The redundancy can therefore only be diminished by shortening each code drastically. This can be done either by following the structure trees up to the first or second sphere, or (as we do) taking only that part of a code which exactly fits into a computer word. Up to that point we are still using, except for some changes in the priority rules and numerical codes, a copy of the HOSE-coding. This code is fully sufficient for searching for a complete structure (identity search), a structure match being indicated when all the test codes coincide with those of a stored structure.

4.4.3 Structure search

If we search for a part of a structure (substructure search) we can run into problems. Substructures are incomplete structures because they include undefined remainders. This results in incomplete codes, which break at the position of the unknown remainder. To compare these incomplete codes with the complete ones stored in our library we first have to shorten the latter to the length of the incomplete codes and then compare them. We can prove this by the simple example of an ester of acetic acid with an unknown alcohol group:

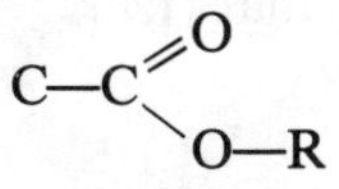

```
       O
      //
C—C
      \
       O—R
```

where R represents the unknown remainder. The corresponding code for the first carbon atom is

C/C/=O−O/

If we compare this with the already derived code of the methyl ester

C/–C/=O–O/–C,/

We see that indeed the first parts are the same. We can also see that any other group instead of the methyl group will give the same result, since this part is not taken into account in the comparison. It is easy to recognize that this is also valid for the other codes of the substructure, the only difference being that they become shorter the closer the control atom is to the remainder. For the single-bonded oxygen atom the code breaks immediately after the first neighbour:

O/–C

and this is our problem. The shorter the code the less specific it is and the higher is the probability of finding this code in other parts of a stored structure which have nothing to do with our substructure. The effect is that we find non-valid structures in addition to the valid one.

Although this is better than finding too little, there is a simple way to make the search perfect. We only need to keep track of the connections so that we know which EVIC codes belong to the next partners of the particular central atom.

We know for example that 'our' atom, in the substructure for which we find an identical code in the library, is connected to atoms m, n and o. If the structures are identical then the codes for these atoms m, n and o must be identical with the codes for neighbours of the 'library' atom, etc.

Although this solution requires a quite complicated search procedure the search is still very fast because most of the structures are dropped after the first step, in which the longest EVIC code of the substructure is searched for in the library.

4.5 CONCLUSION

I will conclude this discussion with a schematic display of the system (Fig. 4.9) and a comprehensive list of its features [26].
Features of the system are:

- — spectrum similarity search
- — search for compound mixtures
- — search for absorption bands
- — search for compound information
- — structure/substructure search

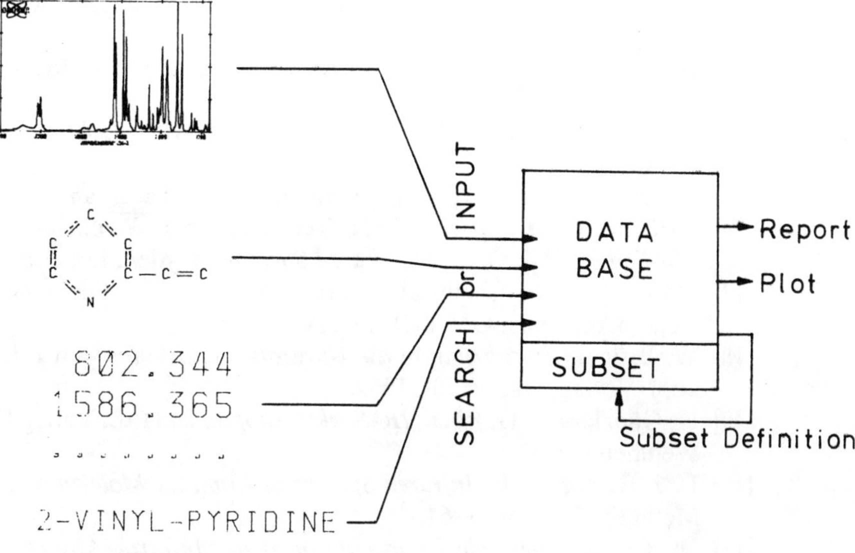

Fig. 4.9 — Block diagram of the BIRSY®-system: complete infrared spectra, structure formulas, absorption bands and compound information can be input (stored) in the database. All of the stored species can be searched either in the full database or a subset of it. The result of a search is the search report and a newly defined database subset. All stored information can be printed, displayed or plotted after a search.

— combination of different search modes
— high flexibility for user's own libraries

The aim of this system is to give the spectroscopist a tool for documentation of his work, for identification of compounds which are present in his own or one of the commercially available databases, and also to assist him in the elucidation of the structure of an unknown compound. Certainly our system only falls into the class of search systems and cannot perform a classical spectrum interpretation. However, the fact that the spectrum comparison is a similarity search and not only an identity search, can lead to results comparable with an interpretation based on certain rules. These rules are themselves ultimately derived from the same spectral information.

I hope this chapter can help in crossing the border which often prevents the use or implementation of such a system on small computer systems. The implementation is indeed long and difficult, but feasible.

REFERENCES

[1] Bruker Analytische Meßtechnik GmbH, Wikingerstr. 13, D–7500 Karlsruhe 21, FRG.

[2] *CRC Atlas of Spectral Data and Physical Constants or Organic*

Compounds, 2nd Ed., The Chemical Rubber Company, Cleveland, Ohio, USA, 1975.
[3] *Beilstein–Handbuch der organischen Chemie,* Beilstein Institut, 6000 Frankfurt 90, FRG.
[4] *Chemical Abstracts,* Chemical Abstracts Service, Columbus, Ohio, USA.
[5] W. Bremser, L. Ernst, B. Franke, R. Gerhards and A. Hardt, *Carbon–13 NMR Spectral Data,* Verlag Chemie, Weinheim, 1981.
[6] *The Sadtler Handbook of Infrared Spectra,* Heyden, London, 1978.
[7] *CAS ONLINE,* Chemical Abstracts Service, 2540 Olentangy River Road, Columbus, OH 43210, USA.
[8] W. Brügel, *Einführung in die Ultrarotspektroskopie,* 4th Ed., Steinkopf–Verlag, Darmstadt, 1969.
[9] H. Günzler and H. Böck, *IR–Spektroskopie,* 2nd Ed., Verlag Chemie, Weinheim, 1983.
[10] L. J. Bellamy, *The Infrared Spectra of Complex Molecules,* 2nd Ed., Methuen, London, 1964.
[11] W. Otting, *Spektrale Zuordnungstafel der Infrarot–Absorptionsbanden,* 1st Ed., Springer Verlag, Berlin, 1963.
[12] *The Aldrich Library of Infrared Spectra,* Aldrich Chemical Company, USA, 1970.
[13] A. J. Luft, *DMS–Arbeitsatlas der Infrarot-Spektroskopie,* Verlag Chemie, Weinheim; Butterworths, London, 1972.
[14] Sadtler Research Laboratories, 3314 Spring Garden Street, Philadelphia, PA 19104, USA.
[15] Perkin–Elmer Corp., 06856 Norwalk, Conn., USA.
[16] Nicolet Instrument Corporation, 118 Warwick Street, Leamington Spa, England.
[17] Digilab, 237 Putnam Avenue, Cambridge, Mass 02139, USA.
[18] International Union of Pure and Applied Chemistry, *Nomenclature of Organic Chemistry,* Butterworths, London, 1971.
[19] M. F. Lynch, J. M. Harrison, W. G. Town and J. E. Ash, *Computer Handling of Chemical Structure Information,* MacDonald, London; Elsevier, New York, 1971.
[20] W. T. Wipke, S. R. Heller, R. J. Feldmann and E. Hyde (eds.), *Computer Representation and Manipulation of Chemical Information,* Wiley, New York, 1974.
[21] E. G. Smith and P. A. Baker, *The Wiswesser Line Formula Chemical Notation (WLN),* Chemical Information Management Inc., Cherry Hill, New Jersey, USA, 1975.
[22] D. O. Hummel and F. Scholl, *Atlas of Polymer and Plastics Analysis,* Vol. 2, 2nd Ed., Carl Hauser Verlag, München; Verlag Chemie, Weinheim, 1984.
[23] I. Köhler and H. J. Opferkuch, Deutsches Krebsforschungszentrum, Heidelberg, FRG, unpublished work.
[24] W. Bremser, E. Frank, B. Franke and H. Wagner, *J. Chem. Research (M),* **1979,** 1401.

[25] W. Bremser, *Anal. Chim. Acta,* 1978, **103,** 355.
[26] BIRSY®, The Bruker Infrared Library Search and Documentation System.

5

IDIOTS — structure-oriented data bank system for the identification and interpretation of infrared spectra

Michael Passlack and Wolfgang Bremser
Department of Molecular Spectroscopy, Central Research Laboratory, BASF Aktiengesellschaft, D-6700 Ludwigshafen, FRG

5.1 INTRODUCTION

The structure-elucidation of organic compounds is one of the most important tasks of spectroscopy, the principal analytical methods used being nuclear magnetic resonance spectroscopy, infrared spectroscopy and mass spectrometry. The interpretation of the spectra is almost always based on reference spectra and semi-empirical interpretation models; that is, it relies on the evaluation of available spectroscopic data. A computerized data collection and the programs required for its design, maintenance and application combine to form a single unit that constitutes the analytical tool for spectral interpretation.

Infrared spectroscopy is a very powerful tool for establishing the identity of a compound for which a reference spectrum is available for comparison. Consequently, ever since the application of data-processing to spectroscopy, library searching has grown in importance as the number of spectral libraries available has increased. Library searching has thus become the most common method of interpretation. Even when a positive identification is not possible by reference to the library, valuable clues to the nature of the structure of the unknown compound are obtained by location of the most closely corresponding spectra.

For the interpretation of spectra with the aid of interpretation rules, nuclear magnetic resonance spectroscopy, like atomic spectroscopy, is superior because of the relatively simple relationship between structure and spectrum.

In contrast, infrared spectra are based on the vibrations of the whole molecule and the relationship between structure and spectrum is essentially more complex. Many empirical rules exist, of course, but there are so many exceptions to them that only experienced spectroscopists are able to apply them. Data-processing makes it possible for us to manipulate a structure-oriented databank of spectra to derive, improve and assess the applications of statistically based interpretation rules.

We have been able to construct a search and interpretation system for infrared spectra — Infrared Spectra Documentation and Interpretation Operating with Transcripts and Structures (IDIOTS) — that makes independent suggestions for the substructures contained in a compound and is a considerable aid in the identification of unknown substances.

I nfrared spectra
D ocumentation and
I nterpretation
O perating with
T ranscripts and
S tructures

5.2 THE CONCEPT BEHIND THE DATA BANK SYSTEM IDIOTS

5.2.1 A logical approach

For many years conventional spectroscopic data collections have been an important aid for the interpretation of spectra. These collections range from tables [1,2], through recorded spectra [3,5] in book or chart form, right up to the modern microfiches [6], which are produced by computers (for a survey of these see [7]). The spectra have mostly been collated in haphazard sequence and their greatest restriction lies in accessing them. Access is normally by indexes which sort the data according to certain criteria, such as formula or spectroscopic properties. Thus the biggest disadvantages of conventional data collections are the very restricted access, the time-consuming searches, the lack of scope for multidimensional searches and finally the tendency to become obsolete quickly.

All of these disadvantages could be overcome with computerized spectroscopic data collections. Even instrument manufacturers supply appropriate libraries and spectral search programs with their software. All the data in a data-bank system can now be interlinked as desired; access is possible through any number of characteristics; improvements and corrections can be made immediately, thus ensuring that the data are up to date. Several starts have already been made on the development of spectroscopic data systems, e.g. CASE [8], CHEMICS [9], DENDRAL [10], PAIRS [11] and others [12, 13]. The infrared spectroscopic system IDIOTS described here will in the future be supplied with the FIZ–CNMR program (INKA) packet SPIN [14] as a combined system, via Euronet.

It is intended to connect the infrared data-bank system to the ^{13}C data-bank system [6] available and possibly with other components to form a comprehensive spectroscopic system [14]. The infrared system is totally independent and consists of different building blocks, each of which builds on its predecessor(s) to finally yield interpreted spectra. Special importance is attached to its being a simple-to-operate tool for the chemist involved in elucidating organic structures. The data bank also serves as the basis for systematic spectroscopic research.

Below are listed the individual building bricks that were necessary for the concept of IDIOTS.

- A Design of an infrared spectral data file with topologically encoded structures and additional information
- B Spectra search and other search methods, intersecting search
- C Substructure search
- D Substructure statistics
- E Frequency distribution of the infrared bands
- F Automatic production of TRANSCRIPTS (interpretation rules)
- G Testing and optimization of TRANSCRIPTS
- H Interpretation system

5.2.2 Formal organization of the infrared data bank

Definition of data bank

A data bank comprises systematically collected data files and the data management necessary for their organization, access and protection [15]. The user programs have only indirect access to the data file. Access is governed by the management program. This distinct separation of application from data protects the data better against abuse or erasure, even if the applications change in the course of time.

Requirements

Spectroscopic data collections can only be established and maintained on computer systems with sufficient storage capacity. We had at our disposal for the design and development of the system a large Honeywell–Bull Computer with which we operated via terminals on a time-sharing basis. The design, maintenance and editing of workfiles of large data banks really require large computers, especially for data security. All the data are copied daily onto tape and there is no problem in ascertaining the former state of a data file for error debugging.

The data bank and the corresponding programs can be transferred, however, to a suitable personal computer with corresponding storage capacity, if the application and not the design of the data-bank system is the main consideration.

The data files of the infrared data bank

Library data files. The data bank consists of two library data files:

(1) the spectral data file, into which the information is fed from the spectrometer;
(2) the structure data file, which contains the chemical structure and other compound-specific additional information.

The data are linked by a common reference number.

Alterations to these data files are principally done with carefully tested programs by batch processing from the source data files.

Work files. Work files are created from library files in order to handle frequently occurring or expensive inquiries. They are constructed to allow efficient access and only the data necessary for access are stored in them. Examples of work files would be an auxiliary file for spectra searches, or index files for substructure searches, name searches etc.

Source files. Source files are files that contain the data necessary for the design, extension and correlation of library files. Thus the peak lists of all spectra from the spectrometer are sent via modem to the large computer and the raw data are stored in a source file. Similarly, the structures entered from the terminal are first stored temporarily in a source file. Source files are temporary and are erased after they have been processed.

Exchange files. Exchange files are used to exchange data between different computer systems. A universal format is selected and the file is copied onto magnetic tape. One such exchange file was submitted to the FIZ Physik in Karlsruhe in order to make our data bank accessible to the public.

5.3 STRUCTURE-ORIENTED INFRARED SPECTRAL FILE

5.3.1 Contents and presentation of the file

The heart of the system is a digital reference library of 17000 spectra with topologically encoded chemical structures. All of the spectra have been measured on Fourier instruments in the Central Research Laboratory of BASF.

The spectra must first be standardized to obtain digitized spectra that correspond as closely as possible to the actual spectrum. We mainly use spectra with about one point per wavenumber and a resolution of $2\,cm^{-1}$ in the region from 4000 to $400\,cm^{-1}$. Our infrared spectra are represented in negative extinction. 'Negative extinction' means that the measured transmission spectrum is first converted into an extinction (absorption) spectrum, which is then reflected with respect to the wavenumber axis. In this way a spectrum is obtained that is independent of the concentration and yet qualitatively still compares well with the usual concentration-dependent transmission spectra because the bands point in the same direction. The baselines of these spectra are then corrected so that, despite the varying dispersion in spectra of compounds in KBr discs, comparable spectra can be obtained.

Figure 5.1 shows one of the 17000 references in the spectra library. For the purposes of the data bank, the spectrum is reduced to a peak list containing the position, intensity and width of all bands. This reduces the storage space necessary for a fully resolved spectrum by about 90%, whilst still retaining almost all of the relevant information in the spectrum. With the aid of a reconstruction program, a spectrum which is almost identical to the original can be regenerated from the unintelligible peak list. For comparison purposes, Fig. 5.2 shows an original spectrum and the corresponding reconstruction spectrum. Despite the fact that the total information has been reduced to approximately one tenth of the original, it is clear that hardly any of the *relevant* information has been lost. The chemical structures can also be depicted graphically beside the alphanumeric representation.

The decisive factor in the use of the data bank for routine analysis is the link between the spectral data and the topologically encoded structures. To ensure an unambigous characterization, the reference contains the CAS registry number and the name it has been assigned in *Chemical Abstracts*. There are also cross-references to reference spectra in the literature [5] or to spectra of the same compound in other spectroscopic data banks (e.g. [6], ^{13}C-Datenbank, Verlag Chemie; W. Bremser, BASF).

The individual data records of a reference are listed in Table 5.1.

5.3.2 Data input

Input of spectral information

All recorded spectra are stored daily in a source data file on the main computer system. When the spectra have been evaluated and the choice of those suitable for the library has been made, the data are fed into the spectral file by a batch program.

Input of structural information

The structures are input interactively via a terminal into the source file of the main computer. They are checked and then transmitted by batch processing to the structure file. At the same time, the codes for the substructure search (HOSE and HORD codes [16]) and the identification search (DAMI and DAMJ codes [17]) are produced and stored, just as are the formulas and the relative molecular weights. The DAMI code makes it possible to check in

C6 H7 N1 O3 S1 115* 68* 56 IR 19649

BENZENESULFONIC ACID, 4-AMINO-
SULFANILIC ACID
ANILINE-4-SULFONIC ACID

CA: 121-57-3 MW: 173.01

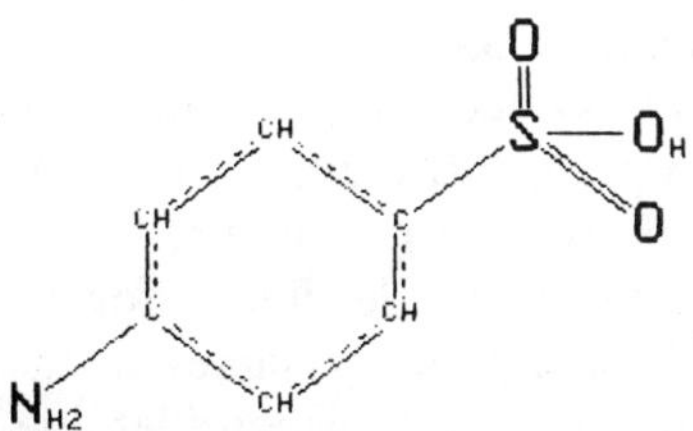

IR-Reference: SADTLER 21035K MP: 290°C
Source : MERCK-SCHUCHARDT HOHENBRUNN
Identicals : IR 19649
C13-Isomers : CNM24961 SULFANILIC ACID;P-AMINO-BENZENESULFONIC ACID
C13-Isomers : CNM29042 SULPHANILIC ACID ANION

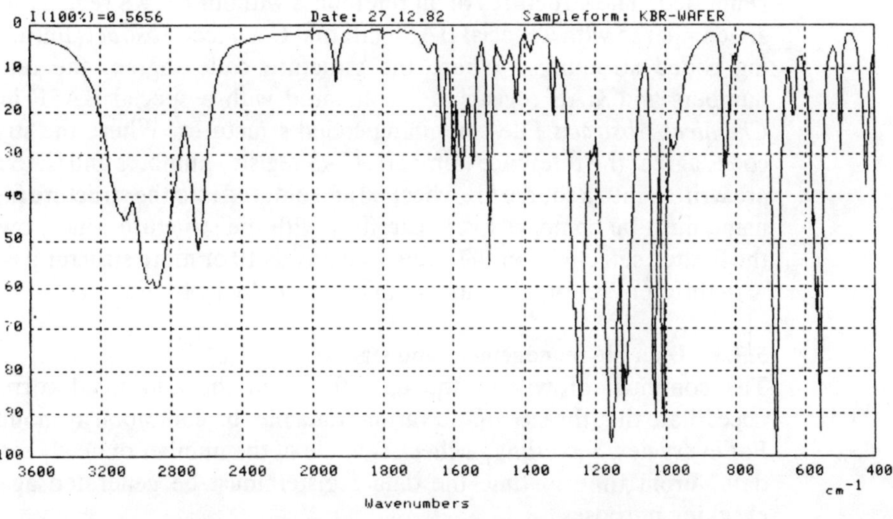

Position, width and intensity of the ir-bands [1/cm , %] :

No.	Position	Width	Int.	No.	Position	Width	Int.	No.	Position	Width	Int.
1.	3086.9	239	43	15.	1498.6	11	53	29.	1008.7	21	93
2.	3062.8	138	45	16.	1458.1	70	12	30.	979.8	85	39
3.	3045.4	225	43	17.	1424.3	17	22	31.	846.7	8	15
4.	2923.0	295	57	18.	1383.8	52	10	32.	836.1	8	41
5.	2879.6	298	58	19.	1319.2	15	27	33.	829.3	14	40
6.	2647.1	136	51	20.	1260.4	33	68	34.	818.7	14	27
7.	2378.1	39	5	21.	1245.0	43	87	35.	801.4	33	13
8.	2322.2	70	4	22.	1211.2	61	37	36.	712.7	14	17
9.	1933.5	22	13	23.	1184.2	27	57	37.	684.7	24	92
10.	1672.2	29	7	24.	1157.2	60	100	38.	634.5	19	21
11.	1631.7	19	29	25.	1123.5	23	89	39.	570.9	31	65
12.	1601.8	14	37	26.	1114.8	54	86	40.	560.3	14	91
13.	1577.7	39	35	27.	1038.6	10	84	41.	500.5	11	30
14.	1547.8	24	33	28.	1033.8	14	92	42.	427.2	21	35

Fig. 5.1 — Listing of a typical reference with spectrum reconstruction.

the course of recording a new reference whether it is already present in the library. If so, several spectra can be assigned to one structure as, for example, with different preparation forms of the same compound.

The DAMI code is used to assign the corresponding references to the ^{13}C library.

Input of additional information

After the structure has been entered, additional information is read into a source file by two procedures, either line by line or via a form, than all is checked and transferred to the structure file.

A special technique was developed for ascertaining the CAS registry numbers and the corresponding names so that these data could be read digitally. This not only saves a considerable amount of work but also decreases drastically the number of input errors. The procedure is as follows.

At intervals of several months, comfiches, containing details of the current state of the infrared data file and the relevant inverted files are generated. The structures of all references without a CAS registry number are compared with a special BASF internal *Chemical Abstracts* File containing coded structures. Where the structure codes agree, the reference numbers and CAS registry are compared with a special BASF internal *Chemical Abstracts* File containing coded structures. Where the structure codes agree, the reference numbers, CAS registry numbers and CAS names are written into a source file, checked and entered into the structure file. The name must be compared very carefully with the structure, since, owing to the limited selectivity of the code, as many as 10 or more structural isomers with different registry numbers can occasionally be found.

5.3.3 Data file management and statistics

The continual growth of the data files and the additional corrections necessitate that the size of the various data files be continuously monitored. For every new recording, a check is made of the number of newly recorded data. From time to time the data register must be generated again for checking purposes.

The various inverted files and other work files, such as the search file, must be generated afresh from the library files approximately every month so that they are up to date. With the program package it is possible to derive and display graphically the desired relationships. Thus, we determined the frequency distribution of the intensity or the width of all bands (Fig. 5.3) and the distribution of the bands over the wavenumber region (Fig. 5.4). This knowledge helped during the development of the interpretation program.

5.3.4 Data correlation

For a good data bank, the correction of errors is much more important than the input of new references, because quality and reliability are fundamental to correct evaluation. Errors can creep in at practically every place where

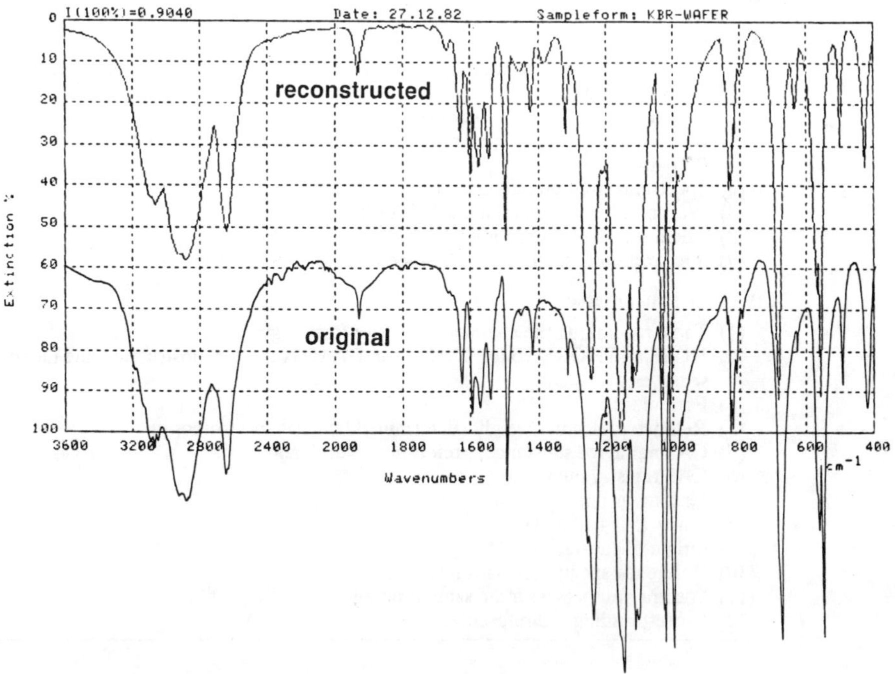

Fig. 5.2 — Comparison of a reconstructed and an original spectrum.

there are data, and it is therefore necessary to maintain a constant and systematic check of the existing material.

Basically there are two types of errors. The one kind consists of duplicated references or incomplete information and the other of erroneous data.

Duplicated references

A unique 'DAMI' and 'DAMJ' code is stored for every structure and ion [17]. A program has been written to call the DAMI codes in order to periodically generate a list of identical structures. The relevant spectra are compared to decide whether they are identical (in which case all but one will be eliminated) or show variations due to different preparation techniques or different diastereomers. In the latter cases we create one master reference with the structure, and the other reference spectra are linked to this structure to avoid duplicated topologies in the library.

If the spectra, however, show so much difference that they cannot be regarded as spectra of the structure in different preparations, stereoforms etc., then one or more of the spectra will not belong to the same structure and must be checked and assigned to the correct corresponding structure.

Table 5.1 — Data records of the structure-oriented data bank of the Central Research Laboratory on BASF AG.

(a) In the spectral file

(1) Spectra bands with location (cm^{-1}), peak width (cm^{-1}) and relative intensity (%)
(2) Number of bands
(3) Absolute intensity of the strongest band (in extinction)
(4) Recording date of the spectrum
(5) Preparation form
(6) Spectral resolution (standard resolution, cm^{-1})
(7) Wavenumber region (standard 4000–400 cm^{-1})
(8) Chemist's sample description
(9) Spectrometer (standard FT-IR spectrometer IFS 85, Bruker)

(b) In the structure file

(1) Table for linking the chemical structure (topology vector)
(2) HOSE and HORD codes, DAMI and DAMJ codes for substructure and identification searches
(3) Formula
(4) Relative molecular weight (determined by mass spectroscopy)
(5) CAS name for substance, preferably several names
(6) CAS registry number
(7) Melting or boiling point (if known)
(8) Purity (%) (if known)
(9) Origin of substance
(10) Reference spectra (cross-reference)
(11) Spectra numbers with the same topology
(12) Corresponding ^{13}C references

Incomplete information

Since the spectra and structures are entered separately, the data bank often contains spectra without corresponding structures or vice versa. These references are printed out with the aid of a program. Since our internal spectra numbers are generated by the FT–IR spectrometer, transmitted digitally with the spectrum and entered into the data bank, such spectra can only be missing or have been recorded by mistake and they can either be entered or erased accordingly. In contrast, the reference numbers of the structures are input by hand, thus making it possible that structures which have been entered with a wrong number do not bear any relation at all to the spectrum. Careful input of data and a thorough check of the input logs help to prevent a very time-consuming search for the correct number.

Erroneous information

A very effective albeit unsystematic check is the constant critical use of the data bank in the course of daily routine searching, with subsequent printing out of located references. Despite careful input of data, a 'new' mistake is discovered and corrected almost every day.

On the other hand, there is a specific method for recognizing errors in nearly every type of data record. Every deletion from and correction to the data bank is automatically registered together with the date in a special correction file so that alterations can be made later.

Errors in spectral information. There are relatively few problems here

(a)

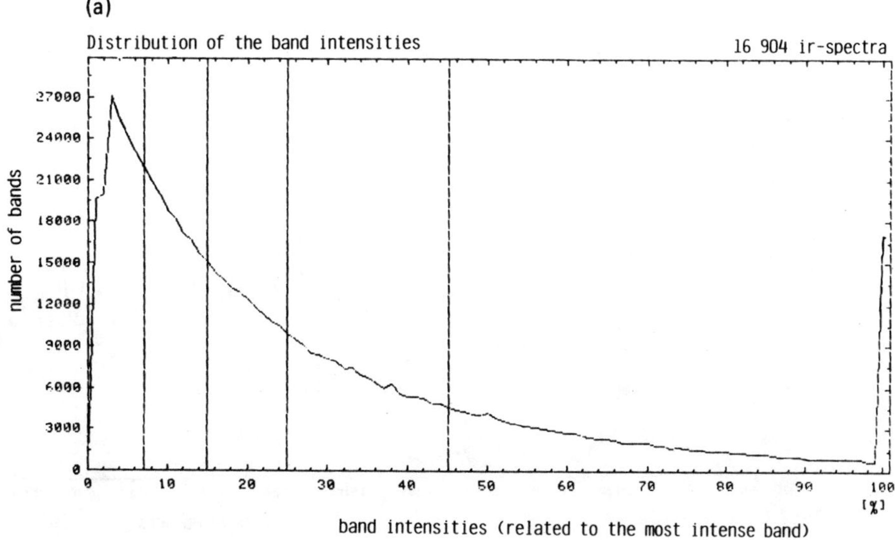

(b)

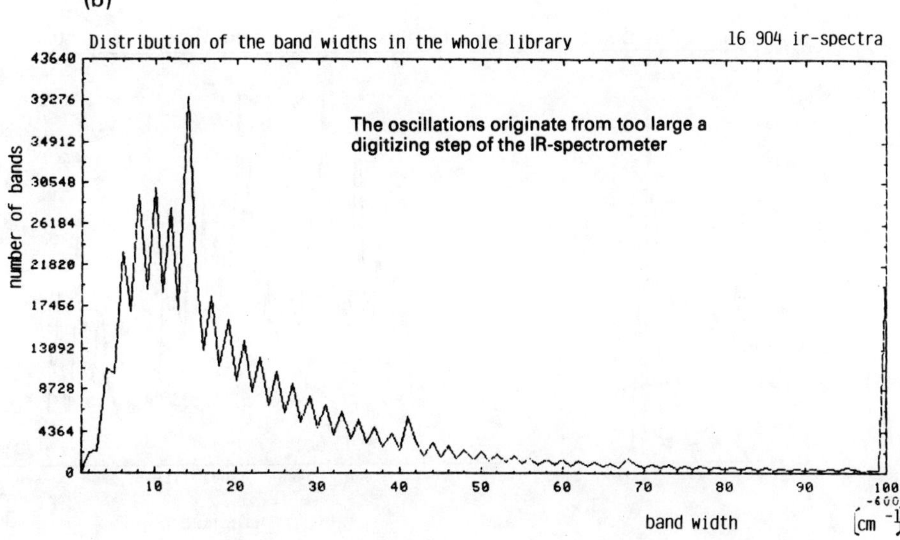

Fig. 5.3 — Distributions of (a) band intensities; (b) band widths in the whole library (16904 infrared spectra).

because the information is measured and transmitted digitally. Errors can only arise during the automatic generation of the peak list, but a great deal of work and time was invested to exclude errors here. Differentiation between bands and noise is the only problem, because it cannot always be made reproducible. However, all programs make allowances for the differences in the peak list. An unrecognized impurity in the recorded compound can, of course, cause the spectral information not to be totally correct.

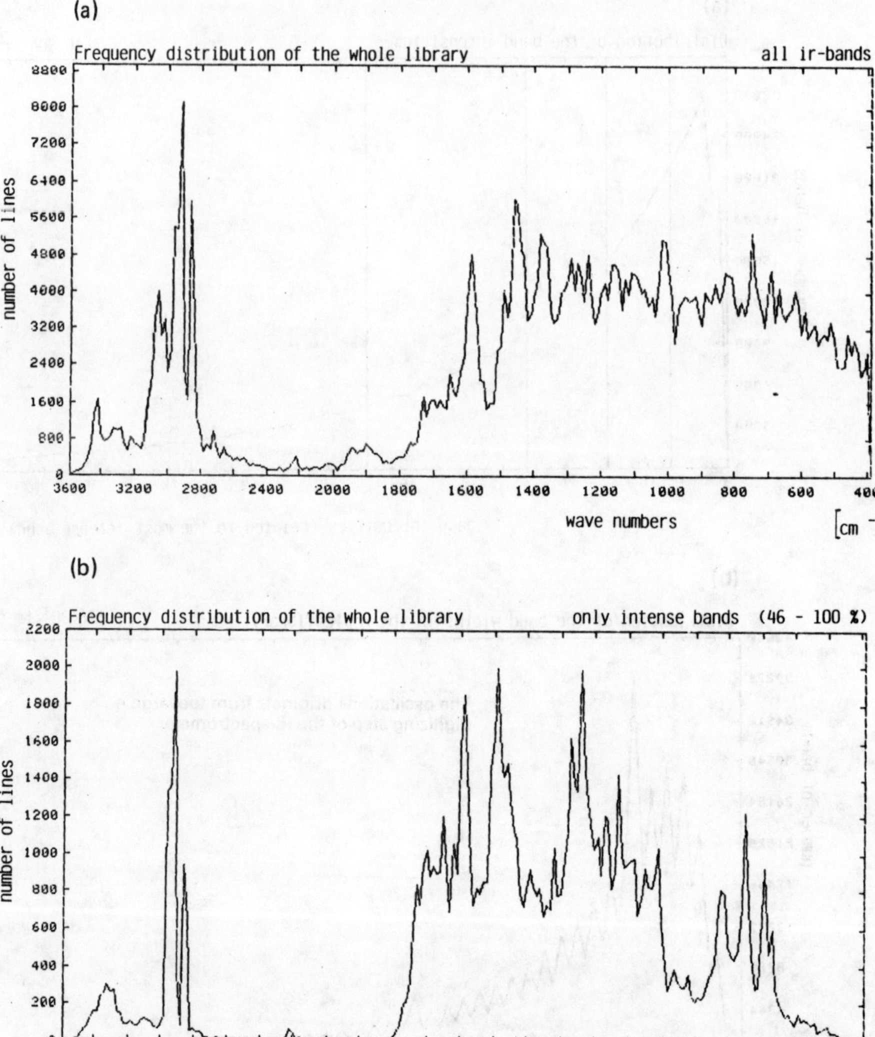

Fig. 5.4 — Frequency distribution of the whole library (a) all infrared bands; (b) only intense bands with relative intensity 46–100%.

Errors in structures. Since the structures are entered by hand there is much scope here for errors. For this reason, there are several monitoring stages for checking the structures. Painstaking checks, backed up by other spectroscopic methods, are made even at the interpretation stage to ensure that spectrum and structure agree. When the structure has been encoded in the computer, the bonds are checked for accuracy, the molecular formula is worked out and compared with that calculated previously, and the structure is again matched with the original. The final step, which is not applied at present, is the use of the interpretation rules (transcripts; see Section 5.5.3), which are generated automatically by the program, to see whether the functional groups are reflected in the spectrum.

Errors in the additional information. To avoid errors in the nomenclature and CAS registry numbers, we employ the method of data transfer described in Section 5.3.2. Nevertheless, since the names are input partly by hand, errors must be looked for here. A check of the sorted name index facilities the search for erroneous nomenclature. The additional information generated from the structures, such as the HOSE, HORD, DAMI and DAMJ codes, the molecular formula and the relative molecular weight, can only be as error-free as the basic structure.

Additional information such as melting and boiling point, purity, origin and classification of the literature spectra, can still only be checked according to formal criteria after their careful input.

5.4 SEARCH PROGRAMS

5.4.1 Identification and similarity searches with the aid of spectra

One of the main objectives of the data bank is to use the spectra library as a basis for a routine search for the best references. It is very important for informative interpretation in the field of infrared spectroscopy to have the spectrum of a similar compound if a reference spectrum of the test compound is not available. The references are all encoded in one search file [18] and are searched sequentially. Depending on the problem, preliminary research may or may not be done, and the agreement of the number of bands can be taken into account in the evaluation. On average, every day we obtain 60 new spectra and make two searches in the library for interpretation in the course of routine work. Figure 5.5 shows the result of a spectra search in which the spectrum was identified on the basis of a points score of 95 points out of a possible 100. In Fig. 5.6 we show a search result with an identification (95/100 points) and two 'possibles'. Even the two 'possibles' (with 66/100 and 61/100 points) are *para*-substituted acetophenones, which indicates the presence of this substructure. The search can cope with up to 60 unknown spectra, and names in each case the most similar reference spectra and their structures.

5.4.2 Fragment and substructure search

By virtue of the storage of all the substructures of a chemical structure (HOSE and HORD codes) [16]) and their sorting in an inverted register file, there are no problems in conducting substructure searches (see Fig. 5.8, p. 108). The spectra of compounds having any desired structural properties can thus be located by combined searches and compared with an unknown spectrum.

The substructure search is the first step in the development of the

```
IR - HAUPTLABOR  SUCHE  11.05.1984
==================================
( IDENTITAETSSUCHE )

2. H-36207        VON NICKELS        MIT  26 BANDEN FAND  1 REFERENZEN
-----------------------------------------------------------------------

1.  H-65078        95 PKTE.   24 BANDEN   23 TREFFER

              GOETZ          28.12.83       KBR-PRESSLING
              17041/146                     WZ 4000.-398.

REFERENZ   65078      VOM 13.01.84
---------------

BRUTTOFORMEL: C16 H16 O2                       MOLEKULARGEWICHT:     240.1146
```

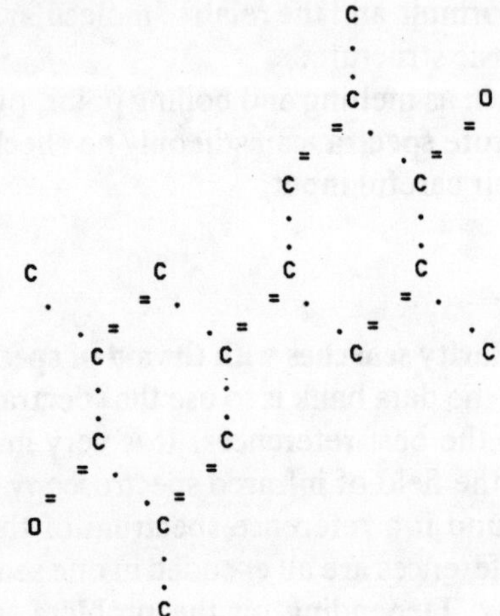

```
NAME = 2,5-CYCLOHEXADIEN-1-ONE, 4-(3,5-DIMETHYL-4-OXO-2,5-
       CYCLOHEXADIEN-1-YLIDENE)-2,6-DIMETHYL-
       3,3',5,5'-TETRAMETHYL-DIPHENO-QUINONE

CAS-NUMMER:  4906-22-3          LITERATURSPEKTRUM:  12077K
SCHMELZPUNKT:   224 GRAD C

LAUFZEIT DIESER SPEKTRENSUCHE       54.7 SEK. INKLUSIVE    0.7 SEK.OVERHEAD
--> 18.2 SEK./ANFRAGE BEI   12401 REFERENZ-SPEKTREN.

97.72% DER SPEKTRENVERGLEICHE NACH VORRECHERCHE ABGEBROCHEN
```

Fig. 5.5 — Library search for reference spectrum.

computer-generated interpretation rules (TRANSCRIPTS) (see section 5.5.3), by which the computer derives structure–spectra relationships from the data bank.

In addition a special substructure search was developed, which allows search for a full structure with unknown substituents. The corresponding possible structure codes are generated by the program and compared with all reference structures.

```
                IR - HAUPTLABOR  SUCHE  18.05.1983
                ==================================
                      ( IDENTITAETSSUCHE )

H-61713        VON MUELLER J.   MIT  45 BANDEN FAND  3 REFERENZEN
-----------------------------------------------------------------

  1.  H-05005        90 PKTE.   38 BANDEN   38 TREFFER

           MUELLER J.    22.01.81      KBR-PRESSLING
           15412/36                    WZ 4000.-398.

      BRUTTOFORMEL: C15 H12 O3          MOLEKULARGEWICHT:   240.0783
```

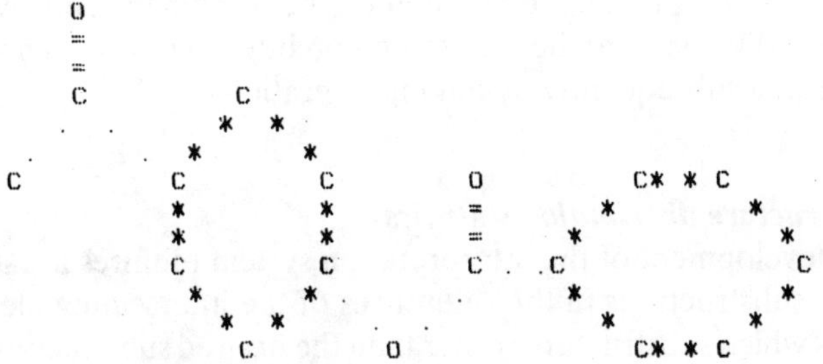

```
      NAME = ETHANONE, 1-[4-(BENZOYLOXY)PHENYL)-
                 4-HYDROXY-ACETOPHENONE, BENZOATE
      CAS-NUMMER = 1523-18-8


  2.  H-51234        66 PKTE.   46 BANDEN   37 TREFFER

           SAUTER         13.01.82     KBR-PRESSLING
           15771/163                   WZ 4000.-398.
    BRUTTOFORMEL: C10 H11 BR1 O2        MOLEKULARGEWICHT: 241.9939
```

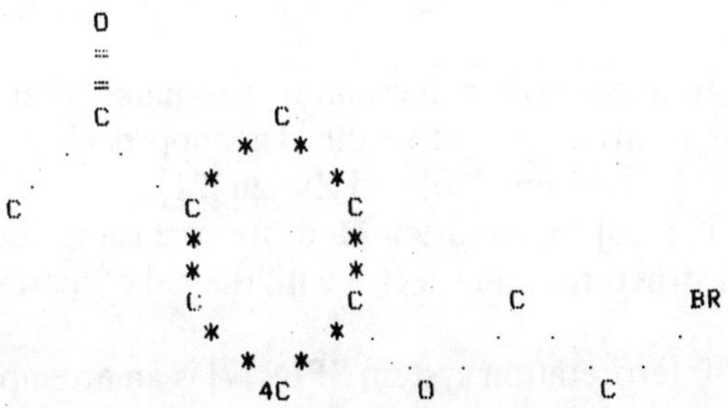

```
      NAME = ETHANONE, 1-[4-(2-BROMOETHOXY)PHENYL]-
      CAS-NUMMER = 63557-10-8

  3.  H-22247        61 PKTE.   38 BANDEN   33 TREFFER

           PA MERCK-SCH 15.04.83       KBR-PRESSLING
           4150580                     WZ 4000.-398.

      NAME = ETHANONE, 1-(4-METHOXYPHENYL)-
                ACETOPHENONE, P-METHOXY-

   LAUFZEIT DIESER SPEKTRENSUCHE    24.5 SEK. INKLUSIVE  0.3 SEK.OVERHEAD
    --> 24.5 SEK./ANFRAGE BEI    9314 REFERENZ-SPEKTREN.
```

Fig. 5.6 — Result of a library search with three references.

5.4.3 Other searches and utilities

Single line search, formula search, name search

All three searches are based on inverted registers. The programs must be flexible enough in practice to allow scope for a direct approach to the problem.

'Intersecting' search

An intersecting search is a search conducted later that allows all the search programs instigated up to that point to be combined in any way. The results of the individual searches are stored on intersecting search files and can be connected subsequently by linking-operations.

Substructure distribution statistics

The development of the interpretation system requires a statistical analysis of the substructures in the references of the intersecting files. This process shows which substructures other than the desired substructure are present in greater numbers than would be expected statistically (see Fig. 5.9, p. 110).

5.5 INTERPRETATION SYSTEMS

5.5.1 Possible approaches

There are currently three main approaches to interpreting spectra with the aid of a computer.

1. The program employs a decision tree to make a series of yes-or-no decisions to arrive at the result. This approach was suggested by Woodruff [19], Hippe [20] and Zupan [21].
2. Others [22–26] have attempted to ascertain the relationships between structures and spectra with the aid of 'pattern recognition' methods.
3. The ^{13}C-interpretation system SPIN [7] is an attempt to imitate the decision-making process of a human, where the computer has, in the form of a data bank, a tool to carry out more qualified assessments of its own suggestions by comparisons with similar spectra. ^{13}C-spectroscopy provides the possibility of checking a proposed structure by calculation of the spectra [14].

In infrared spectroscopy the first steps [27] have already been taken towards calculating a spectrum, but another process must be chosen for checking the interpretation results.

We tried initially to apply the program of Merck, Sharp and Dohme [19] to our aims (approach 1) and subsequently developed our own system based on our experiences [7] with the ^{13}C-interpretation system.

5.5.2 Attempts with decision trees

The system employed by Merck, Sharp and Dohme [19] is described in detail in the literature. We made a lot of modifications in order to arrive at an informative interpretation for infrared spectra, once we had integrated the program into our system. The results (an example is shown in Fig. 5.7) were in part very unsatisfactory and we abandoned this approach. The main problem with this method is the inflexibility of its decisions. Attempts are being made to include a minor evaluation of deviations by additional inquiries but the system is too inflexible and too intricate to incorporate knowledge gained from experience.

5.5.3 Transcript generation from frequency distribution

After our experiences with the interpretation program of Merck, Sharp and Dohme, we wanted to develop a system that evolves its own interpretation rules and is flexible and capable of learning. The program incorporates the following steps.

1. A substructure search is conducted to list all spectra with a special substructure (Fig. 5.8).
2. The substructure-distribution program (Section 5.4.3) checks whether in these references other substructures occur frequently that could influence the spectral characteristics. References are then eliminated until only one characteristic substructure is contained in the references (Fig. 5.9).
3. The frequency distribution of these references' bands is calculated, i.e. the number of bands for each wavenumber is calculated. This is the stage where the crucial correlation between spectral and structural information is made.

   Figure 5.10a shows the frequency distribution of the spectra of those compounds containing a trifluoromethyl group. When the normalized average frequency distribution of the whole library has been subtracted (see Fig. 5.4), characteristic bands for the substructure remain (Fig. 5.10b). The more bands there are found in a wavenumber region, the more characteristic is the corresponding band. Intense, weak, broad and narrow bands can be differentiated by classification in any of five different intensity classes and five width classes (classified along the lines of the distribution in Fig. 5.3).

   Figure 5.11 shows the very intense characteristic bands of the trifluoromethyl group and Fig. 5.12 shows the bands with a bandwidth of 11–25 cm^{-1}.
4. All this spectral information is drawn up automatically according to defined rules into a set of interpretation rules, known as the transcript. An excerpt from the tables is shown in Fig. 5.13 and illustrates how the bands are arranged according to regions, intensities and widths and finally condensed into the rules. It is not necessary to go into any more detail in order to be able to see what can be varied in the

I R - I N T E R P R E T A T I O N :   S U C H L A U F

TELL ME THE NAME OF THE BRUKER-LIKE-FILE
=888888

SUCHE ? (J,N,E)
NR: 61713 MUELLER J. DATUM: 18.05.83 KBR-PRESSLING 16883/36/2
=J

DO YOU WANT A SUMMARY OF THE DATA (N OR Y)
=Y

SPECTRAL DATA SUMMARY FOR:

NR: 61713 MUELLER J. DATUM: 18.05.83 KBR-PRESSLING 16883/36/2

THE SOLVENT IS: NACL

NO EMPIRICAL FORMULA GIVEN

NR	BR	IN	LINE	NR	BR	IN	LINE	NR	BR	IN	LINE	NR	BR	IN	LINE
1.	B.	5	3450	13.	A.	2	1430	24.	S.	4	1105	35.	S.	1	729
2.	S.	1	3066	14.	S.	4	1411	25.	S.	6	1082	36.	S.	9	711
3.	S.	1	3007	15.	S.	1	1376	26.	S.	10	1060	37.	S.	1	685
4.	A.	1	2923	16.	S.	4	1358	27.	S.	6	1024	38.	S.	5	661
5.	A.	10	1736	17.	S.	4	1313	28.	S.	6	1015	39.	S.	1	630
6.	A.	10	1733	18.	A.	4	1301	29.	S.	5	1002	40.	S.	2	617
7.	A.	10	1676	19.	B.	10	1262	30.	A.	4	954	41.	S.	5	592
8.	B.	4	1640	20.	B.	10	1258	31.	S.	2	939	42.	S.	4	579
9.	A.	8	1596	21.	A.	10	1203	32.	A.	4	885	43.	S.	3	498
10.	A.	6	1584	22.	S.	7	1174	33.	S.	4	817	44.	S.	2	484
11.	S.	5	1503	23.	A.	9	1167	34.	S.	3	800	45.	S.	2	464
12.	S.	4	1453												

DO YOU WANT TO CHANGE ANY DATA (N OR Y)
=

EINGABE-KOSTEN: 0.31 DM

*** STARTING SPECTRAL ANALYSIS ***

INTERPRET.-KOSTEN: 1.34 DM

NR: 61713 MUELLER J. DATUM: 18.05.83 KBR-PRESSLING 16883/36/2

FUNKTIONELLE GRUPPEN, SORTIERT NACH GROESSTER WAHRSCHEINL.

1.	ESTER-SATURATED	1.00	7.	KETONE-SATURATED	0.60
2.	ESTER-LACTONE-6-SAT	1.00	8.	KETONE	0.60
3.	ESTER-(OF-CO2H)	1.00	9.	IMIDE-ACYC	0.60
4.	ALCOHOL	1.00	10.	IMIDE	0.60
5.	AROMATIC	0.90	11.	AMINE-TERTIARY	0.60
6.	AROMATIC-(MONOSUBST)	0.60	12.	AMINE	0.60

NICHT VORHANDENE FUNKTIONELLE GRUPPEN

SULFONE	SULFONATE	SULFONAMIDE
OXIME	NITRO	NITRILE
NH3+	NH2+	NH+
CARBAMATE	ACID	ACETYLENE

Fig. 5.7 — Interpretation program of Merck, Sharp and Dohme.

```
----------------------------------------
   B A S F   IR - INFORMATIONSSYSTEM
----------------------------------------

          VERSION  08/84

IHREN NAMEN, BITTE
=PASSLACK

WELCHES SYSTEM WOLLEN SIE BENUTZEN

   1. LIST REFERENZ  (111=AWETA)          8. SPEKTREN-PLOT
   2. SPEKTRENSUCHE                       9. STRUKTUR-PLOT
   3. EINZELLINIENSUCHE                  10. MULTI-PLOT ->GRAPH.DRUCKER
   4. TEILSTRUKTURSUCHE                  11. SPEKTRENINTERPRETATION
   5. BRUTTOFORMELSUCHE                  12. HORD-/HOSE-CODE VERTEILUNG
   6. NAMENSSUCHE                        13. HORD-/HOSE-CODE KOMBINATION
   7. SCHNITTMENGENBILDUNG               14. ENDE

NUMMER
=4


------------------------------------------------
    SUCHE NACH STRUKTUREN UND STRUKTURTEILEN
------------------------------------------------

      HOSE/HORD - TEILSTRUKTUR-DATEI MIT
       67786 KODES VON 13580 STRUKTUREN


UND WEITER?
=>CF3,2LLO,1.PH
```

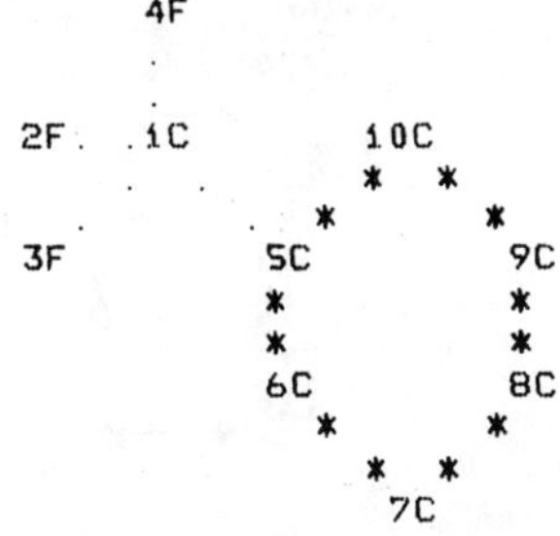


```
UND WEITER?
=T1

STRUKTURKODE:    CFFF(*C*C,,,/*C,*C/*C,*&)

STRUKTURKODE:    CFFF(*

 546 REFERENZEN GEFUNDEN

WELCHE FILENUMMER ? (1-20,L)
=3

TEXT ?
=TRIFLUORMETHYL AN AROMATEN

UEBERTRAGEN
```

Fig. 5.8 — Computer plot of the substructure search for trifluoromethyl on aromatics.

```
-------------------------------------------------
H O S E -   U N D   H O R D - C O D E - V E R T E I L U N G
-------------------------------------------------

STRUKTUR-DATEI  FILE-VERWALTUNG  08.10.84
---------------------------------------

ANZAHL STRUKTUREN, SPEKTREN-ZUORDNUNGEN 13719 13954

CODE-VERTEILUNG BEI:TRIFLUORMETHYL AN AROMATEN

                    OHNE SUBTRAKTION: 546    MIT SUBTR.:246
----------------------------------------------------------------------

HORD-CODE                               ANZAHL          ANZAHL
---------                               ------          ------
R6#(C,N$$,,,O,)                             38               -
R6#(C,,C,,,)                                36              28
R6#(C,,O,,,)                                36              16
R6#(C,,N,,,)                                51              31
▶R6#(C,,X,O,,)                             223              49  ◀—
R6#(C,,,C,,)                                38              32
R6#(C,,,O,,)                                37              24
R6#(O,,N,N$$,,)                             72               -
R6#(O,,S,N$$,,)                             63               -
R5==N.N.N(,,,,C)                            36              28

HOSE-CODE                               ANZAHL          ANZAHL
---------                               ------          ------
*C*CC(*C,*C,FFF/*CX,*&,,,/*                235              51
*C*CO(*CX,*C,C/*C,,*&,*C*C/*               230              51
*C*CX(*CO,*C,/*C,C,*&C/*&,                 222              47
*C*C(*CC,*CX/*C,FFF,*&O,/*                 223              49
*C*C(*CC,*C/*C,FFF,*&O/*&X                 223              64
*C*C(*CO,*C/*CX,C,*&C/*&,,                 222              49
CFFF(*C*C,,,/*C,*C/*CX,*&)                 235              51
CL;C(*C*C/*CO,*C/*C,C,*&C)                 222              56
F;C(CFF/*C*C,,/*C,*C)                     1413             612
O;CC(*C*C,*C*C/*CX,*C,*C,*C/*C             207              42

HOSE-CODE                               ANZAHL          ANZAHL
---------                               ------          ------
*C*CC(                                     757             370
*C*CO(                                     664             196
▶*C*CN$$(                                  300               -  ◀—
*C*CN(                                     292             125
*C*CX(                                     363             115
*C*C(                                     3444            1486
CC(                                        349             177
CFFF(                                      562             254
C(                                         349             169
CL;C(                                      426             142
F;C(                                      1746             794
O;=C(                                      401             163
O;CC(                                      446             149
▶N;=O=OC(                                  300               -  ◀—
```

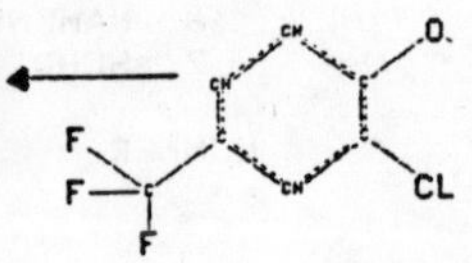

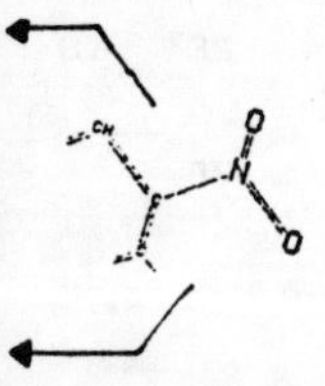

Subtraction of 300 references with substructure 'aromatic nitro'

Fig. 5.9 — Determination of substructure distribution and subtraction of aromatic nitro-compounds.

transcripts: band region, intensity, width, number of lines, conditions and evaluation numbers.

5.5.4 Transcript testing and design of the interpretation system

The critical and most important work now begins, because all the transcripts must be thoroughly tested, and either improved or rejected. It is important during the substructure search that only substructures are selected which are very characteristic for infrared spectroscopy.

(a)

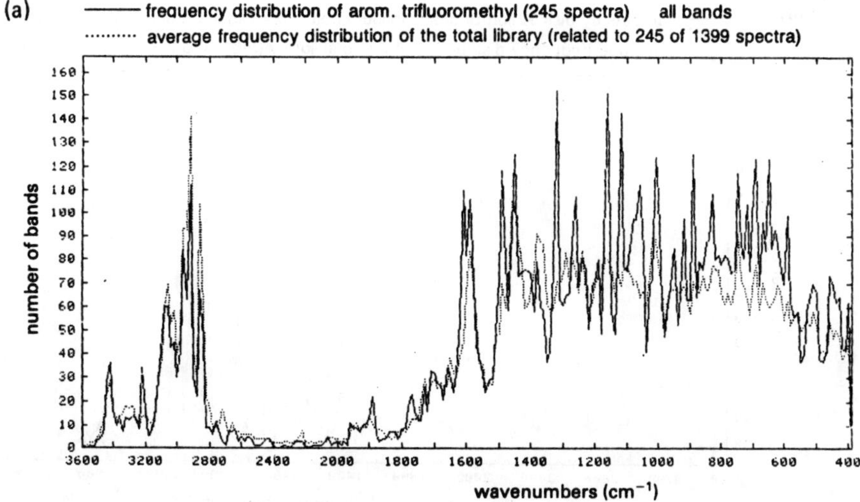

(b)

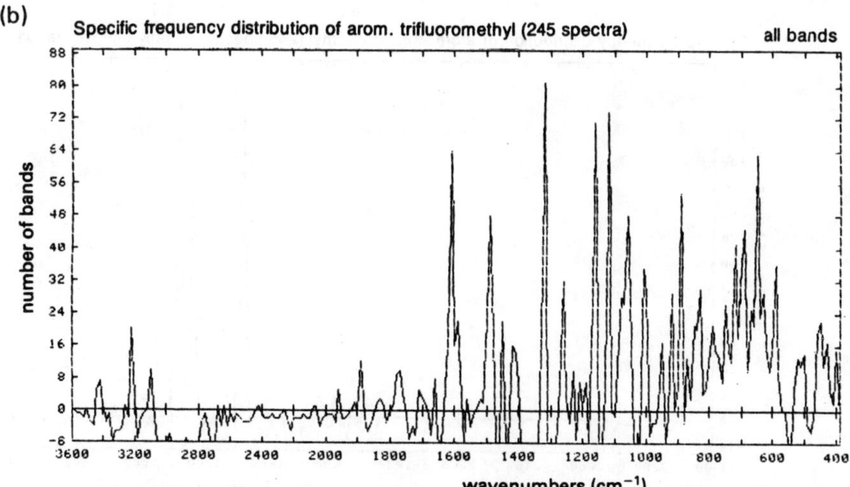

Fig. 5.10 — Frequency distribution of all bands of aromatic CF_3 spectra: total (a) and specific (b).

The program works with two reference groups, only one of which contains the CF_3 group. It is thus possible to ascertain for each transcript the proportion of those that match and those that do not.

Figure 5.14 is a graphical representation of such a test and demonstrates clearly the differentiation between both reference groups.

From the numbers in the middle, it is also possible to identify which lines of the transcript make a pronounced or less pronounced contribution to the differentiation. In addition, the percentage figures for the positive evaluation for both reference groups are listed on the right and on the left. The

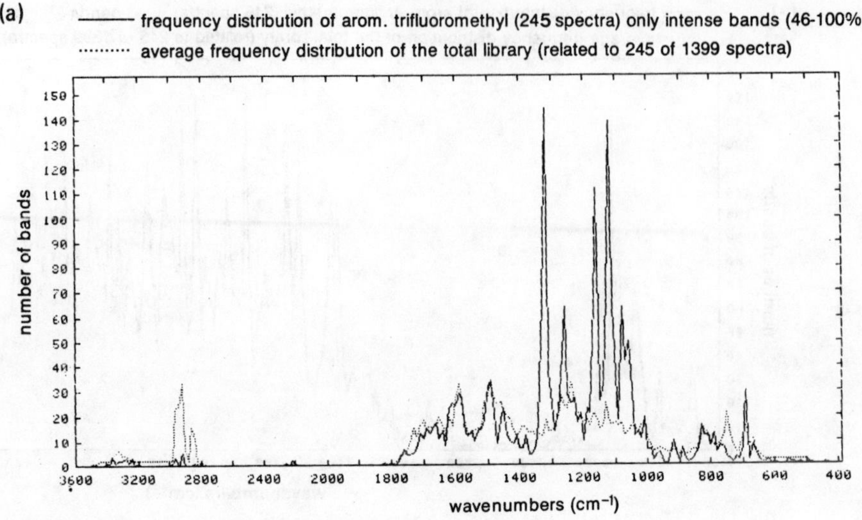

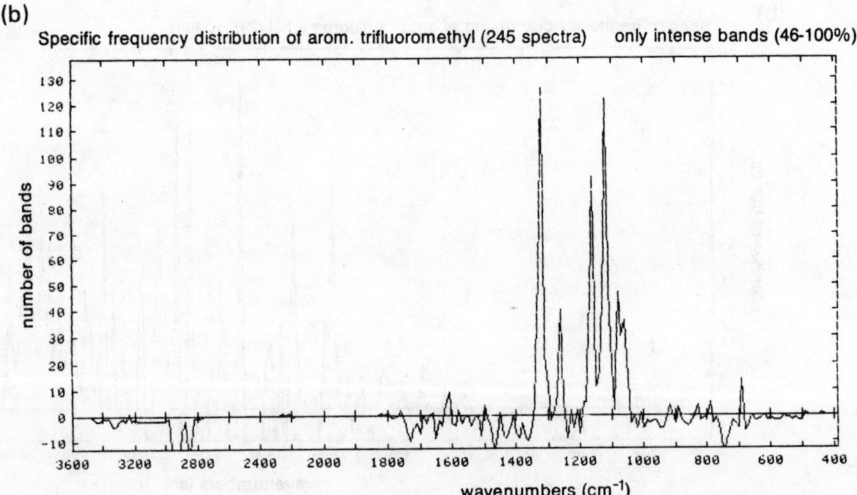

Fig. 5.11 — Frequency distribution of the intense bands of aromatic CF_3 spectra: total (a) and specific (b).

effect of an alteration to the transcript, as shown in the lower half of Fig. 5.14, demonstrates the feasibility of optimizing it. Figure 5.15 shows two tests where an alteration was made, so that in the first example practically all references without the CF_3 group were rejected, whilst in the second example almost all references with the CF_3 group were positively evaluated.

We have not yet been able to compile a comprehensive transcript library, although initial tests with the interpretation system have produced encouraging results. Figure 5.16 shows the result of one such spectra interpretation

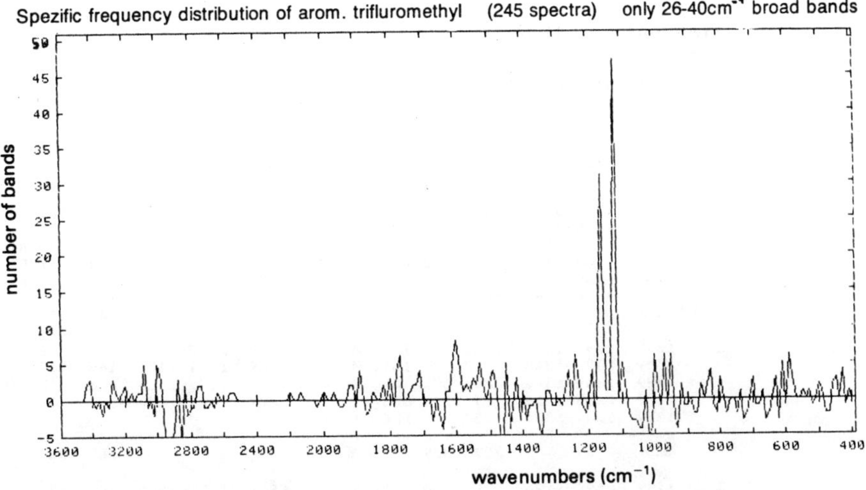

Fig. 5.12 — Specific frequency distribution of the 26–40 cm^{-1} broad bands.

where all four of the substructures present were identified. A spectrum interpretation based solely on infrared spectroscopy will obviously not always be so successful, but in combination with a second spectroscopic method IDIOTS should prove to be an indispensable aid for the elucidation of unknown compounds.

5.6 FUTURE DEVELOPMENTS

For more than three years now we have benefited from the 17000 reference spectra at present in the library and are constantly optimizing the whole data bank system IDIOTS through its continuing use. The various search programs are an important base for our spectral evaluation.

After the TRANSCRIPT library has been completed, the interpretation program itself will be employed routinely to make a preliminary interpretation by computer and to provide the user with unprejudiced proposals for structures. Our aim here is to create a spectroscopic interpretation system, incorporating other spectroscopic methods, that will eventually make and critically evaluate its own structure proposals [14].

The data bank system IDIOTS will be made available to the public via the Fachinformationszentrum Physik in Karlsruhe (INKA).

Frequency distribution

AROM. TRIFLUOROMETHYL **245/13999**

			No of bands					No of bands		
	maximum	region	subt.	all	class	maximum	region	subt.	all	class
1.	1099	1109-1090	31	70	INT. 4	1129	1139-1110	50	136	BR 2
*	1129	1159-1100	265	371	INT. 5	1129	1159-1120	63	98	BR 3
	1129	1139-1110	82	302	GESAMT	1109	1119-1090	7	33	BR 3
	1139	1139-1130	1	13	BRE. 1	1129	1149-1110	20	41	BR 4
	1109	1109-1100	4	16	BRE. 1	1129	1129-1120	1	1	BR 5
	Sum		296	441				146	338	
2.	1349	1349-1340	6	17	INT. 4	1309	1319-1300	5	24	BRE. 1
	1309	1309-1300	1	21	INT. 4	1329	1349-1300	148	282	BRE. 2
*	1329	1349-1300	220	291	INT. 5	1329	1339-1320	3	18	BRE. 3
	1329	1339-1320	99	230	GESAMT	1299	1309-1290	3	16	BRE. 4
	1339	1349-1330	3	15	BRE. 1					
	Sum		227	329				162	355	
3.	1199	1199-1190	5	20	INT. 3	1169	1189-1160	81	171	BRE. 2
	1169	1189-1150	47	120	INT. 4	1199	1209-1190	5	23	BRE. 3
*	1169	1199-1160	146	224	INT. 5	1169	1179-1160	44	62	BRE. 3
	1199	1209-1190	8	152	GESAMT	1199	1199-1190	5	11	BRE. 4
	1169	1179-1160	98	260	GESAMT	1159	1179-1150	10	24	BRE. 4
	1169	1169-1160	1	14	BRE. 1	1169	1169-1160	2	2	BRE. 5
	Sum		198	364				148	307	
4.	1069	1069-1060	6	18	INT. 3	1069	1099-1050	117	181	BRE. 1
	1079	1089-1050	60	124	INT. 4	1089	1109-1050	101	271	BRE. 2
*	1069	1079-1050	80	122	INT. 5	1079	1089-1070	2	2	BRE. 5
	1069	1079-1050	89	294	GESAMT					
	Sum		146	264				220	454	

:
and so on

TRANSCRIPT

```
N, AROM.  TRIFLUOROMETHYL              (2, 245/13999)
B,
K,
I,  1, 1639-1590,    10 / 10,        , 1-4     , 133/ 57
I,  2, 1529-1480,    20 / 10, 1-4    , 1-3     , 120/ 53
I,  3, 1349-1300,    10 / 10,   5,     2       , 134/ 93
I,  4, 1199-1160,    10 / 10, 4-5    , 2-3     , 149/ 81
I,  5, 1159-1100,    10 / 10, 4-5    , 2-3     ,  90/121
I,  6, 1099-1080,    10 / 10, 3-5    ,         ,  43/ 54
I,  7, 1079-1050,    30 / 10, 4-5    , 1-2     , 108/ 60
I,  8, 1019-1000,    20 / 20, 1-4    , 1-4     ,  98/ 33
I,  9,  919- 880,    10 / 10,        ,         , 116/ 41
I, 10,  859- 810,    10 / 20, 2-5    , 1-4     , 189/ 58
I, 11,  779- 740,    10 / 10, 1-3    , 1-2     , 120/ 54
I, 12,  719- 690,    20 / 10,        ,   1     , 142/ 58
I, 13,  669- 630,    20 / 20, 1-4    , 1-2     , 173/ 68
I, 14,  609- 580,    20 / 10, 1-3,   , 1-4     , 109/ 35
I, 15,  549- 500,    10 / 10,   1    , 1-2     ,  98/ 35

          region   tolerance  inten-   width    qualification
                              sity               factor
```

Fig. 5.13 — (a) Cut of the list of frequency distribution. (b) Automatically generated TRANSCRIPT.

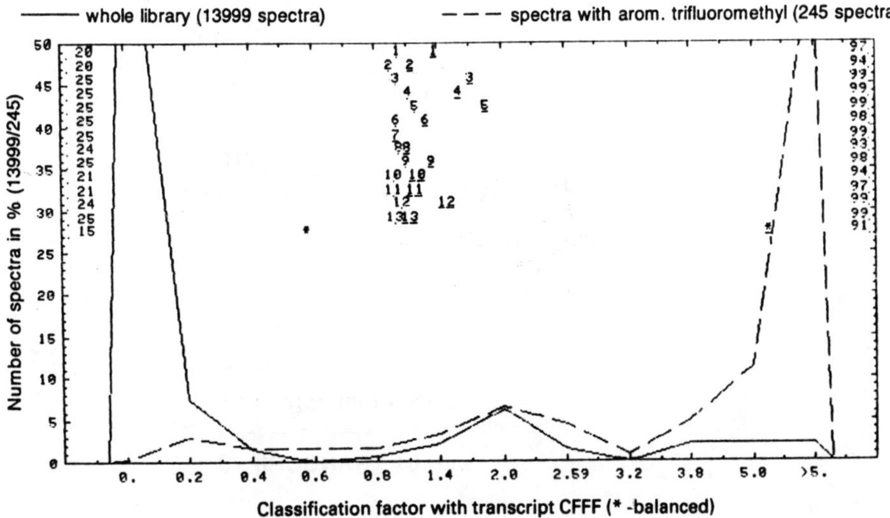

Fig. 5.14 - Test of the balanced TRANSCRIPT.

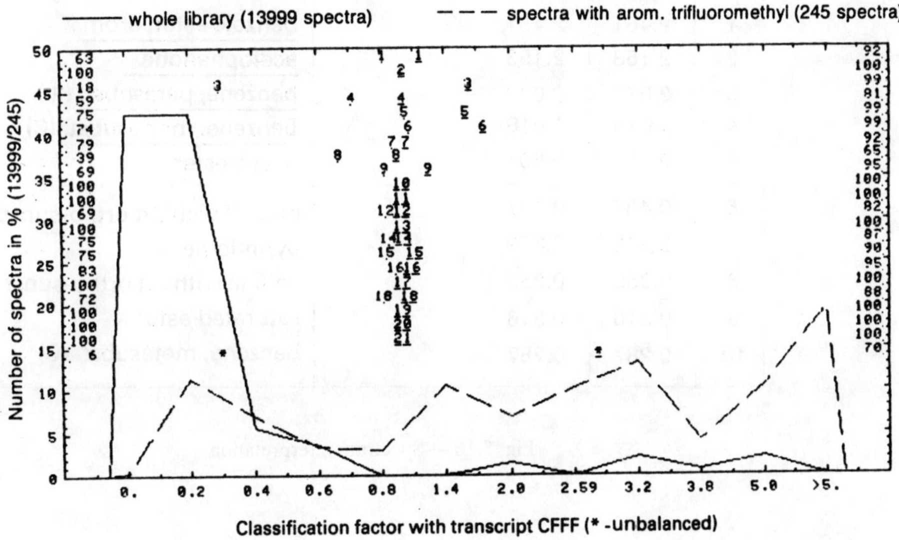

Fig. 5.15 — Test of the unbalanced TRANSCRIPT.

ACKNOWLEDGEMENTS

The authors wish to thank W. Fachinger and H. Wagner for developing the necessary software and M. Beckmann and D. Arndt for organizing the data base. The research work leading to this paper was supported by the Federal Minister of Research and Technology of the FRG.

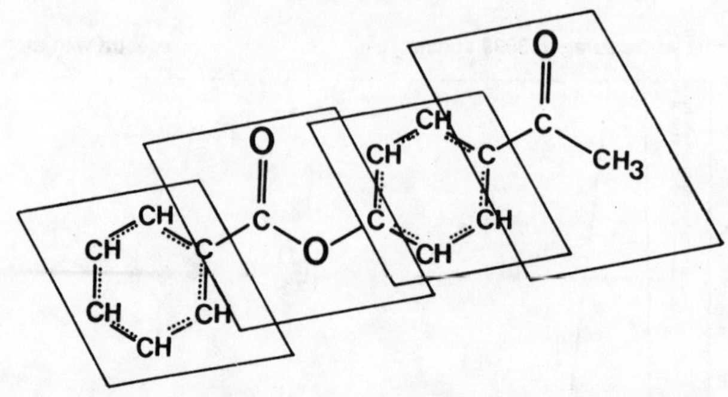

Spectra interpretation

with 61 TRANSCRIPTS

Query: 19632/19 P from Dr.Lauer

Result: 5 Substructures

	classification factor	IR	CNMR	HNMR	Substructure
1.	2.461	2.461			benzoic ester, arom.
2.	2.153	2.153			acetophenone
3.	2.077	2.077			benzene, parasubst. (+)
4.	1.016	1.016			benzene, monosubst. (C)
5.	0.501	0.501			acetic ester
6.	0.487	0.487			phenol without ortho-subst.
7.	0.379	0.379			pyrimidine
8.	0.353	0.353			aniline without ortho-subst.
9.	0.316	0.316			saturated ester
10.	0.287	0.287			benzene, metasubst. (C)

Fig. 5.16 — Spectrum interpretation.

REFERENCES

[1] D. Dolphin and A. Wick, *Tabulation of Infrared Spectral Data*, Wiley, New York, 1977.

[2] *CRC Atlas of Spectral Data and Physical Constants of Organic Compounds*, The Chemical Rubber Company, Cleveland, Ohio, USA.

[3] *The Aldrich Library of Infrared Spectra*, Aldrich Chemical Company, USA, 1970.

[4] *DMS, Dokumentation für Molekülspektroskopie*, Verlag Chemie, Weinheim, 1956–1973.

[5] *The Sadtler Standard Infrared Grating Spectra*, Sadtler Research Laboratories, Philadelphia, 1968–1985.
[6] W. Bremser, L. Ernst, B. Franke, R. Gerhardts and A. Hardt, *Carbon-13 NMR Spectral Data*, Verlag Chemie, Weinheim, 1981.
[7] W. Bremser, *Nachr. Chem. Techn. Lab.*, 1983, **31**, 456.
[8] C. A. Shelley and M. E. Munk, *Anal. Chim. Acta*, 1981, **133**, 507.
[9] I. Fujiwara, T. Okuyama, T. Yamasaki, H. Abe and S. Sasaki, 1981, **133**, 527.
[10] D. H. Smith, N. A. B. Gray, J. G. Nourse and C. W. Crandall, *Anal. Chim. Acta,* 1981, **133**, 471.
[11] H. B. Woodruff and G. M. Smith, *Anal. Chim. Acta*, 1981, **133**, 545.
[12] L. A. Gribov, M. E. Elyashberg and V. V. Serov, *Anal. Chim. Acta, Comp. Techn. Opt.*, 1977, **95**, 75.
[13] J. Zupan, M. Penca, D. Hadži and J. Marsel, *Anal. Chem.*, 1977, **49**, 2141.
[14] W. Bremser and W. Fachinger, *Magn. Res. Chem.*, 1985, **23,** 1056.
[15] H. Wedekind, *Datenbanksysteme I*, Bibilographisches Institut, Mannheim, 1974.
[16] W. Bremser, *Anal. Chim. Acta*, 1978, **103**, 355.
[17] W. Bremser, E. Frank, B. Wagner and E. Wagner, *J. Chem. Research (M)*, **1979**, 1401.
[18] B. Franke, H. Pekar, H. Schweppe and H. Wagner, *Z. Anal. Chem.*, 1980, **303**, 349.
[19] H. B. Woodruff and G. M. Smith, *Anal. Chem.*, 1980, **52**, 2321.
[20] Z. Hippe, R. Hippe and J. Duliban, *Z. Anal. Chem.*, 1982, **311**, 440.
[21] J. Zupan, *Anal. Chim. Acta*, 1982, **139**, 143.
[22] L. A. Gribov and M. E. Elyashberg, *CRC Crit. Rev. Anal. Chem.*, 1979, **8**, 111.
[23] K. Varmuza, *Anal. Chim. Acta*, 1980, **122**, 227.
[24] J. C. W. G. Bink and H. A. Van't Klooster, *Anal. Chim. Acta*, 1983, **150**, 53.
[25] D. S. Frankel, *Anal. Chem.*, 1984, **56**, 1011.
[26] W. Bremser, *Chem.-Ztg.*, 1980, **104**, 53.
[27] A. Gribov, *J. Mol. Struct.*, 1983, **100**, 13.

6

Mass spectrometry databases and search systems

Stephen R. Heller
Agricultural Research Service, US Department of Agriculture, Beltsville, MD 20705 USA

6.1 INTRODUCTION

This chapter will provide the reader with a discussion of mass spectrometry databases and some examples of library search systems used in mass spectrometry.

The development of mass spectral databases started in the 1940s with the American Petroleum Institute (API) Project 44 activities. The reason that mass spectrometry database activity goes back so far is, no doubt, the nature of mass spectral data. The mass spectrum of a chemical compound produces data which are ideally suited for representation and manipulation in digital form. Compared to infrared and nuclear magnetic resonance (NMR) spectral data, mass spectra are extremely simple, consisting just of peaks and intensities. However, this is not to say that the data are simple or easy to understand, interpret or correlate.

While the API Project 44 continued over the years, other groups began to initiate their own mass spectral data collections. It was not until 1965 that the British Government initiated funding their Atomic Weapons Research Establishment (AWRE) at Aldermaston to create a world-wide database of mass spectra. This project funded a group which became known as the Mass Spectrometry Data Centre (MSDC) at Aldermaston. A few years later, the US National Institutes of Health (NIH) Laboratory of Chemistry, which was heavily involved in mass spectrometry, began the development of a computer-based library retrieval system using this MSDC database and one provided by Professor Biemann at MIT.

As the computer system developed (and this will be discussed in detail later in this chapter), it became clear that there were a number of problems with the database, both in quantity and quality. It is likely that these became noticeable only because the database was being used every day in an on-line system by practising mass spectrometrists. The result of this computer retrieval project led the NIH, and in later years the US Environmental Protection Agency (EPA), along with the US National Bureau of Standards (NBS), and the US Food and Drug Administration (FDA) to begin work with the MSDC in enlarging the database and bringing quality assurance and quality control into the database activity project [1].

In addition to these Anglo-American efforts, a second major effort was initiated by Stenhagen and Abrahamsson in Sweden, and was later joined by McLafferty. As Stenhagen, and then later Abrahamsson, died, McLafferty took over this database development and maintenance. Today this database is known as the Mass Spectrometry Registry and is distributed by the publisher John Wiley and Sons.

Other activities in database development have taken place at the Atomic Energy Laboratory in Grenoble, France under the direction of Cornu and Massot. A small database of 2000 mass spectra of chemicals of biological interest was compiled by Markey. Cairns and Jacobson of the US FDA compiled a database of some 2000 mass spectra of pesticides and industrial chemicals. Sorenson at Agriculture Canada compiled 300 mass spectra of drugs used in horse racing. The API Project 44 collection continued for many years under the direction of Zwolinski at Texas A&M as part of the Thermodynamics Research Centre data-collection activities. Shackelford at the US EPA collected a database of some 1500 mass spectra of pollutants which had been found in water analyses. Ryhage at the Karolinska Institute in Sweden collected about 2500 mass spectra of chemicals studied in research activities in this research centre in Stockholm.

The list goes on, but by now the reader should easily see that mass spectrometry data-collection was very much a cottage industry for the most part, with just two major efforts, by the US–UK group and the McLafferty group. Over the past decade this has remained the case, and today there are two major collections of mass spectral databases in the world. Of course there are many mass spectral database collections which can be found in industrial laboratories throughout the world, but these collections, a number of which are reported to contain over 10^5 spectra of different compounds (such as would be expected in the flavour and fragrance industry) will never become public, owing to the need for corporate secrecy. Because of intense concern over trade secrets and intense competition in many industries, corporate lawyers see no reason to be generous and donate useful mass spectral data to the scientific community.

6.2 NBS AND WILEY MASS SPECTRAL DATABASES

The first of these two major efforts to be discussed in some detail is the NBS mass spectral database, which contains some 43000 mass spectra of an equal number of chemicals. Only one spectrum per compound is to be found in this database. All repetitive (but not necessarily exactly duplicate) spectra have been removed, by a process described later. All labelled compounds have been removed from the database, so no spectra of deuterium derivatives and the like will be found. Each spectrum has had a Chemical Abstracts Service (CAS) Registry number assigned to the chemical which produced it. Each chemical has a CAS name, and as many other names as could be found, both formal (i.e. IUPAC) and trivial, and in English and foreign languages (but not in Japanese, Arabic, Cyrillic, etc.). Each spectrum has a quality index (QI), which ranges from 0 to 999, calculated and assigned to it. When a new spectrum is received for a given chemical, a QI is calculated and compared with the one already in the file. If the new QI is higher than the current QI, the new spectrum replaces the current spectrum in the database, and the current spectrum is placed in an archive file. This archive file, which is not available at present to users, contains well over 75000 spectra, and includes all the multiple copies of spectra and all labelled spectra [2].

The Stenhagen, Abrahamsson and McLafferty mass spectral database, hereafter called the Wiley database, is similar to the NBS database in many ways, but is larger, containing some 80000 spectra. The main reason for this is that the Wiley collection includes more than one version of the mass spectrum of a chemical when these are considered different (as judged qualitatively by the author of the database). The database also includes the spectra of labelled chemicals which have been left out of the NBS collection. The Wiley collection uses the Wiswesser Line Notation (WLN) as the method of trying to uniquely identify the structure of the chemical associated with each spectrum. The word 'trying' is correct in this context, since WLN is not a canonical notation (i.e. one that will produce a unique structure from a given structure representation). A WLN, used to represent a chemical structure, can and does give rise to more than one structure. That is, two different structures can and do have the same WLN. For this reason modern structure representation systems no longer use WLN as their primary structure representation. Today, connection tables are used for structure representation. It should be noted that though the NBS database has a CAS Registry number for every entry, the Wiley database does not. Somewhat over two thirds of the entries in the Wiley database have CAS Registry numbers. The situation for the WLN in the Wiley collection is somewhat worse. There are WLN structure notations for slightly over half of the spectra in the database. The NBS database, which uses the CAS Registry number (and associated connection table–structure record), does not contain the WLN, except as a synonym along with other chemical names. The Wiley collection also has a QI for every spectrum, although the method used to calculate it differs slightly from the one used by the NBS project [3].

Before leaving the subject of databases, it is worthwhile to mention a third database from the MSDC, which is their eight-peak spectra database. As the name implies, the database is comprised of the eight largest peaks in each spectrum, not the entire spectrum. (Of course, if a spectrum consists of eight or fewer peaks, the spectrum in the MSDC database will be the complete spectrum; except for methane, ethane, water, and a few other very simple compounds, this is not the case.) The eight-peak database from MSDC contains some 70000 spectra, including duplicates, and is available from the MSDC. The older MSDC complete spectra are also available [4]. A summary of the electron impact (EI) mass spectra databases is given in Table 6.1.

Table 6.1 — Summary of EI mass spectral databases

Source	Approximate size	CAS RN	Quality Index	Hard copy	Cost (Dollars)
NIH/EPA/NBS	40,000	Yes	Yes	Yes	3,000
Wiley/US Govt	60,000	Some	No	No	5,000
MSDC—All data	25,000	No	No	No	1,600
MSDC—8 peak	70,000	No	No	Yes	NA

6.3 QUALITY CONTROL AND QUALITY EVALUATION

An obvious concern of the scientific community regarding these mass spectral databases is the quality of the spectra contained in the files. As the US National Bureau of Standards Office of Standard Reference Data (OSRD) was one of the early participants and sponsors of one of the major database efforts in mass spectrometry, this issue arose early. Methods were quickly devised to control the quality of the chemical nomenclature and structure associated with each spectrum. The Chemical Abstracts Service (CAS) Registry number, a sort of social security number for a chemical, was accepted as the unique identifier, and CAS nomenclature was used for the primary names. In the development of the method or algorithm used to determine the quality of a spectrum, a semi-qualitative method was devised, as no absolute measurement of a mass spectrum is known [5,6].

In 1974 the US–UK group decided to remove redundant or multiple copies of spectra from the file. This decision was reached as it was felt by almost everyone that these spectra served little purpose and were taking up valuable storage space and computer search time. The names of every compound in the file were sent to the Chemical Abstracts Service where, under contract to the US EPA, the CAS Registry number for each compound was identified. The first step in the process was to perform a simple name match. When this did not succeed, the structure of the chemical was matched against the structures in the CAS file of a few million chemicals. If this second step failed, then it was decided that the chemical was not in the CAS file (which numbered some 4–5 million at the time), and a new CAS registry number was assigned to the chemical.

When this CAS registration step was complete the next step was to devise a method to decide which of several spectra for the same compound was the best. The approach taken was to use the experience of practising mass spectroscopists. As the mass spectrometry of organic compounds developed during the 1960s and early 1970s, spectroscopists became familiar with the types of errors that occur frequently in recorded mass spectra. Responses ranging from modification of experimental procedures to redesign of spectrometers were adopted to eliminate or minimize these errors. The result is that a conscientious analyst using a modern mass spectrometer can produce mass spectra which rarely, if ever, contain such errors. Thus the US EPA funded a project to develop an algorithm which examines a mass spectrum for the occurrence of such standard errors. The program computes a number, which is called the Quality Index (QI), and is a measure or indicator of the quality — in terms of the absence of standard errors — of the spectrum.

The QI algorithm employs seven quality factors (QF), each having a value between zero and unity. Multiplication of all these quality factors and further multiplication of the product by 1000 leads to the quality index (QI) for the spectrum. The quality factors now being used by the NBS Office of Standard Reference Data are as follows.

QF1 The electron voltage
QF2 Peaks at *m/z* above that corresponding to the molecular weight
QF3 Illogical neutral losses
QF4 Isotopic abundance accuracy
QF5 The number of peaks in a spectrum
QF6 Lower mass limit of the spectrum
QF7 Sample purity
QF8 Calibration date
QF9 Similarity Index of calibration mass spectrum

Details of the method for determining the QI from QFs can be found elsewhere [6]. Only a few points will be noted here. The first is that the NBS QI procedure uses these nine factors, whereas the McLafferty QI uses only the first six of them together with a seventh QF, which is called the source of the spectrum.

The second point is that the last three QFs are based on experience gained in developing a contract by the US EPA for obtaining new mass spectra. The cost of running some 1000 new spectra a year has been found to be almost $250 per spectrum. As much of this cost is that of acquiring and purifying the sample ($61), and that of laboratory overheads, including calibration ($130), these additional QFs were considered important enough to be used in modifying the original method for calculating the QI. As the Wiley effort does not involve any activities in running new spectra, these QFs were not added to their QI calculation.

The last point to be made is that QF9, which is the quality of the reference spectrum, is a very important factor for ensuring that only the best data are added to the database. To obtain this QF, at the time of calibration the calibration spectrum is stored and the similarity between it and the standard library spectrum of the compound bis(pentafluorophenyl)phenylphosphine is computed by the Similarity Index program within the Mass Spectral Search System (MSSS) [1] of the NIH/EPA Chemical Information System (CIS). This number, which lies between zero and unity, becomes QF9, which is an indicator of spectrometer performance.

All the quality factors are automatically calculated by means of a computer program which also computes the Quality Index (QI) for each spectrum. Whenever spectra associated with the same CAS Registry number are encountered, the one with the highest QI is retained, and the remaining spectra are put into an archive file. When this process was completed with one version of the database, about 22% of the entire database was consigned to the archive file. For the spectra in the current NBS database, the average QI is slightly over 500. For spectra such as these, both QF8 and QF9, which relate to calibration of the spectrometer, were arbitrarily assigned values of 0.90.

As new spectra are assimilated into the database, each is assigned the appropriate CAS Registry number and the database is scanned for the presence of this number. The QI is then computed and, if the compound is new to the file, the entry is simply added to the database. If the CAS Registry number is already in the file, then the spectrum with the higher QI is retained and the other spectrum is archived. This process has led to a great improvement in the database, as many duplicates have been removed and the quality of the data has been defined (whether high, low or medium quality) for the first time. In addition, each spectrum, after this process was completed, was guaranteed to be cited only once and with its CAS Registry number, standard nomenclature, standard Hill notation molecular formula, and QI.

It should clearly be understood that creating a QI and saying the database has a QI for each spectrum does not necessarily mean that the database is a quality database. The QI only defines the quality of the database. In addition, though no new spectra are created by this process, the fact that each spectrum has a CAS Registry number, standard notation molecular formula, and a standard chemical name, gives the file a certain level of quality and acceptance as a result of this standardization. To show clearly this point of the actual quality of the database, a check was made of an older version of the database to see how many spectra had a QI of zero. Of 33898 spectra of different compounds, 1353, or slightly under 4% of the entire working database had a QI of zero. When the 1353 spectra were examined in some detail, the reasons for the assignment of a zero for the QI emerged from a few of the quality factors. The QFs which most often cause the QI to be zero (remember that the QI is a multiplicative quality, so if any QF is zero, QI will automatically be zero) were the lowest mass reported and the presence of impurity peaks at m/z greater than that for the molecular ion of the test compound. While the lowest mass value has no real bearing on the correctness of a spectrum, it does bear very heavily on the usefulness of the spectrum, and the constant need to remind scientists to report *all* the data.

Scientists are tending to report fewer and fewer raw data (with the approval of those journal editors who appear more concerned about printing costs than science), and seem to be beginning to select the data which support their explanation or interpretation of the experimental results. This is clearly not in the best interest of the scientific community. It may be hoped that with use of QIs it will occur less often in mass spectral data reporting in the future.

Again, the reader should remember that the QI is not really an indicator that a spectrum is in fact a good one. Rather it is an indication of problems with a spectrum. The QI is more reliable in telling a scientist that a spectrum is poor, which means, from the QFs above, that the spectrum is incorrect and/or lacking in certain areas.

6.4 MASS SPECTRAL SEARCH SYSTEMS

The mass spectral library search, started in the 1960s, continues to be of interest to many research groups around the world. There are probably dozens of different approaches to mass spectral library searching, and a few hundred papers written on the subject. While the numbers of these have been decreasing in the last few years, they are not likely to end. Minor enhancements and slight refinements will continue, and hence additional publications will result.

It is not the purpose of this chapter to go over this long history of library search systems; rather it is desired to highlight the major ones being used today, and briefly discuss some of the more recent research results. The reader is referred elsewhere for more detailed presentation and reviews of library search systems [7,8].

There are four main computer systems in which library search systems are to be found.

1. Large time-sharing systems
2. Dedicated laboratory or mini-computer systems
3. Instrument-manufacturer computer data systems
4. Microcomputer library search systems

It can be argued that 2 and 4 are the same, or will be, as microcomputers grow in size, speed, capability, and readily available large disk storage. Thus only three main areas will be covered.

For the large time-sharing systems there is really only one system, the Mass Spectral Search System (MSSS) which is part of a larger Chemical Information System (CIS), developed by the US Government from about 1970 to 1984 [9]. The MSSS was first made available to the public in late 1972, when it was introduced to the mass spectrometry community at the International Mass Spectrometry meeting in Scotland, by means of the General Electric (GE) computer system and corresponding GE telecommunications network. The original MSSS was sponsored by the UK Government, which later bowed out and the US Government took over the running and support of this system. The MSSS has the most extensive list of search and plotting options of any mass spectral search system on any computer system. It was meant to serve as broad a community of mass spectroscopists as possible. Since the system used a large time-sharing computer, disk space was not the problem it was with laboratory computer or instrument data systems. Thus, considerable capabilities could easily be built and made available to the user. However, as laboratory computers grew in size and capability, and their costs began to decrease, the MSSS became relatively less powerful. Furthermore, the decision of the US Government, through the National Bureau of Standards Office of Standard Reference Data (as discussed above), to distribute the database to mass spectrometer manufacturers, led to a considerable decline in the usage of the MSSS.

Notwithstanding all these developments, coupled with the NBS publishing what is now a six-volume set of books of the mass spectral database, the MSSS is alive and running, and being used by many scientists on a regular daily basis. The MSSS main search is a variation of a procedure devised by Hertz *et al.* [10] and redesigned by Heller [1] for use in an on-line time-sharing system.

Searches through the MSSS database can be made in a number of ways. With the mass spectrum of an unknown substance in hand, the search can be conducted interactively, as is shown in Fig. 6.1. In this example the user finds that 91 database spectra have a peak (minimum intensity 60%, maximum intensity 100%) at an m/z value of 224. When this subset is examined for spectra containing a peak at m/z 207 with intensity between 80 and 100%, only 3 spectra are found. The entering of a third peak, at an m/z value of 73 (with an intensity between 10 and 40%) narrows the search down to just 1 answer, which is then printed out. In this example, the answer 2,3,6-trichlorobenzoic acid is shown with a number of synonyms used in naming this chemical, as well as other identifying information. If there had still been a large number of answers after entering the three peaks used in this example, the search could have been reduced further to a manageable number of spectra by entering further peaks. In addition, the database could be examined for all occurrences of a specific molecular weight or a partial or complete molecular formula. Combinations of these properties can also be used in searches. Thus, all molecules containing, for example, five chlorine atoms and having mass spectra with a base peak at a particular m/z value can be identified.

In contrast to these interactive searches, which are of little appeal to those with large numbers of searches to make, two batch-type searches are available which accept the complete spectrum of the unknown substance and examine all spectra in the file sequentially to find the best fits. These are the KB (forward search) [10] and PBM (reverse search) search algorithms [11–13]. The spectra can be entered by teletype, but in a more powerful approach the user's data system can be connected to the network and the unknown spectra down-loaded into the network computer for searching. An example of a Biemann (KB) search is given in Fig. 6.2. The search is for dioxin, and the data entered are underlined in the figure. The result of the

```
Option? PEAK

Type peak,min int,max int
CR to exit, 1 for CAS RN, QI, MW, MF and Name

User:224,60,100

File 8 contains 91 references to m/z 224

Next request: 207,80,100

File 9 contains 3 references to m/z 224 207

Next request: 73,10,40

File 10 contains 1 references to m/z 224 207 73

Next request: 1

     CAS RN     QI     MW   Formula, Names
     50-31-7    507    224  C7H3C1302
                            Benzoic acid, 2, 3, 6-trichloro- (8CI9CI)
                            Benzac
                            Benzac 1, 281
                            HC 1281
                            T-2
```

Fig. 6.1 — Typical MSSS PEAK search.

search is three spectra with similarity values greater than 0.10. Of the three, the first, which is dioxin, has the highest similarity index (SI). Once an identification has been made and the name and CAS Registry Number of the database compound are reported to the user, the database spectrum can be listed or, if a CRT terminal is being used, plotted, to facilitate direct comparison of the unknown and standard spectra.

Before we leave the area of mass spectral search systems it should be noted that today virtually every mass spectrometer which runs electron impact (EI) spectra has both a search program and a database provided as part of the system package. The search programs are usually variations of the Biemann and McLafferty PBM algorithm search routines. The database is usually the NBS database, although not usually the latest version. The reason why the database may not be the latest version is twofold. First, not everyone gets a frequent update of a system disk, and secondly, and more critically, not many disk systems installed on old, or even new, computer

KB Search

Option? ENTER

Input 2 Title lines
Line 1: SPECTRUM OF DIOXIN, 1746-01-6

Line 2:

Enter M/Z, Intensity (PBM search requires complete spectrum)
50,7; 62,8; 63,5; 73,6; 74,15; 85,7; 97,14; 109,8; 113,9
160,15; 161,15; 162,7; 194,19; 196,12; 257,27; 259,26; 261,8; 320,82
321,10; 322,100; 323,13; 324,50; 325,6; 326,10; 0,0

Data OK (Y/N)? Y

Option? SEARCH KB

Complete Spectrum Search

Searching has begun
15000 spectra searched
33898 spectra searched

SI	REGN	QI	MW	MF, Names
.617	1746-01-6	563	320	C12H4Cl402
				Dibenzo[b,e] [1,4]Dioxin, 2,3,7,8-tetrachloro- (9Cl) Dibenzo-p-dioxin, 2,3,7,8-tetrachloro- (8Cl) Dioxin Dioxin (herbicide contaminant) (VAN) Tetrachlorodibenzodioxin
.507	33423-92-6	53	320	C12H4Cl4O2
				Dibenzo[b,e] [1,4]dioxin, 1,3,6,8-tetrachloro- (9Cl) Dibenzo-p-dioxin 1,3,6,8-tetrachloro- (8Cl) 1,3,6,8-Tetrachlorodibenzo-p-dioxin
.289	30746-58-8	691	320	C12H4Cl4O2
				Dibenzo[b,e] [1,4]dioxin, 1,2,3,4-tetrachloro- (9Cl) Dibenzo-p-dioxin, 1,2,3,4-tetrachloro- (8Cl) 1,2,3,4-Tetrachlorodibenzo-p-dioxin

File 2 contains the 3 references retrieved
in CAS Registry Number sequence.

Fig. 6.2 — Typical search using the Biemann search procedure.

systems have sufficient disk capacity for the entire library of over 40000 spectra. Even when the entire 40000-plus library is installed on a manufacturer's data system, it is soon discovered that some of the original database is missing. In particular, the information normally left out, owing to space limitations on the disk, will be many (if not all) of the chemical names and synonyms, and details of the source of the spectrum. Thus going to an on-line system for complete details may still be necessary. (In connection with incomplete data, it is useful to mention that the six-volume set of books published by the US Government Printing Office does not have spectral source information, such as is shown in Fig. 6.3.) An example of a typical

CAS RN QI MW MF,Name
50-31-7 507 224 C7H3C1302
Benzoic acid, 2,3,6-trichloro- (8CI9CI)
Instrument: MAT CH5 ; Inlet: DIRECT ; Source temp.: 200 C; eV: 70
Contributor: CATALOGUE OF MASS SPECTRA OF PESTICIDES, APRIL 1975;

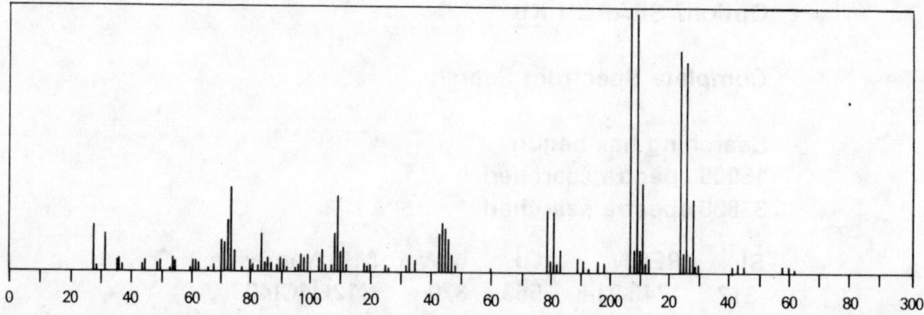

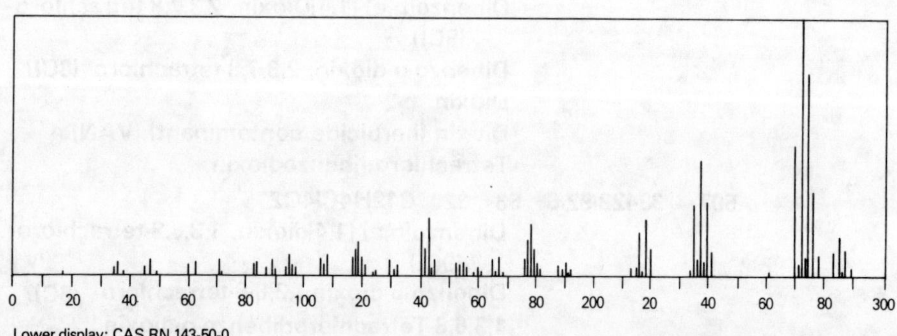

Lower display: CAS RN 143-50-0

Fig. 6.3 — Plot for compound identified in PEAK search in Fig. 6.1.

plot of a spectrum is given in Fig. 6.3, and a sample page from the six-volume set of books is given in Fig. 6.4. In Fig. 6.3, the spectrum of 2,3,6-trichlorobenzoic acid (the result of the search in Fig. 6.1) is plotted on an expanded scale.

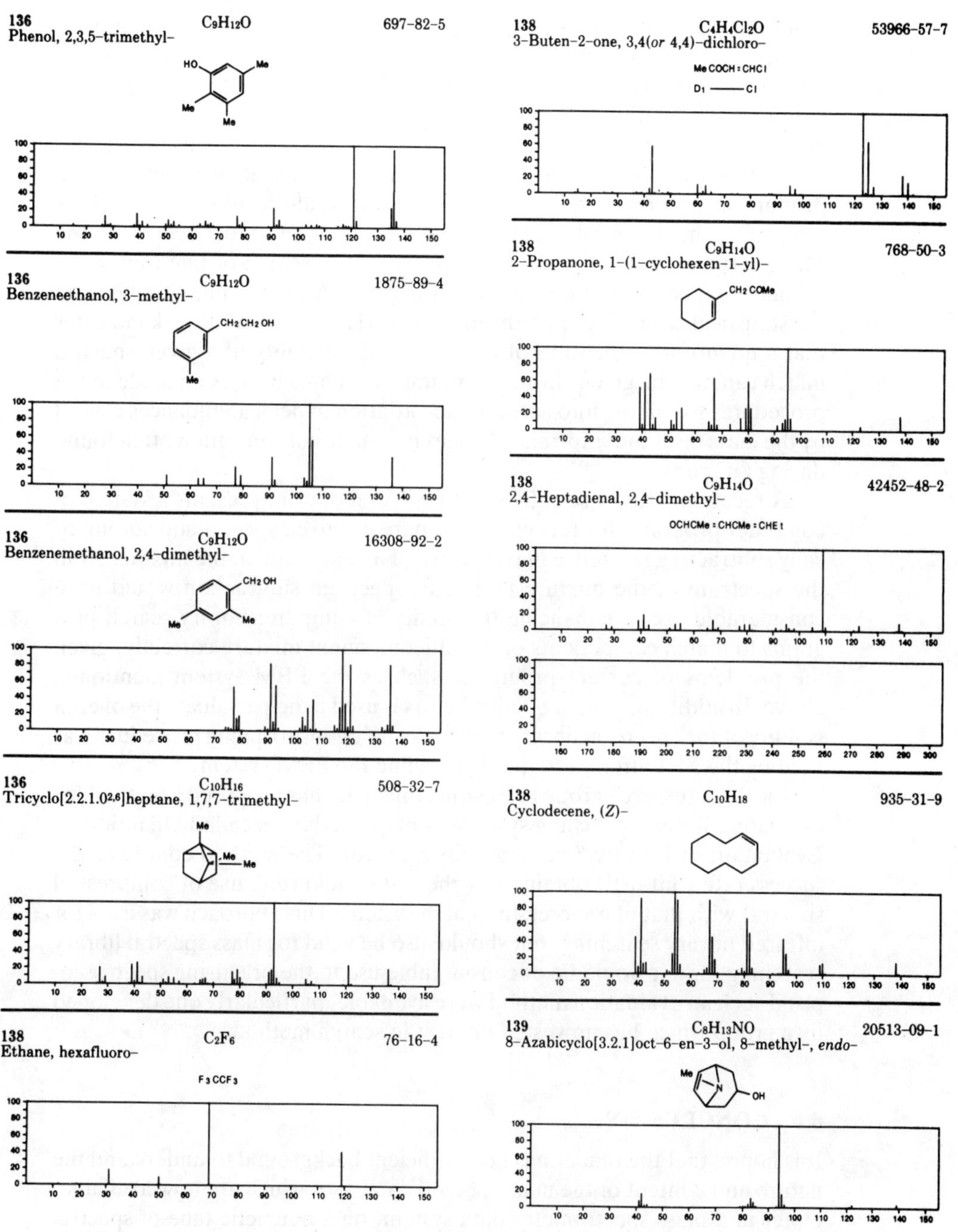

Fig. 6.4 — Sample page from the six-volume set of mass spectral books [2].

6.5 RECENT ACTIVITIES IN LIBRARY SEARCHING

One important aspect of library searching which is attracting continued attention is that of how to analyse and search for compounds found in mixtures. The PBM method, mentioned before, is one good approach, although it encounters problems when some components are present in large amounts, and others in only much smaller or trace amounts. PBM does best when the compounds in the mixture are present in roughly equal proportions, which is not always the case in real-life problems, such as samples from dump sites and polluted waters. The most recent of the McLafferty papers (stretching over a decade) in search of fine tuning the ultimate search program, is one which deals with further improvements in the statistical reliability of predicted matches [13]. This latest work indicates that a quantitative measure of the predicted reliability of a given spectral match can now be given. In addition, improvements have been made in the procedures for taking into account the variation in peak abundances caused by the mass discrimination and changes in sample concentration often found during GC runs.

A recent article by scientists at an EPA laboratory presents a system of computer programs for recognizing impure or mixed spectra and automatically subtracting reference mass spectra of a compound in the mixture from the spectrum of the mixture [14]. This spectrum subtraction would have considerable use in enhancing the ability of computer library search programs to match components of a multicomponent mixture correctly, given the problems of current programs, such as the PBM system mentioned above. In addition, a set of quality factors is used to help evaluate the overall validity of the spectrum library match. A analogous stripping procedure was used by the McLafferty group [15] to refine the PBM system.

Lastly, a research group at Boston University has proposed a method for evaluating library searching systems. The procedure is called Quantitative Evaluation of Library Searching (QELS) [16]. The method compares the success rate ('hit-list') obtained by the test system (e.g. use of compressed spectra) with that of a successful search system. This approach was used for infrared library searching, but should also be valid for mass spectral library searching, and it would be of considerable use to the practising spectroscopist if such an evaluation method were available, particularly one developed by a group which has no vested interest in search methods.

6.6 CONCLUSION

It is hoped that the reader has now sufficient background to understand the nature and content of the mass spectral databases which are now available, either in a mass spectrometry data system, on a magnetic tape of spectral data, or in an on-line system. The most important point to realize from this chapter is that the mass spectral databases are small in size (60000 spectra out of over 7×10^6 reported chemicals is well under 1% of known chemicals) and not of the highest quality. However, what has been read about here is what is available, so it is best to learn to work with it. A critical point, which all scientists should remember, but most often forget, is that structure elucidation is not founded upon one technique. Mass spectral data are very valuable, but not absolute and not unique. Other confirmatory evidence, whether chemical or spectral (e.g., infrared, NMR, and so forth) is absolutely necessary for good science. One reason why there continues to be further work on library search systems to fine-tune them and squeeze out the last drop of information, is simple: mass spectral data alone are not enough, but some still try to make them so. Good scientists use *all* the tools that are available to solve a problem. In most cases this means more than mass spectrometry.

REFERENCES

[1] S. R. Heller, *Anal. Chem.*, 1972, **44**, 1951; G. W. A. Milne, S. R. Heller, R. S. Heller and D. P. Martinsen, *Adv. Mass Spectrom.*, 1980, **8B**, 1578; S. R. Heller, *Kemia-Kemi*, 1984, No. 1, 15.

[2] The NIH/EPA/MSDC database is available for lease on computer tape from the US National Bureau of Standards (NBS), Office of Standard Reference Data, Physics Building, Room A-320, Gaithersburg, Maryland 20899, USA (Telephone 301-921-2228). The database is also available in printed form (currently six volumes and an index volume), available from the US Government Printing Office Washington, DC 20402. The MS books are available as the first four-volume set (stock number 003-003-01987-9), Supplement Number 1 (stock number 003-003002268-3), and Supplement Number 2 (stock number 003-003-02514-3). For prices and details of how to order, please contact the Government Printing Office.

[3] The Wiley/NBS Mass Spectral Database is available from John Wiley & Sons, Electronic Publishing Division, 605 Third Avenue, New York, NY 10158.

[4] Mass Spectrometry Data Centre, UKCIS, The University, Nottingham, UK.

[5] J. G. Dillard, S. R. Heller, F. W. McLafferty, G. W. A. Milne and R. Venkataraghavan, *Org. Mass. Spectrom.*, 1981, **16**, 48.

[6] G. W. A. Milne, W. L. Budde, S. R. Heller, D. P. Martinsen and R. G. Oldham, *Org. Mass Spectrom.*, 1982, **17**, 547.

[7] D. P. Martinsen, *Appl. Spectrosc.*, 1981, **35**, 255.

[8] Finnigan MAT, *Spectra*, 1984, **10**, No. 1.

[9] S. R. Heller, *J. Inform. Processing and Management*, 1984, **27**, 19; *Drexel Library Quarterly*, 1983, **18**, No. 3/4, 39; G. W. A. Milne, R. Potenzone Jr. and S. R. Heller, *Science*, 1982, **215**, 371.

[10] H. S. Hertz, R. A. Hites and K. Biemann, *Anal. Chem.*, 1971, **43**, 681.

[11] F. W. McLafferty, R. H. Hertel and R. D. Villwock, *Org. Mass Spectrom.*, 1974, **9**, 690.

[12] G. M. Pesyna, R. Venkataraghavan, H. E. Dayringer and F. W. McLafferty, *Anal. Chem.*, 1979, **48**, 1362.

[13] B. L. Atwater, D. B. Stauffer, F. W. McLafferty and D. W. Peterson, *Anal. Chem.*, 1985, **57**, 899.
[14] W. M. Shackelford and D. M. Cline, *Anal. Chim. Acta*, 1985, **164**, 251.
[15] B. L. Atwater, R. Venkataraghavan and F. W. McLafferty, *Anal. Chem.*, 1979, **51,** 1945.
[16] J. R. Hallowell and M. Delaney, *Trends Anal. Chem.*, 1985, **4**, No. 3, IV–VII.

7

^{13}C and ^{1}H NMR spectra collections as a base for the retrieval system SPIRES

Shin-ichi Sasaki, Tohru Yamasaki, Kazuo Tanaka and **Hidetsugu Abe**
Department of Materials Science, Toyohashi University of Technology, Tempaku Toyohashi 440, Japan

7.1 INTRODUCTION

We have been developing an automated organic structure elucidation system named CHEMICS [1]. Since CHEMICS is a fully automated system, spectral data (infrared, ^{1}H and ^{13}C NMR) of an unknown compound are analysed by formalized empirical rules for spectral data interpretation. CHEMICS uses these formalized empirical rules as a table containing substructure–subspectra correlations, a simple and effective form for rule representation. In CHEMICS, a set of substructures is defined and each substructure in the set is strictly defined in accordance with its environment. Unfortunately, such a correlation table containing all the substructures defined in the system was not available to us.

Therefore, we have constructed a ^{13}C NMR spectral database in which all signals in the spectral data are assigned to corresponding atoms of structural formulas. Using this database, we have developed a retrieval system named SPIRES (SPectral Information REtrieval System) for making the correlation table for CHEMICS. SPIRES has been designed not only for CHEMICS but also for general spectral information retrieval and is found to be very useful for this purpose.

Additionally, we plan to build a 90-MHz ^{1}H NMR spectral database. Generally speaking, the proton-noise decoupled ^{13}C NMR spectrum of an organic compound displays single well separated lines for each carbon nucleus and it is easy to represent it in a coded form. In contrast to the ^{13}C spectrum, the ^{1}H spectrum is generally much more difficult to represent in a coded form because of its complex signal pattern. Moreover, the signal pattern will vary severely according to measurement frequency, even for the same compound.

Since it is well known that the chemical shift and the coupling constant for a nucleus are both independent constants with respect to the measurement frequency, they are most suitable for encoding ^{1}H spectral data. However, it is virtually impossible to obtain these constants routinely for a spectrum. Therefore, we have employed a simple and practical encoding format in which every signal group of a spectrum is represented by positions (ppm) and intensities (proton units). These values can easily be read out from a spectral chart. Additionally, by employing this encoding method for ^{1}H NMR spectral data, the work in modification of the original SPIRES system can be minimized and users can access both ^{13}C and ^{1}H data files in the same manner.

Both ^{13}C and ^{1}H NMR data files are at present independent because of the limitations of the computer facility, so there is some inconvenience when it is wished to access both data files at the same time. This inconvenience will be resolved in the near future.

7.2 SPECTRAL DATA COLLECTION AND FILE ORGANIZATION

7.2.1 Collection of spectral data

The ^{13}C NMR data of SPIRES originate from two sources. One is NIH-EPA [2], which was used in developing the original system. The second is a collection published in microfiche form [3]. The data on the microfiche were rewritten on coding sheets and structural formulas in CANOST notation [4] were added. All ^{1}H spectra were recently recorded in our laboratory with a 90-MHz spectrometer.

Both kinds of spectral data were compiled independently and supplemented with other information (compound name, molecular formula, structural formula, etc.). We have both kinds of spectra for about 1000 compounds, but only one of them for others.

The present status of the data collection is as follows. The ^{1}H spectra for over 10000 organic compounds have been measured and about 8000 converted into computer-readable form, accompanied by names, molecular formulas, structural formulas, assignments, and sample source. Among them, 400 have passed detailed inspection and are now ready to be added to the database. In addition, the ^{13}C spectra of over 15000 compounds have been converted into computer-readable form, and their inspection is now under way. Figure 7.1 shows the data collection schemes for ^{1}H and ^{13}C NMR spectra.

As shown in Fig. 7.1, various error checks were made in every step of the data collection process. The quality (resolution, noise level, phase, and so on) and consistency checks were made on the measured spectral chart. For the assigned spectra, the following checks were made.

Does the number of signal groups correspond to the number of assignments?
Have all protons or carbon atoms been assigned?
Are all the assignments appropriate in a chemical sense?

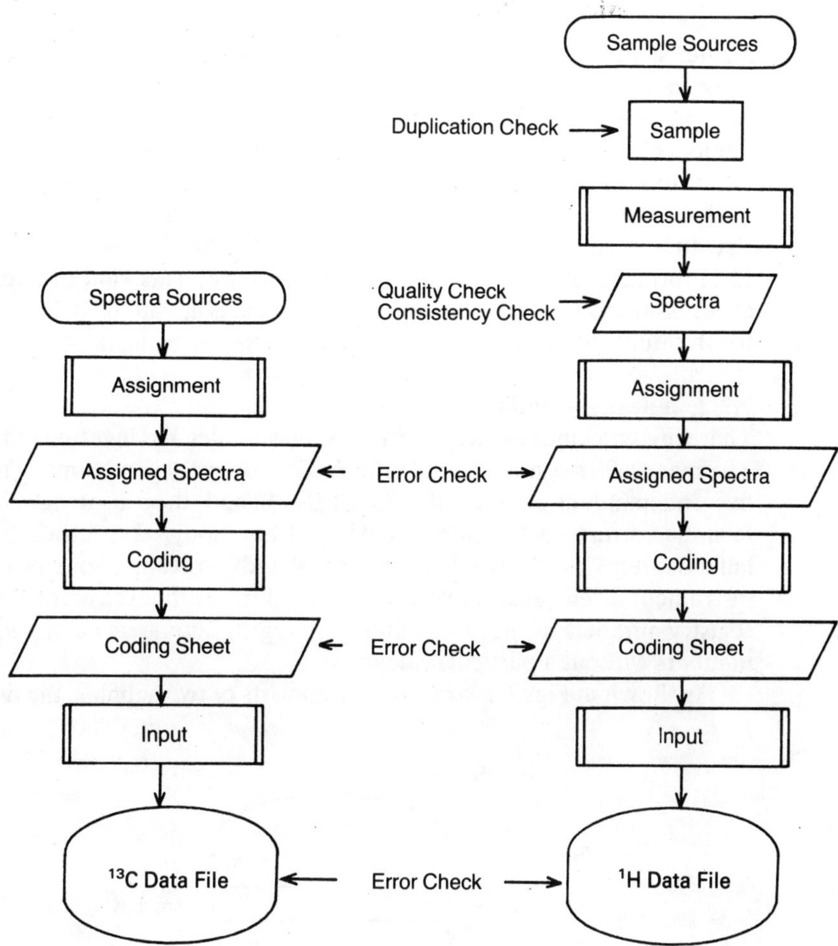

Fig. 7.1 — Schematic diagram of ^{13}C and ^{1}H NMR spectral data collection at Toyohashi University of Technology.

For some compounds, it is very difficult to ensure the correctness of the last check, so it takes much time to do it.

Since not all coding sheets could be checked thoroughly by hand, the following checks were done by using a computer program which checks various coding and typing errors.

Are all coding data in the correct columns?
Have all protons been assigned?
Is the molecular formula in accordance with the structural formula?
Is the valency of each CANOST symbol in a coded structure correct?

There still remain some errors which cannot be detected by the various checks mentioned above. Most of those errors are due to misassignments.

As mentioned above, ^{13}C and ^{1}H data were collected independently. Name, structural formula and molecular formula for a compound appear twice in the SPIRES data files when both ^{13}C and ^{1}H data for the compound are present. Furthermore, the compound has two different registry numbers, one for the ^{13}C data file and the other for the ^{1}H file. This kind of duplication is inevitable in compilation of a vast amount of spectral data.

For resolving this undesirable duplication, high-speed matching of structural formulas is required. Standardized CANOST notations of structural formulas are very suitable for this purpose. This kind of duplication check is always required whenever the database is updated. Utility programs for this duplication check and database update are being developed.

7.2.2 File organization

There are two kinds of files in SPIRES: master files and inverted index files. The master files contain actual information for every compound. There are five independent master files in SPIRES and they contain molecular formulas, structural formulas in CANOST notation, ^{13}C spectra and miscellaneous items (such as names of compounds, solvents, sources of data, instruments used), respectively. All master files are indexed according to the registry numbers of the compounds, the registry numbers being sequential numbers without a particular meaning.

As shown in Fig. 7.2, a master file consists of two subfiles, the directory

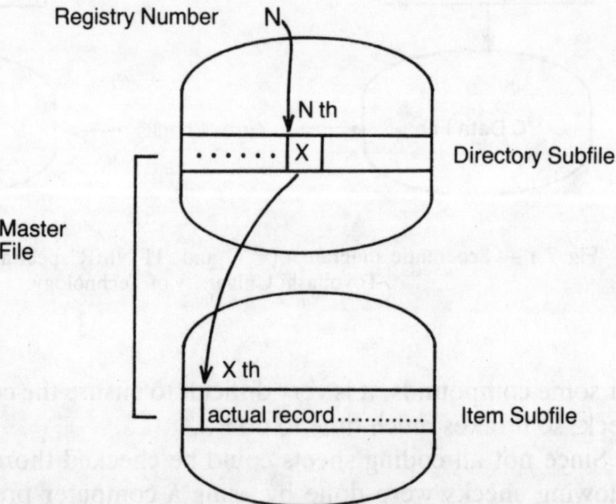

Fig. 7.2 — File organization of master files. A master file consists of two subfiles, the directory subfile and item subfile.

subfile and item subfile, respectively. For a compound with the registry number N, the Nth record of the directory subfile is referred to for obtaining the address of the item subfile where the actual information is stored. The structural formula file and two spectral files are linked by pointers to allow mutual retrieval.

For improving the efficiency of retrieval, four inverted index files pointing to molecular formulas, ^{13}C peaks, ^{1}H peaks and substructures were prepared.

Addressing the molecular formula file. A certain numerical value is required as the key for addressing the molecular formula inverted file. The molecular weight is a first candidate for the key because it can be calculated easily from a given molecular formula, but an integral representation of the molecular weight will correspond to many molecular formulas, for example, the integer 156 corresponds to molecular formulas such as C_2H_5I, $C_7H_8O_2S$, $C_9H_{13}Cl$, and many others. Therefore, some other procedure is required for the addressing.

The so-called hashing method [5] is applied to address an objective molecular formula in the inverted file. The hashing value 'N' is calculated from the accurate molecular weight of a given molecular formula according to the procedure shown below

$$N = \mathrm{MOD}(\mathrm{BAS}, 2099) + 1 \text{ (2099 being a prime number)}$$

where

$$\mathrm{BAS} = a_i \times 3^{i-1}$$

and a_i is the ith numeral (numbered 0–9 from *right* to *left*) of the accurate molecular weight multiplied by 10^4.

For example, the 'N' value for molecular formula C_2H_5I is calculated as follows:

$$C_2H_5I \rightarrow 1559435 \; (= 155.9435 \times 10^4)$$

$$1 \times 3^6 + 5 \times 3^5 + 5 \times 3^4 + 9 \times 3^3 + 4 \times 3^2 + 3 \times 3 + 5 \times 1 = 2642$$
$$N = \mathrm{MOD}(2642, 2099) + 1 = 544$$

When the hashing method is used, it is inevitable that the same value is sometimes obtained for two or more different molecular formulas, as shown in Fig. 7.3.

These are called synonyms and for discrimination between them the gate value G (G = carbon number × 100 + hydrogen number) is used, as shown in the figure.

Though the two molecular formulas C_2H_5I and C_8H_9OCl give the same value, 544, the gate value 205 corresponding to the former and a pointer value for the latter are sequentially stored at the address 544 in the inverted index file.

This means that the master file address stored at the addıess 544 of the

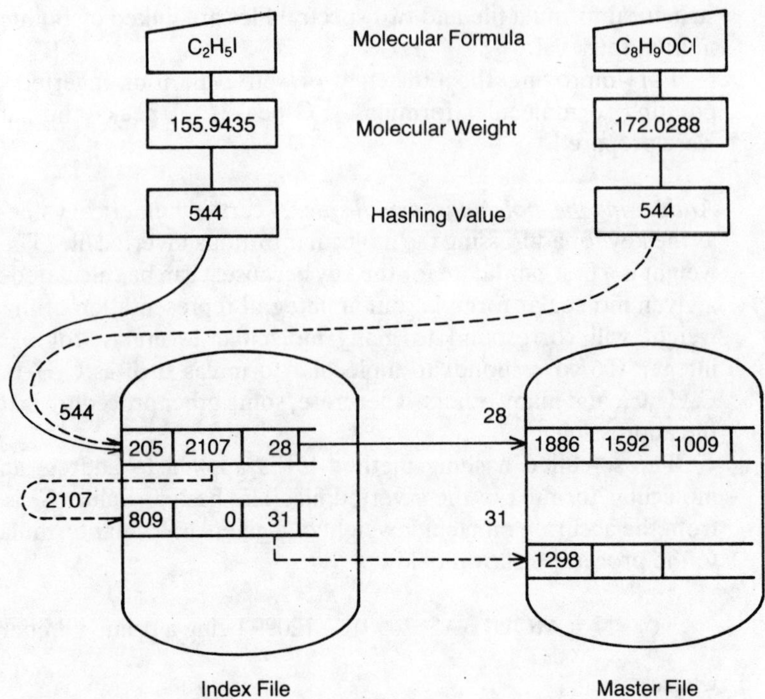

Fig. 7.3 — Hash addressing method for molecular formula file. In this case, two different molecular formulas, C_2H_5I and C_8H_9OCl, gave the same hashing value, 544. However, they could be discriminated by use of the gate values, 205 and 809, respectively.

index file corresponds to the molecular formula C_2H_5I and the address which corresponds to the other molecular formula will be found where the pointer indicates.

The example shown in Fig. 7.3 is taken from the original data file which contained about 1500 ^{13}C data. This hashing method can be applied for enlarging the data file with only minor modification.

Addressing the peak file. As mentioned above, there are two peak index files and two peak master files in SPIRES. They were prepared for ^{13}C and ^{1}H spectra, respectively.

As shown in Fig. 7.4 a peak index file is addressed by the values Ac or Ah calculated by either formula (1) or (2). The addressed records contain the registry numbers of compounds having spectra which exhibit these peaks.

$$Ac = 1000+(Sc\times10) \quad (1)$$

$$Ah = 1000+(Sh\times100) \quad (2)$$

where Sc or Sh is the chemical shift value (ppm) of the corresponding peak of

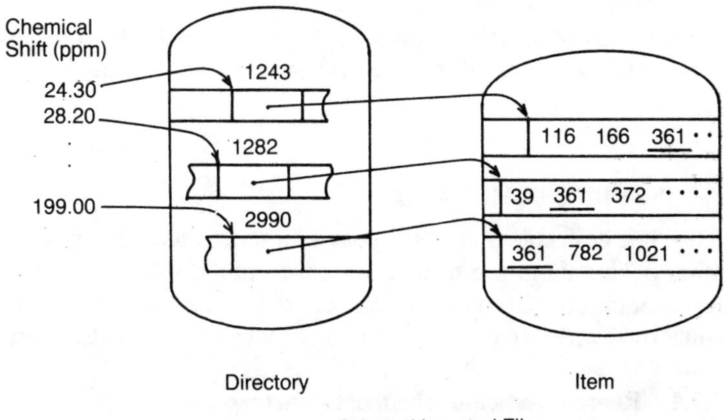

Fig. 7.4 — Addressing method for spectral inverted file. This example shows how the ^{13}C spectral data for a compound (registry number 361) were inverted.

the ^{13}C or ^{1}H spectrum, respectively. For example, the registry number of a compound having a peak at 24.30 ppm in its ^{13}C spectrum is stored at a certain position of the item subfile, the address of which is recorded at the 1243rd position of the directory subfile according to formula (1).

Temporary file. The temporary files are created for storing the primary search results and the results of logic operations. As shown in Fig. 7.5, a

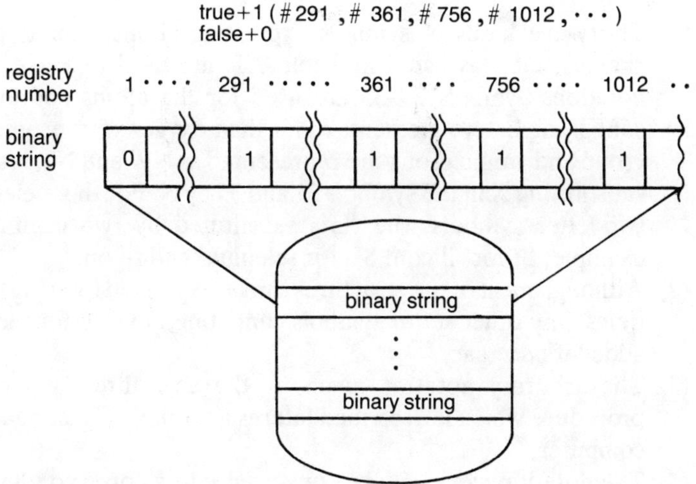

Fig. 7.5 — The temporary file organization. Every position and every element of a binary string correspond to the registry number and its status (true or false), respectively, for a query.

temporary file is a bit array in which each bit corresponds to a registry number. Those array elements displayed as 1 mean that the corresponding compounds give a positive response to the query executed.

7.3 STRUCTURAL DATA

Since it is desirable that every peak of a spectrum is assigned to at least one atom or atomic group of a structural formula, the choice of the structure representation method is one of the most important points for a database concerned with organic compounds, especially for spectral databases.

7.3.1 Representation of chemical structure

There are several computer-oriented methods for representation of chemical structural formulae. Linear notations and connection table methods are two major techniques for the topologically unambiguous and unique representation of structural formulas. Generally speaking, the linear notation for a structural formula requires much less storage area in computer files than does the connection table. Because of this compactness, use of linear notation seems preferable to use of connection tables for compilation of a vast amount of structural formulas to be treated in a computer. However, the procedure for standardization of a linear notation is generally so tedious and complicated, that users hesitate to adopt the method.

For SPIRES, a new linear notation system named CANOST [4] which does not require standardization work by the user was developed and adopted.

The following features describe the CANOST notation system.

(1) Thirty-five kinds of symbols expressing atoms, atomic groups, ionic charges, etc., as listed in Table 7.1, are used to make the arbitrary notation. Symbols 29–35 are used for the atoms and atomic groups containing hetero elements other than oxygen. For example, the nitro group and amino group are represented as NW and N2, respectively, by substituting X in the symbols 31 and 35 by N. For those elements having two-letter symbols, the X is substituted by two capital letters, for example, SI for silicon, SE for selenium and so on.
(2) Although most of the structures can be expressed by using the thirty-five items, any other set of symbols consisting of up to four letters may be added if necessary.
(3) The arbitrary notation given by the user through a rather simple procedure which is described later is automatically standardized by the computer.
(4) The notation can easily be converted into a corresponding connection table. The latter, in some cases, is more useful and convenient than the linear notation for computer-aided manipulation of structures.
(5) For a beginner, two or three hours are usually sufficient to learn how to encode chemical structural formulas.

The general procedures for encoding chemical structural formula into CANOST notation is as follows.

Step 1 Select proper symbols from Table 7.1 for the atoms and/or atomic groups in a given structural formula. If two or more alternative encodings are possible for the formula, choose the one consisting of the smallest number of symbols.
Step 2 Number the symbols consecutively. Since there is no particular rule for the numbering, it is allowed to start at any symbol.
Step 3 Place all the symbols in a line according to the increasing order of the numbers assigned above.
Step 4 For expressing the connections of symbols, arrange the corresponding numerals in a line in the next row of the symbol strings. There are two rules for arranging the numerals; first, continuous arrangement of the numerals indicates the connection between the corresponding symbols, and second, zero is used when the connection is suspended and a new connectivity is cited by numerals, starting with one of the already cited numerals.

Figure 7.6 illustrates the process of arbitrary and non-canonical notation of a

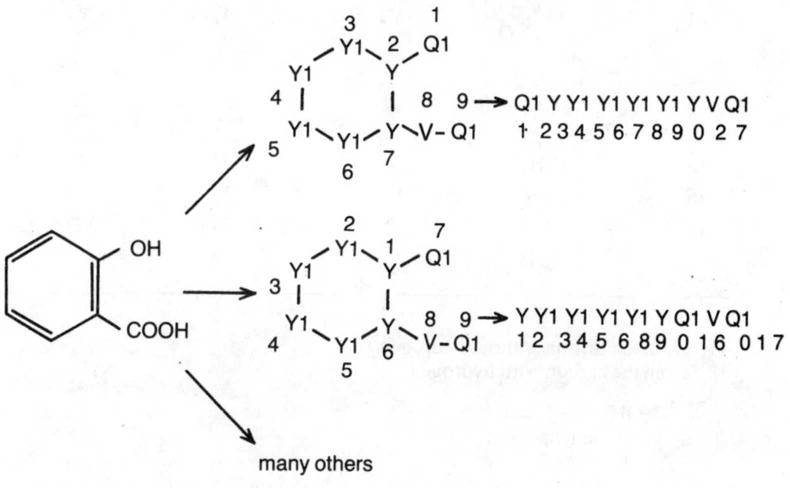

OH
COOH
(a)
Q1 Y Y1 Y1 Y1 Y1 Y V Q1
1 2 3 4 5 6 7 8 9 0 2 7
(b)
Y Y1 Y1 Y1 Y1 Y Q1 V Q1
12 3 4 5 6 8 9 0 1 6 0 1 7
many others

Fig. 7.6 — Coding procedure with CANOST notation system. This example shows only two arbitrary notations for salicylic acid, but there may be many possible alternatives.

structural formula. As shown in the figure, four aromatic carbon atoms carrying a hydrogen atom, two aromatic carbon atoms without hydrogen, two hydroxy groups and one carbonyl group of the structure are replaced by the corresponding symbols, four Y1, two Y, two Q1 and one V, respectively, selected from the symbols in Table 7.1. Then, numerals (1, 2, 3, ..., 9) are

Table 7.1 — Code of substructure in CANOST

No.	substructure	code	No.	substructure	code
1	–C≡	T	19	=O	QD
2	HC≡	T1	20	–F	LF
3	=C=	DD	21	–Cl	LC
4	>C=	DS	22	–Br	LB
5	–CH=	D1	23	–I	LJ
6	$H_2C=$	D2	24	single bond	SG
7	>C<	C	25	cation	+
8	>CH–	C1	26	anion	–
9	$–CH_2–$	C2	27	radical	.
10	$–CH_3$	C3	28	chelation	/
11	–C(aromatic ring)	Y	29	other atom	X
12	HC(aromatic ring)	Y1	30	X(aromatic ring)	XR
13	(7-membered ring) C–OH, C=O	YT	31	X(=O)=O	XW
14	>C=O	V	32	=X	XD
15	–CHO	V1	33	=X=	XX
16	=C=O	VD	34	≡X	XT
17	–O–	Q	35	XH_p	XP
18	–OH	Q1			

11: aromatic carbon without hydrogen
12: aromatic carbon with hydrogen
13: >C–OH | >C=O in troponoid

24: prepared for connecting D1 to clearly express conjugated double bond (see Fig. 7.3)
30: non-carbon atom in aromatic structure

assigned arbitrarily to all the symbols. Two arbitrary numberings are shown under (a) and (b) in Fig. 7.6.

Secondly, the symbols are placed linearly in ascending order of their numerals. To express connections between the symbols, the numerals are placed as shown in Fig. 7.6. The connection of Q1, Y, Y1, Y1, Y1, Y1, Y, V and Q1 in (a) is indicated by a continuous arrangement of the numerals, 1–9. After 9, 0 (zero) indicates that the connection is suspended. Then numerals 2 and 7 are used again to show two Y2 and Y7 are connected to each other. Another arbitrary numbering and the notation used are shown in (b).

Of course many other numbering orders and notations are possible for the structural formula, according to arbitrary choice by the user. Any arbitrary notation can be transformed into a canonical one by using the CANOST standardization program.

7.3.2 Addressing the structure file

As described above, structural formulas are encoded in SPIRES by using the CANOST notation system. Every symbol of the CANOST notation for a compound has an entry in the inverted substructure file. Each symbol for the CANOST notation consists of up to four ASCII characters. All the distinctive symbols in the structural formulas are sorted and arranged in dictionary order and numbered sequentially. For example, the methyl group is symbolized as C3 in the notation and numbered 28 in the SPIRES index.

As shown in Fig. 7.7, the 28th record of the directory part of the

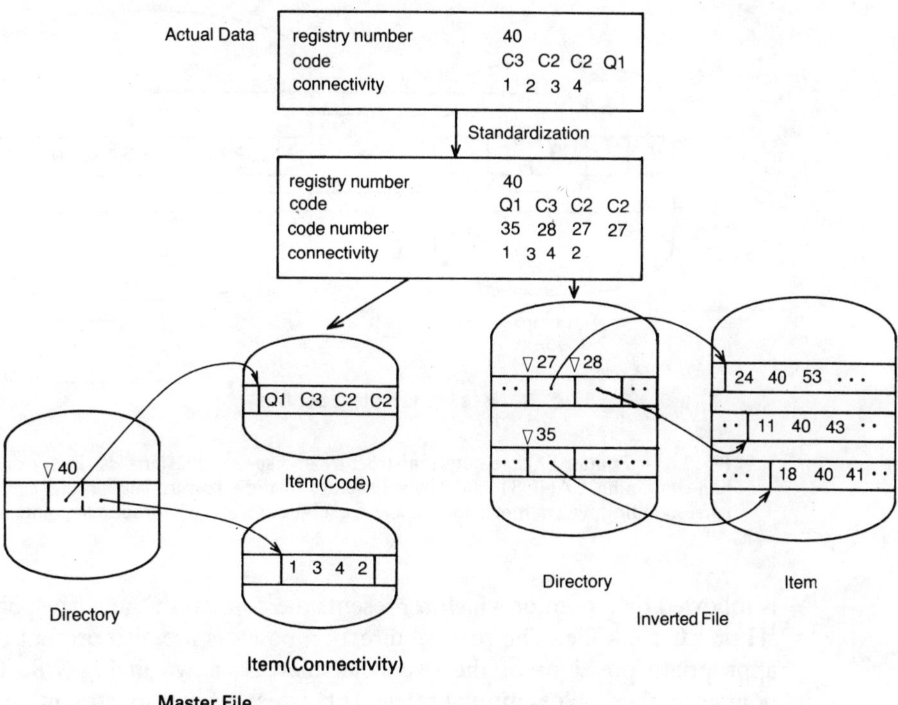

Fig. 7.7 — Organizations of master file and inverted file for structural records.

substructure index file contains the file address for the record, with the registry numbers of the compounds containing the methyl group.

The structural master file is further divided into three subfiles, the directory subfile, the CANOST code subfile and the CANOST connectivity subfile, respectively. The directory subfile is addressed by the registry number and the contents are the file addresses for the code subfile and connectivity subfile.

As shown in Fig. 7.8, every symbol record of the CANOST code subfile

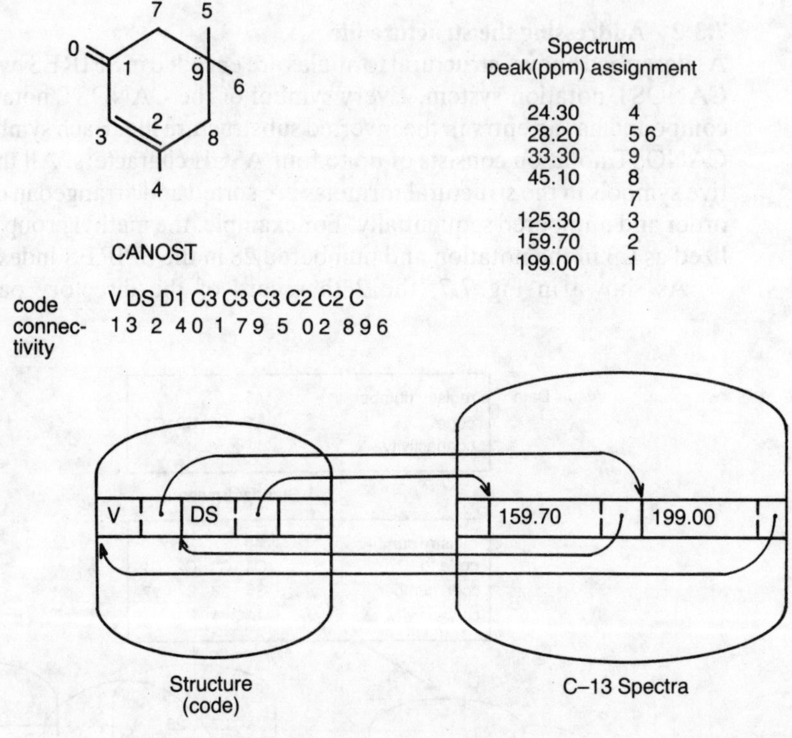

Fig. 7.8 — Pointer linkage between structure and spectra master files. Every carbon-containing CANOST code in a structure in the structure subfile and every corresponding peak datum in the ^{13}C spectra subfile are linked with address pointers.

is followed by a pointer which represents the address of the corresponding ^{1}H or ^{13}C peak file. The reverse direction pointers are also present at the appropriate positions of the two peak files as shown in Fig. 7.8. These pointer linkages allow mutual retrieval between partial spectra and partial structures (actually represented by CANOST codes).

In the near future, the address pointer in the code subfile will be doubled, one for ^{1}H spectra and the other for ^{13}C spectra.

7.4 RETRIEVAL PROCEDURE

As SPIRES is designed to perform retrieval tasks interactively, a variety of commands are prepared. They are listed in Table 7.2.

Table 7.2 — Commands for SPIRES

Command	Description
SEARCH Commands	
CPEAK	search with ^{13}C peak position e.g. CPEAK 125.20 2.00
PPEAK	search with ^{1}H peak position e.g. PPEAK 1.50 0.10
STRUCTURE	search with structure e.g. STRUCTURE C3 C2 1 2 (CH3CH2—)
FORMULA	search with molecular formula e.g. FORMULA C9 H14 O
LOGIC commands	
AND	Boolean AND operation e.g. AND 1 2
IOR	Boolean inclusive OR operation e.g. IOR 1 2
EOR	Boolean exclusive OR operation e.g. EOR 1 2
NOT	Boolean AND NOT operation e.g. NOT 1 2
DISPLAY Commands	
PSTRUCTURE	Display partial structure e.g. PSTRUCTURE 5 1 2 (set no. displaying range)
SSPECTRA	Display partial spectrum e.g. SSPECTRA 5 (set no.)
LIST	Display file record(s) e.g. LIST NAME SSHOW
MISCELLANEOUS Commands	
RESET	initialize the system status
HELP	afford information on how to use the system
END	close the system

The ordinary searching procedure is separated into two phases: primary and secondary search.

As shown in Table 7.2, four commands, CPEAK, PPEAK, STRUC-

TURE and FORMULA are used for making access to the inverted index files.

In the case of the primary search, one of these four commands is used. The result of a primary search is a set of registry numbers, which is stored in a temporary file. After several primary searches have been performed, the sets of registry numbers are treated by using four logic commands, AND, IOR, EOR and NOT for targeting the objective more precisely. Then, by use of the LIST, PSTRUCTURE or SSPECTRA commands, all or partial lists of the file records, arbitrary size of substructures or partial spectral data are output.

Detailed explanations for individual commands are given below. A shortened form of every command is allowed for execution, For example, CPE or CPEA could be used instead of CPEAK, and so on.

CPEAK and PPEAK. As the names indicate, these two commands are used for peak search in the ^{13}C (Carbon) and ^{1}H (Proton) spectral data. The necessary parameter is a peak position value in ppm units. As an additional parameter, a tolerance value in ppm may be input. For example, a command CPEAK 120 5 will yield a set of registry numbers corresponding to those compounds with ^{13}C spectra which contain peaks in the range between 115 and 125 ppm. The system will give the number of compounds and the serial number of the temporary file containing the corresponding registry numbers.

STRUCTURE. This command is used for searching with partial structures. The input partial structures should be represented by the CANOST notation system. Non-standardized notation of the partial structure is also allowed.

The procedure for matching the input partial structure to structures in the file is as follows.

(1) For every CANOST code in the partial structure, independent sets of registry numbers are found by using the structural inverted index file.
(2) A Boolean AND operation is performed on these sets to obtain a set of registry numbers corresponding to those compounds with structures (notations) which contain all the nodes of the input partial structure.
(3) A connectivity check is performed to examine whether each of the structural formulas corresponding to the remaining registry numbers contains the input partial structure or not.

FORMULA. This is the command for searching for the objective compounds by molecular formula. A complete molecular formula is required as the parameter of this command.

The set of registry numbers obtained by using the CPEAK, PPEAK, STRUCTURE and FORMULA commands is sequentially numbered and stored in temporary files for secondary search.

AND, IOR, EOR and NOT. As the names indicate, these four commands are prepared for Boolean logic operations on two registry number sets in the temporary files.

The result of execution of one of the commands is also a set of registry numbers and the set can be used for further logic operations.

The three commands AND, IOR and EOR execute, respectively, Boolean AND, inclusive OR and exclusive OR operations on two sets.

When the command NOT is executed on sets A and B, the resultant set contains those members of set A which are not members of set B.

The functions of the four logic commands are illustrated in Fig. 7.9.

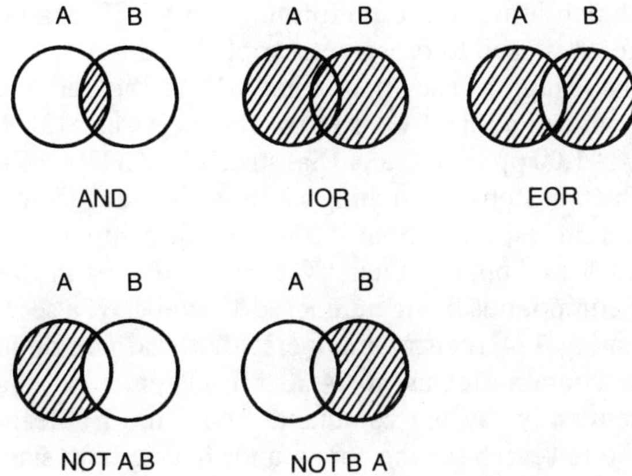

Fig. 7.9 — Functions of logic commands. A and B indicate sets of registry numbers obtained by use of the preceding search commands.

The following three commands are used for displaying the search results obtained by using primary search commands.

PSTRUCTURE. This command is used for displaying partial structures of compounds in the set resulting from the CPEAK or PPEAK search. The partial structures displayed contain carbon atoms or protons which show the particular chemical shift values specified in the previous CPEAK or PPEAK search. The size of the partial structures displayed can be specified with a command parameter. This command also has a histogram option; by use of this option, a histogram is displayed which illustrates what kind of partial structures give signals at the particular position.

SSPECTRA. This is the command for displaying chemical shift data associated with the particular carbon or proton atom of compounds in the set obtained by the STRUCTURE search. This command also has a histogram option.

LIST. This is the command for displaying all or partial records associated with the compound in a registry number set. Items which can be displayed are name, molecular formula, spectral data, solvents, data sources, and structural formula.

7.5 EXAMPLES OF EXECUTION

Examples of SPIRES execution are shown in Figs. 7.10–7.14. These examples illustrate the result obtained by using a small database which contains about 1500 ^{13}C spectra. In the figures, question marks are the prompting symbols from the system. Serial numbers are given to every set of registry numbers obtained by the primary searches and logic operations. To display two-dimensional structural formulas on ASCII character terminals [6], the symbol # is used to represent a triple bond.

The example shown in Fig. 7.10 is the result of searching for the compounds with ^{13}C spectral signals at 125.30 ± 1.00 ppm and 24.30 ± 1.00 ppm, and a partial structure, CH3–C=CH–.

The first step of searching was done by using the command CPEAK and the system responded that it contains 161 compounds which have signals at 125.30 ± 1.00 ppm in their ^{13}C spectra, the set of the registry numbers of these compounds being numbered 1. Similarly, a second set was generated containing 174 registry numbers for those compounds with ^{13}C spectra which contain signals at 24.30 ± 1.00 ppm, and that was numbered 2. Consequently, by the command AND, the Boolean logic operation was applied to search for the compounds having both signals. The resulting set contained 13 compounds and was numbered 3. On the other hand, the compounds with a partial structure CH3–C=CH– were searched for by using the command STRUCTURE, and 13 compounds were picked up from the file (set number 4). As shown in Fig. 7.10, the partial structure is expressed in CANOST notation as C3 DS D1, 1 2 3. Again the Boolean AND operation was applied and the resulting set contained only one registry number for the corresponding compound. Then, the command LIST was used to list all the items specified, with the parameters name, molecular formula, solvent used, data source, full spectrum, and full structure. Numerals given for the carbon atoms of the structural formula corresponded to the numbers of the individual signals in the spectrum displayed.

The next two examples (Figs. 7.11 and 7.12) demonstrate the function of the command PSTRUCTURE. As shown in Fig. 7.11, twenty compounds were extracted from the file by inputting 40.30 ± 0.10 through the command CPEAK (set number 1). The user can request which kind of atoms or atomic groups are at positions alpha- and beta- to the carbon atom, with signals at that position, by inputting 1 and 2, respectively, through the command PSTRUCTURE.

The output consists of the partial structures up to the alpha- and beta-positions, together with their chemical shift values. Because of limitations of space, only two examples for alpha-positions and three for beta-positions are shown in Fig. 7.11.

```
COMMAND ? CPEAK 125.30 1.00
        ENTRY 161
        SET #   1

COMMAND ? CPEAK 24.30 1.00
        ENTRY 174
        SET #   2

COMMAND ? AND 1 2
        ENTRY  13
        SET #   3

COMMAND ? STRUCTURE C3 DS D1  1 2 3
        ENTRY  13
        SET #   4

COMMAND ? AND 3 4
        ENTRY   1
        SET #   5

COMMAND ? LIST 5 NAME MOLECULAR SOLVENT REFERENCE SPECTRA SSHOW


    *** REG.#    361   ***


  1  ISOPHORONE
  2  C9 H14 O
  3  DEUTEROCHLOROFORM
  4  J&J 357

  5  SHIFT      ASSIGNMENT
     199.00      1
     125.30      3
     159.70      2
      45.10      8
      33.30      9
      50.70      7
      24.30      4
      28.20      5  6

  6  MOLECULAR FORMULA
```

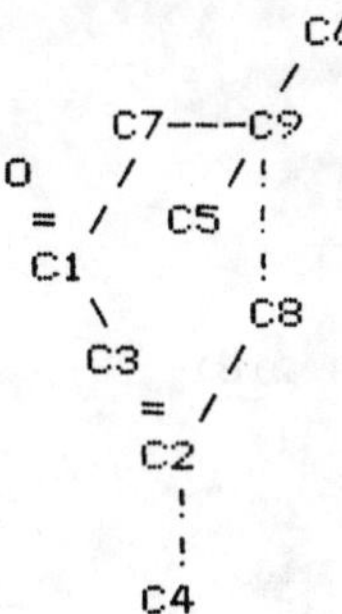

Fig. 7.10 — A typical example of execution of SPIRES. The CPEAK, AND, STRUCTURE and LIST commands were used in this example.

```
COMMAND ? CPEAK 40.20 0.10
        ENTRY  20
        SET #   1

COMMAND ? PSTRUCTURE 1 1 2

          * SUBSTRUCTURE (UP TO ALPHA POS. )

        1 C1= 40.30 PPM(REG.#    2)

            BR
              \
              C1-C--
              /  2
            BR

        2 C1= 40.20 PPM(REG.#  64)

            O       /
             =     /
             C2-C-C3
             /  1  \
            /       \

        3 C1= 40.20 PPM(REG.# 216)

==============================================================

==============================================================

          * SUBSTRUCTURE (UP TO BETA POS.)

        1 C1= 40.30 PPM(REG.#    2)

            BR
              \
              C1-C-BR
              /  2
            BR

        2 C1= 40.20 PPM(REG.#  64)

                     O
                     =
            O        C5
             \      / \
             C2-C-C3   \
             =  1 !
            O     S

        3 C1= 40.20 PPM(REG.# 216)

            N-C-C-C--
              1 3 4
```

Fig. 7.11 — Example of usage of PSTRUCTURE command. Structural environments of the carbon atoms with signals at 40.20 ± 0.10 were displayed.

```
COMMAND ? CPEAK 125.00 2.00
        ENTRY 263
        SET #    1

COMMAND ? PSTRUCTURE 1

 HISTOGRAM FOR TARGET CARBON..... [Y(ES)] ? Y

  >C< ;    2 **
 =CH2 ;    2 **
 =CH- ;   19 *******************
  =C< ;    4 ****
  #C- ;    1 *
 =C=O ;    2 **
 =AH- ;  110 **************************************************
             **************************************************
             **********
  =A< ;   11 ***********
 # AND A INDICATE TRIPLE BOND AND AROMATIC CARBON, RESPECTIVELY

 STATISTICS FOR ; TOTAL= 151, KIND= 8 FOR 123.00 - 127.00 PPM

COMMAND ?
```

Fig. 7.12 — Example of histogram option. Since structural data are not yet recorded for some compounds, the total number of 'target' carbons is less than the number of entries in this case.

As mentioned in the Section 7.4, the command PSTRUCTURE has a histogram option. When only the set number is input as a parameter of this command, the system will inquire whether the histogram is to be displayed or not, as shown in Fig. 7.12. The histogram shows the kinds of carbon nuclei and their appearance frequencies within the range specified in the preceding CPEAK command.

Also, the partial spectrum for any partial structure can be displayed through the command SSPECTRA. An example of displaying the chemical shifts of the methyl group, quarternary carbon and aromatic carbon atoms in partial strucutre A is shown in Fig. 17.13.

The partial structure A is input in the form of non-canonical CANOST notation. That there are three compounds on file with partial structure A is reported after issue of the command STRUCTURE (set number 1). The chemical shifts of the methyl (^{1}C), quarternary carbon (^{2}C) and aromatic carbon (^{3}C) atoms were displayed after input of the numerals 1, 2 and 3, respectively, through the command SSPECTRA as shown in Fig. 7.13.

The example shown in Fig. 7.14 is the result obtained by using another small prototype database in which both ^{13}C and ^{1}H spectral data files are linked with a single structure data file. Therefore, by use of this database it is possible to search for a compound with both ^{13}C and ^{1}H spectral data.

In the first step, those compounds which have signals at 1.02 ± 0.10 ppm in their ^{1}H spectra are searched for with the command PPEAK. There are 83 of those compounds in the file and the registry number set for them is numbered 1. Then, those which have signals at 25.40 ± 1.00 ppm in their ^{13}C

```
COMMAND ? STRUCTURE C3 C Y Y1 Y1 C3 C3 1 2 3 4 5 0 2 6 0 2 7
        ENTRY   3
        SET #   7

COMMAND ? SSPECTRA
  SET # ? 7
VERTEX # ? 1 2 3
  HISTGRAM ONLY [NO] ?

        * REG.#    SHIFT (PPM) FOR VERTEX #  1
           389      29.50
           426      31.40
           429      29.70

  STATISTICS FOR ;     3 SHIFTS FOR VERTEX #  1

        * REG.#    SHIFT (PPM) FOR VERTEX #  2
           389      34.40
           426      34.20
           429      34.40

  STATISTICS FOR ;     3 SHIFTS FOR VERTEX #  2

        * REG.#    SHIFT (PPM) FOR VERTEX #  3
           389     136.10
           426     148.00
           429     135.60

  STATISTICS FOR ;     3 SHIFTS FOR VERTEX #  3

COMMAND ? END
```


Fig. 7.13 — Example of usage of SPECTRA commands. Chemical shift data corresponding to every code in the input partial structure were displayed.

spectra are sought. There are 211 such compounds in the file and their registry numbers are saved as set number 2. The result of the Boolean AND operation on sets 1 and 2 is stored in set number 3, which contains 11 compounds. Again command CPEAK is used to search for those which have signals at 52.60 ± 1.00 ppm in their ^{13}C spectra.

There are 50 such compounds and the resulting set is numbered 4. The second AND operation is performed on sets 3 and 4, and the final set, number 5, contains only one compound. By use of the command LIST, all data of the compound are displayed as shown in Fig. 7.14.

7.6 CONCLUSION

A prototype spectral data retrieval system has been developed as an aid for structure elucidation. The system is based on a newly-constructed database containing both ^{13}C and ^{1}H NMR spectra.

Although the database still requires some unification of structural data files, as mentioned above, the usefulness of the system has been sufficiently demonstrated. There are still some problems to be solved, however, one of

```
COMMAND ? PPEAK 1.02 0.10
        ENTRY   83
        SET #    1

COMMAND ? CPEAK 25.40 1.00
        ENTRY  211
        SET #    2

COMMAND ? AND 1 2
        ENTRY   11
        SET #    3

COMMAND ? CPEAK 52.60 1.00
        ENTRY   50
        SET #    4

COMMAND ? AND 3 4
        ENTRY    1
        SET #    5

COMMAND ? LIST 5 NAME MOLECULAR SOLVENT SPECTRA SSHOW

    *** REG.#  270 ***

  1  2,6-DIMETHYLPIPERIDINE
  2  C7 H15 N
  3  DIOXANE

  4  --- CMR ---                      --- PMR ---

     SHIFT      ASSIGNMENT            SHIFT                ASSIGNMENT
     52.60         7 8                 0.72 - 1.22            4
     34.60         5 6                 1.08                   2 3
     25.40         4                   1.22 - 1.87            5 6
     23.20         2 3                UD.                     1

  5  MOLECULAR FORMULA
```

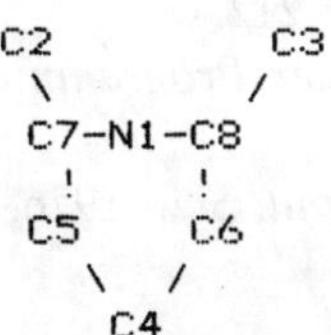

Fig. 7.14 — Example of combined retrieval. The compound which has certain signals in its ^1H and ^{13}C spectral data was retrieved.

them being the encoding format for ^1H spectral data. Most organic chemists would not be satisfied with the present format. However, since 16 kbytes of storage area are required for the complete digitized data of a single spectrum, the full data for all the compounds cannot be stored in the present computer facility of our laboratory. At present they are stored on magnetic tapes. A coding form that will be acceptable for most chemists is now being investigated. When it is completed, those data on magnetic tapes will be easily converted into the new data format.

The next problem, how to keep the database up to date, is a more important and more serious one. Although much of the data collection work can be done by non-chemist assistants, assignments and corrections of misassignments require expert organic chemists, but it is much more difficult to obtain such experts as volunteers.

Therefore, a so-called expert system should be developed to assist the assignment work. CHEMICS itself is an expert system because it interprets spectral data and generates candidate structural formulas.

The larger the database becomes, the more correctly CHEMICS can interpret spectral data. We are planning to develop an integrated system of CHEMICS and SPIRES. Such a system will certainly become a powerful tool for most organic chemists.

ACKNOWLEDGEMENTS

We thank those people who have assisted at various stages in developing the SPIRES system and compiling ^{13}C and ^{1}H spectral data. They are Shizuko Sasaki, Harukazu Okuda, Mikito Takezawa, Tohru Mitsuhashi, Tomiko Kato, Sayuri Hosoi, Akiyo Kawai, Hiroko Kato, Yuko Murata, Kumiko Kato, Atsuko Ishii, Kyoko Yokoyama and Kohtaro Yuta. We also thank the many Japanese chemists who have kindly afforded us their precious samples.

REFERENCES

[1] H. Abe, I. Fujiwara, T. Nishimura, T. Okuyama, T. Kida and S. Sasaki, *Computer Enhanced Spectrosc.* 1983, **1**, 55 and references therein.

[2] S. R. Heller, G. W. A. Milne and R. J. Feldmann, *Science*, 1973, **195**, 253.

[3] W. Bremser, L. Ernst, B. Franke, R. Gerhards and A. Hardt, *Carbon-13 NMR Spectral Data*, Verlag Chemie, Weinheim, 1981.

[4] H. Abe, Y. Kudo, T. Yamasaki, K. Tanaka, M. Sasaki and S. Sasaki, *J. Chem. Inf. Comput. Sci.*, 1984, **24**, 212.

[5] D. E. Knuth, *The Art of Computer Programming*, Vol. 3, Addison-Wesley, Reading, 1973.

[6] R. E. Carhart, *J. Chem. Inf. Comput. Sci.*, 1976, **16**, 82.

8

A conceptual challenge: multi-spectroscopy expert systems in structure eludication

Z. Hippe
Department of Physical & Computer Chemistry, Technical University, 35–041 Rzeszów, Poland

8.1 INTRODUCTION

Identification of the structure of organic compounds plays an important role in many areas of contemporary chemistry — in organic synthesis, toxicology, forensic chemistry, pharmacy, biochemistry, environmental protection, etc. For structure elucidation (identification), the traditional wet methods of making derivatives of an unknown substance or decomposing a molecule into the determinable or predicatable fragments, are now largely replaced by spectroscopic methods. Hence, structure is usually identified by the empirical interpretation of data from fragmentation of the excited molecule (mass spectrometry, MS) or the interpretation of molecular spectra such as the nuclear magnetic resonance (carbon-13 or proton, ^{13}C NMR or ^{1}H NMR, respectively), infrared (IR), Raman or ultraviolet spectra,† or simultaneous use of two or more of these methods to obtain better results.

In any case, the whole process of spectral interpretation may be assisted by the computer. For both approaches, we may exploit computer-supported databases (containing a large collection of spectra of a given type) or a special type of algorithm may be used [1].‡ Here we confine ourselves to

† The entropy of the information on molecular structure obtainable from a given type of spectrum, decreases in the sequence
MS>^{13}C NMR>^{1}H NMR>infrared>Raman>ultraviolet.

‡ In the latter case, much of the domain knowledge (e.g. spectroscopic rules) is usually buried in the code rather than represented as an explicit knowledge base [2].

computer-supported databases, and do not discuss other types of identification algorithms, such as AND/OR algorithms or matrix algorithms [3], since the material presented here is intended to be devoted to the latest developments in use of spectroscopic databases as tools for structural identifcation.

8.2 PRESENT STATUS OF STRUCTURE ELUCIDATION BY SEARCHING SPECTROSCOPIC DATABASES

For many years [4] the procedure of searching through a collection of standard reference spectra of a given type (MS, NMR, etc.), stored on a machine information carrier (e.g. a computer disk), has been used as the simplest algorithm for structure identification. This procedure, called the library-search method, looks for identity or similarity between the spectrum of an unknown substance and one (or more) spectra from the standard collection. As the result of the search, the computer outputs a list (preferably not too extensive) of spectra identical and/or similar to the unknown, according to an *a priori* fixed criteria of similarity. The library-search algorithms thus supply two types of results. When the unknown spectrum has an exact match within the spectra stored in the database, we get exact determination of the unknown structure (i.e. the structure corresponding to the standard reference spectrum retrieved may be assigned to the unknown compound with very high probability). Alternatively, when the unknown spectrum does not have an exact match in the collection of standard reference spectra, we may obtain information about the chemical class of the molecule being investigated and/or substructures contained in it. Experience with the computer-supported spectroscopic databases used as research tools in structure elucidation soon leads to the conclusion that we had arrived at a level where no further progress is possible. In particular, the library-search algorithms (in general) have reached such a degree of maturity [5], that we can hardly expect to obtain better identification with them. Moreover, taking into account that the largest collections (databases) of standard reference spectra amount to less than 0.8% of all known organic substances [6], it is obvious that more general solutions than simple library-search need to be found. The most recent approach uses an entirely different data-structure representation in the data-based computer program system. According to this solution (described in detail later) the new type of spectroscopic database contains not only factual knowledge (purely spectral data) but also (and in many cases, only) *procedural knowledge*. This special type of database (called a knowledge base) thus contains all the domain information (say, about infrared) required for advanced interpretation of a particular spectrum in the sense of structural identification. Besides the novel type of database, new problem-solving algorithms (for structure identification) that embody and reflect the knowledge, experience and intuition of the expert spectroscopist have been elaborated, creating so-called expert systems for problem-solving in structure elucidation.

8.3 PROBLEM-SOLVING AND EXPERTISE

Problem-solving, even when restricted to structure elucidation might seem to be an extremely vague topic. In its broadest sense, it encompasses all of computer science because any computational task can be regarded as a problem to be solved. For our purposes, however, we desire a somewhat narrower definition, that excludes routine computational methods. Hence, we will talk about application of sophisticated software for structural analysis, working in such a way that it plays the role of a real research tool assisting the efforts of the chemist, giving full and multivariant possibility of usage of his/her personal skill, and of any information about the molecule being investigated. Software of this type may be called an intelligent problem-solver, or a *computer program system,*† exhibiting the characteristics we associate with intelligence in human behaviour. One common feature of all intelligent computer programs solving a problem is that they must search for solutions, because in attempting to solve the problem they cannot usually obtain an answer directly. All possible (whether reasonable or irrelevant) solutions of a given problem form the 'solution space'. Problem-solving programs (PS) are able to search only a part of this space, which we may call the 'search space'. In structure elucidation, the solution space is of enormous size, equal to the number of all existing plus the number of feasible (but not yet discovered) organic structures. However, the search space part is very much smaller, and usually restricted to a given class or classes of compounds of interest to the researcher.

To date, a variety of techniques‡ have been developed for space searching until the solution is found. This approach of an exhaustive search through all possible solutions to find the correct one is known as *'brute force'*. But an exhaustive search through the entire space may be applicable to only very simple problems. For this reason, the efficiency of any problem-solving method, particularly in structural analyis, must be improved by endowing the technique with special theoretical tools for the elimination of classes of solutions (called candidate solutions) that cannot succeed in the given class. This type of directed search is frequently called reduction pruning. Additionally, a variety of heuristic (rule-of-thumb) or simple ad hoc programming shortcuts can be used to reduce the size of the search space. Finally, some problem-solving programs can even improve their performance with experience.

Expertise. One special type of problem-solver, (also used in structural elucidation) is that of *expert systems* [8–10], which derive from the observation that the 'old-fashioned programs' (data for processing+knowledge coded within subroutines) are extremely difficult to keep updated with

† The computer program system may be defined as the package of sophisticated utility programs (showing profound logical interconnections) designed for solving the given problem(s).

‡ The most frequently used techniques are: depth-first, breadth-first, best-first, hill-climbing, branch-bound, mini-max, alpha-beta, etc. For details, see [7].

progress in domain knowledge, and have usually been written in outmoded style with very little user-friendliness (if any). Thus, according to recent trends [11], an expert system consists of three main parts: a knowledge base, an inference engine and the user's interface. The *knowledge base* contains, besides the parametric data (for instance, a collection of spectra of a given type), properly structured knowledge obtained from a human expert. This type of knowledge is called the procedural knowledge and is usually stored in the form of *production rules*. A production rule is a connection between two assertions specifying how the presence (or absence) of a piece of evidence affects the truth of a hypothesis, i.e. IF (evidence) is present/absent THEN hypothesis is true/false, within a certain degree of confidence. In structure elucidation such production rules might be a set of well defined spectrum–structure correlations. Almost all of today's expert systems apply knowledge stored in explicitly separated databases, in the form of production rules.

The *inference engine* is a module (also separated) of utility programs which infer suggested solutions from the facts stored in the database(s). Recently, much more sophisticated and powerful algorithms than simple library-search are used in the inference engines of real expert systems for structure elucidation; for example the static/dynamic method of spectrum interpretation [12].

The *user's interface* ensures smooth communication with the system, enabling change of its method of working and sometimes making it possible to explain the suggestions provided or to draw some novel conclusions while the system is running. In structure elucidation, a properly constructed user's interface should accept any information about the investigated molecule, particularly about:

heteroatoms known to be present,
and/or heteroatoms known to be absent,
or qualitative composition,
and/or substructures known to be present,
and/or substructures known to be absent,
or quantitative composition.

This very effectively cuts down the size of the search space.

8.4 THE IIAI-APPROACH TO PROBLEM-SOLVING IN STRUCTURE ELUCIDATION

Let us begin once again with the relation between the solution space in structure elucidation and the search space of the particular identification system, explicitly elaborated for a given spectroscopic method. Using some basic theorems of contemporary artificial intelligence [3], we may draw the obvious conclusion that any identification program package, even an extremely well designed one (that interprets a given type of spectrum) of the old type, or a problem-solver in the form of a modern expert system, has a search space that is many times smaller than the total solution space. In other words, the search space is very restricted, which means that the correct solution(s) may not necessarily belong to the set of solutions actually found. Thus, the structural identification may in some cases be incorrect or even not attainable at all. This is particularly true when a given system was originally designed for the interpretation of only one type of spectral data, for example DENDRAL [13], designed for mass spectrometry. Somewhat better results (because of a more complete search space) are given by the so-called integrated systems such as CASE [14], CHEMICS [15], STREC [16] and SEAC [17]. Here, various spectral techniques are integrated, on the assumption that the increase in the probability of arriving at the correct solution will be larger than the overall increase in the size of the search space. This is because the procedure uses the fact that various spectroscopic methods give structurally significant pieces of information which may confirm, complement and/or eliminate each other. However, all the above-mentioned systems are of the 'old-fashioned' type, so updating of the knowledge (mostly buried within the code) is achievable only by painstaking reprogramming or even by reconstruction of the basic architecture of the system. That is why an entirely novel approach to solving the problem of structure elucidation was developed [18], namely the set of carefully designed expert systems in which all knowledge databases are detached from the program modules (inference engines), and there is a very flexible, clear and consistent user's interface. This approach is called IIAI (Independent Identification by Artificial Intelligence), and features the following properties:

(a) expert systems designed for the interpretation of various types of spectra are fully independent of each other;
(b) the user has a very flexible choice of spectral method(s), according to his/her requirements resulting from the philosophy of the experiment or from the instrumentation available;
(c) the results of the spectral interpretation are loaded onto a common disk for further processing;
(d) the final step in structural identification (structural assembly, i.e. the combination of substructures found by the particular expert systems, into a meaningful total structure) is executed by an independent package of utility programs, stored on the same disk.

The computer program environment called SCANSPEC† is the first reported example of the practical application of the IIAI philosophy [19]. SCANSPEC consists of independent real expert systems for interpretation of mass spectra (MS-SCAN), nuclear magnetic resonance spectra

† Developed in the Department of Physical & Computer Science within the framework of the research project MR-I.32, under the co-ordination of Warsaw University.

(^{13}C NMR and ^{1}H NMR) and infrared spectra (IR-SCAN)†. The structural assembly of the substructures recognized is performed by an independent program package SCANGEN. Hence, the conceptual challenge of multi-spectroscopy expert systems in structure elucidation has successfully been put into operation.

ACKNOWLEDGEMENTS

Financial support in the years 1981–1985, for development of all parts of SCANSPEC within the mutual research project MR-I.32 of the Polish Academy of Sciences and Ministry of Science and Higher Education (Warsaw), is gratefully acknowledged. I am also specially indebted to my co-workers: J. Duliban, J. Kozioł, R. Licbarska, M. Mazur and the guest-researchers H. Barańska, M. Jamróz and Z. Latek for devoted work during the last five years.

REFERENCES

[1] Z. Hippe, *J. Chem. Inf. Comp. Sci.*, 1985, **25**, 344.
[2] A. Barr and E. Feigenbaum (eds.), *The Handbook of Artificial Intelligence*, Vols. 1–3, Kaufman, Los Altos Cal., 1981–192.
[3] Z. Hippe, *Anal. Chim. Acta*, 1983, **150**, 11.
[4] J. T. Clerc and F. Erni, *Fortschr. Chem. Forsch.*, 1973, **39**, 91.
[5] A. Kaczmarek, *Ph.D. Thesis*, Mining and Metallurgy Academy, Kraków, 1985.
[6] J. Hilsenrath, *Summary of On-line or Interactive Physiochemical Numerical Data Systems*, National Bureau of Standards, Washington DC, 1980.
[7] P. H. Winston, *Artificial Intelligence*, Addison-Wesley, Reading, 1979.
[8] R. E. Dessy, *Anal. Chem.*, 1984, **56**, 1200A.
[9] M. R. Detaevernier, Y. Michotte, L. Buydens, M. P. Derde, M. Desmet, L. Kaufman, G. Musch, J. Smeyers-Verbeke, A. Thielemans, L. Dryon and D. L. Massart, *J. Biomed. Pharm. Anal.*, 1986, **4**, 297.
[10] R. Benares-Alcantara, A. W. Westerberg and M. D. Rychter, *Comput. Chem. Eng.*, 1985, **9**, 127.
[11] F. Hayes-Roth, *Computer*, 1984, **17**, 11.
[12] M. Jamróz, Z. Latek and Z. Hippe, *Anal. Chim. Acta*, 1986, **181**, 65.
[13] D. H. Smith, N. A. B. Gray, J. G. Nourse and C. W. Crandell, *Anal. Chim. Acta*, 1981, **133**, 471.
[14] C. A. Shelley and M. E. Munk, *Anal. Chim. Acta*, 1981, **133**, 507.
[15] S. Sasaki, H. Abe, I. Fujiwara and T. Yamasaki, in *Data Processing in Chemistry*, Z. Hippe (ed.), p. 186. PWN, Warsaw, Elsevier, Amsterdam, 1981.
[16] L. A. Gribov, *Anal. Chim. Acta*, 1980, **122**, 249.
[17] Z. Hippe, in *Data for Science and Technology*, P. S. Glaeser (ed.), p. 107. North-Holland, Amsterdam, 1983.

† Two independent AI-interpreters, of Raman and ultraviolet spectra, are also included in SCANSPEC. Neither RA-SCAN nor UV-SCAN has the structure of a real expert system, because of the low importance of Raman and ultraviolet spectra in structural analysis.

[18] Z. Hippe, in *Proc. Euroanalysis V,* A. Hulanicki (ed.), Akadémiai Kiádo, Budapest.
[19] Z. Hippe, J. Duliban, R. Licbarska, J. Kozioł and M. Mazur, *Anal. Chem. (Warsaw),*.

Index